W9-BLY-420

Fodor's InFocus

TURKS & CAICOS ISLANDS

Welcome to the Turks & Caicos Islands

With picture-perfect white-sand beaches and breathtaking turquoise waters, the Turks and Caicos Islands are a Caribbean paradise. There's much to explore across the varying landscapes, from the caves of Middle Caicos to the beautiful beaches of Providenciales. Whether you come to partake in the many outdoor activities or simply sit with your toes in the sand, you're sure to find natural beauty at every turn.

TOP REASONS TO GO

★ **Beautiful Beaches:** Even on Provo, there are miles of deserted beach without any umbrellas in sight.

★ **Excellent Diving:** The third-largest coral reef system in the world is among the world's top dive sites.

★ **Easy Island-Hopping:** You'll find excellent fishing and boating among the uninhabited coves and cays.

★ **The Jet Set:** Destination spas, penthouse suites, and exclusive villas and resorts make celebrity spotting a possibility; keep your eyes open!

★ **Outdoor Adventures:** Horseback riding, whale-watching, golfing, and exploring caves are just the beginning.

Contents

1 EXPERIENCE THE TURKS
  AND CAICOS ISLANDS ..7
  17 Ultimate Experiences... 8
  Welcome to the Turks
  and Caicos Islands.......... 16
  What's Where 18
  10 Best Beaches
  in the Turks and
  Caicos Islands................. 20
  Best Outdoor Activities
  in the Turks and Caicos
  Islands 22
  Top Hotels for Families
  in the Turks and Caicos
  Islands 24
  Geography, Flora,
  and Fauna 26
  What's New 27
  Kids and Families............. 28

2 TRAVEL SMART
  TURKS & CAICOS 29
  What to Know
  Before You Visit the Turks
  and Caicos Islands.......... 30
  Getting Here 32
  Before You Go 37
  Essentials......................... 38
  On the Calendar.............. 43
  Great Itineraries 44
  Contacts........................... 47

3 PROVIDENCIALES 49
  Welcome To
  Providenciales 50
  Planning 53
  Grace Bay 61

The Bight.......................... 85
Turtle Cove....................... 89
Leeward 91
Long Bay 97
Venetian Road.................. 98
Turtle Tail........................ 98
Discovery Bay.................. 98
Downtown 100
Airport............................. 102
Five Cays 102
Chalk Sound 103
West Harbour.................. 106
Blue Mountain 107
Blue Hills 107
Northwest Point............. 108
Activities 109

4 THE CAICOS
  AND THE CAYS............123
  Welcome To The Caicos
  and the Cays................... 124
  Planning 126
  Little Water Cay 130
  Pine Cay 131
  Fort George Cay............. 132
  Dellis Cay 132
  Parrot Cay 133
  North Caicos 134
  Middle Caicos 143
  South Caicos 149

5 GRAND TURK...............157
  Welcome To
  Grand Turk 158
  Planning 161
  Cockburn Town 165

North Ridge 173
Pillory Beach 174
Grand Turk
Cruise Terminal 176
Activities 179

6 SALT CAY 183
Welcome To Salt Cay 184
Planning 186

INDEX 196

ABOUT OUR WRITER .. 204

MAPS

Grace Bay
and The Bight 64–65
The Bight
and Turtle Cove 87
Providenciales 94–95
The Caicos
and the Cays 128–129
Grand Turk 162
Cockburn Town 169
Salt Cay 189

Chapter 1

EXPERIENCE THE TURKS AND CAICOS ISLANDS

17 ULTIMATE EXPERIENCES

The Turks and Caicos offer terrific experiences that should be on every traveler's list. Here are Fodor's top picks for a memorable trip.

1 Stay in a Dreamy Resort

From the all-inclusive Alexandra Resort to the luxurious Seven Stars on Grace Bay Beach, there's no shortage of fine hotels to choose from—and never a bad view. *(Ch. 3–6)*

2 Family Fun on Provo

Shallow waters, fine sand, and loads of kid-friendly activities make Providenciales one of the Caribbean's best family destinations. *(Ch. 3)*

3 Spas

The spas in the Turks and Caicos are some of the Caribbean's finest. Many feature invigorating local conch scrubs and relaxing open-air massages. *(Ch. 3, 4, 5)*

4 Local Music

Celebrated local musician Quinton Dean performs at different venues around Provo. Catch a performance if you can. *(Ch. 3)*

5 Scuba Diving

Long before luxury resorts attracted beachgoers, divers came to the Turks and Caicos for superb reefs. *(Ch. 3, 4, 5, 6)*

6 Half Moon Bay

Accessible only by boat, this natural sandbar rivals Grace Bay for beauty. Go with Caicos Dream Tours for a great experience. *(Ch. 3)*

7 French-West Indies Food at Coco Bistro

This elegant Providenciales restaurant is popular with vacationers and locals alike for its French-Caribbean cuisine. *(Ch. 3)*

8 Exploring Grand Turk

The atmospheric capital of the Turks and Caicos brims with old Caribbean charm and has beautiful beaches protected by magnificent reefs. *(Ch. 5)*

9 Grace Bay Beach

One of the world's best beaches, Grace Bay has 12 miles of powdery white sand that frame a calm stretch of turquoise sea. Despite its popularity, you're sure to find some solitude. *(Ch. 3)*

10 Island Culture at Bugaloo's

To see real island culture, go where the locals go: Bugaloo's in Five Cays. Here, you can feast on conch with your feet in the sand and hear live music on Sundays. *(Ch. 3)*

11 Whale-Watching

From January through April, humpback whales pass so close to Salt Cay that you can see them from the beach. On some days, you can even snorkel with them. *(Ch. 6)*

12 Stand-Up Paddleboarding

The latest rage on Providenciales is the perfect way to explore the island's lush mangroves. You can also rent a board on Grace Bay. *(Ch. 3)*

13 Sunsets at Amanyara

Gorgeous sunsets can be experienced all over, but the poolside view from Amanyara, a Fodor's Choice resort on Providenciales' far west end, is especially spectacular. *(Ch. 3)*

14 Stingray Encounter

Wade into the shallow waters around Gibbs Cay, a small, uninhabited islet off Grand Turk, to swim with stingrays in a natural environment. *(Ch. 5)*

15 Thursday Night Fish Fry

On Thursday nights everyone in Provo heads to the Fish Fry to taste the real food and culture of the islands. Local entertainers keep the party going from 5:30 to 9:30. *(Ch. 3)*

16 Cave Exploring in Middle Caicos

The Conch Bar Caves in Middle Caicos is one of the largest above-ground cave systems in the Caribbean. You'll see stalactites and stalagmites, bat colonies, and tidal pools. *(Ch. 4)*

17 Glowworm Cruise

If you time your vacation right, you may have a chance to experience a most incredible natural phenomenon: glowworms that illuminate the ocean. It happens following a full moon. *(Ch. 3)*

Welcome to the Turks and Caicos

The Turks and Caicos are made up of more than 40 islands cast upon breathtakingly beautiful cerulean waters. Although white, soft-sand beaches and calm, warm waters are shared among all the islands, their landscapes vary. The flatter, more arid islands of Grand Turk, Salt Cay, South Caicos, Pine Cay, and Providenciales are covered with low-lying bush and scrub, whereas the islands of Middle Caicos, North Caicos, and Parrot Cay are greener, with more undulating landscapes. In addition to these eight inhabited islands, there are the many smaller cays and uninhabited East Caicos that help make up this southern tip of the Lucayan Archipelago, just 575 miles (862 km) southeast of Miami on the third-largest coral reef system in the world.

DISCOVERY

Although the first recorded sighting of the Turks and Caicos Islands was in 1512, there is a much-disputed possibility suggesting that Columbus first made landfall on Grand Turk on his voyage to the New World in 1492. Today this delightful string of islands has become an exclusive and highly prized destination, perhaps because of their history of anonymity.

CHANGING HANDS

The Turks and Caicos Islands were controlled by France and Spain in the past, and then indirectly through Bermuda, the Bahamas, and finally Jamaica before becoming a separate autonomous British Overseas Territory with its own governor in 1973. These islands were initially desirable because of their salt production. In fact, there was a time when Salt Cay provided much of the salt that supplied the whole of the United States and Canada.

REEFS AND WRECKS

It's estimated that some 1,000 shipwrecks surround the islands. Some island residents may be descendants of those shipwrecked off the Spanish slave ship *Trouvadore,* which ran aground off East Caicos in 1841. But the most famous wreck is probably that of the Spanish galleon *Nuestra Senora de la Concepción,* which sank after hitting a shallow reef in 1641 in the Silver Shoals, between the Turks and Caicos and Hispaniola. William Phips had recovered a small portion of the treasure by 1687. However, Burt Webber discovered the majority of it in 1978. The wreck contained treasure worth millions, as well as priceless artifacts, including Chinese porcelain from the late Ming period.

TUMULTUOUS TIMES

Two female pirates, Anne Bonny and Mary Read, captured a Spanish treasure ship in 1718, then settled on Pirate Cay, which is now known as Parrot Cay. Only two years later a pirate named François l'Olonnais moved onto French Cay, using it as a base from which to raid passing ships. Many say that his treasure is still buried there on the edge of the Caicos Banks. On the south shore of Providenciales carvings can be found among the rocks, supposedly maps to buried treasures.

THE PEOPLE

Only 35,500 people live in the Turks and Caicos Islands. Less than half are "Belongers," the term for the native population who are descendants of loyalist slaves, brought south after the American Declaration of Independence drove the loyalists to seek another haven in which to grow their cotton and sugarcane. The ancestors of those from Grand Turk, Salt Cay, and South Caicos worked in the salt industry, descended mostly from Bermudian slaves who settled here in the 1600s. Nowadays the majority of residents work in tourism, fishing, and offshore finance.

THE RISE OF PROVIDENCIALES

The political and historical capital of the country is Grand Turk, with the seat of government there. Most of the tourism development, however, is on Providenciales, more commonly known as "Provo." Thanks to the beauty of its north shore, visitors may enjoy the miles of ivory sand that stretch along its graceful curve; Grace Bay is consistently rated as the best beach in the world. Provo has become a hub of activity since the 1990s, as resorts, spas, and restaurants have been built and the resident population has grown to some 24,000. It is also the temporary home for the vast majority of visitors who come to the Turks and Caicos Islands.

REMNANTS OF HISTORY

Marks of the country's colonial past can be found in the wood-and-stone Bermudian-style clapboard houses that line the streets on Grand Turk, Salt Cay, and South Caicos. Throughout the Caicos Islands, visitors may explore the ruins of several loyalist plantations now protected by the Turks & Caicos National Trust; slave quarters, a great house, stone pens, wells, and cauldrons all draw us back in time to feel what lives were like for those growing cotton and sisal on these islands.

WHAT'S WHERE

1 Providenciales. Provo has most of the accommodations in the Turks and Caicos and gets the majority of visitors. Come if you are seeking miles of soft sand, luxurious accommodations, crystal-clear water, and a serious foodie scene. But don't come for nightlife—there are only a few hot spots that will keep you out late.

2 The Caicos and the Cays. Although most of the cays are uninhabited, there is the ultra-luxurious private-island resort of Parrot Cay, as well as the laid-back tranquility to be experienced at the Meridian Club on the private island of Pine Cay. South Caicos is all about diving and snorkeling, fishing and exploring, although it now boasts its own luxurious resort, SailRock; on North and Middle Caicos, days can be spent simply beachcombing and sunbathing.

3 Grand Turk. The historic capital of the Turks and Caicos gets many more visitors by cruise ship than as overnight guests. Come here if you like to dive or just relax; and if you're on a budget, you'll find that most prices are more reasonable than those on Provo.

4 Salt Cay. Step off the ferry or plane here, and you may feel as if you've landed in 1950. Come to relax on one of the prettiest beaches in all the Turks and Caicos or go diving. In season you may want to whale-watch.

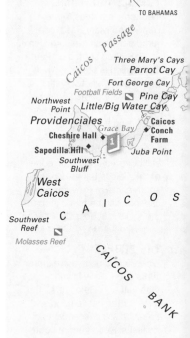

KEY
◤ Dive sites

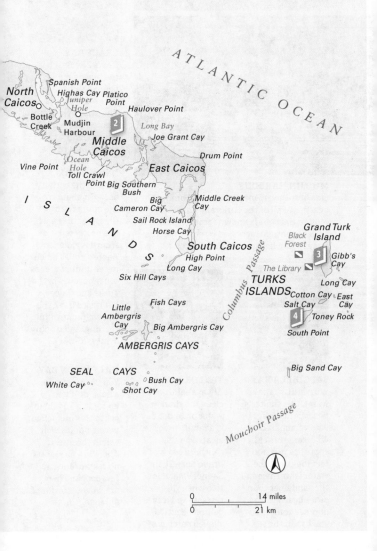

10 Best Beaches in the Turks and Caicos Islands

MUDJIN HARBOUR

One of the most spectacular (and unique) beaches in all of the Turks and Caicos, Mudjin Harbour is known for its cliffs and rock formations, accessed by staircase from Dragon Cay Resort in Middle Caicos. *(Ch. 4)*

SAPODILLA BAY

With still, shallow water, this sheltered beach is not long when compared with some other hot spots (it's just 900 feet long), but the water is warmer and the sand finer than other beaches. You may see conch and starfish in the sea grass. *(Ch. 3)*

TAYLOR BAY

Always calm and clear, the shallow water of Taylor Bay is a family favorite, located on the southern coast of Provo near Chalk Sound. Visit at low tide when the ocean retreats and leaves behind beautiful rippled patches of sand. *(Ch. 3)*

GRACE BAY

Grace Bay Beach is the reason many people visit the Turks and Caicos. The award winning 3-mile stretch of powder-white sand is part of the Princess Alexandra National Park, so despite the activity brought about by the many resorts that line this beach, it is protected from development. There's not as much to see underwater as other beaches in the Turks and Caicos, but Grace Bay can't be beat for strolling, shelling, and sipping drinks. *(Ch. 3)*

HALF MOON BAY

You'll have to take a boat (or if you're up for it, a kayak) to get to this unspoiled beach, but it's well worth the effort. There are no resorts, no restaurants, and few people. There are, however, a lot of iguanas. *(Ch. 3)*

Governor's Beach

LOWER BIGHT BEACH

At this stretch of sand on the northern coast of Provo, the sandy ocean bottom gives way to sea grass and a few small but vibrant coral reefs. You may spot a turtle or even a nurse shark while snorkeling. *(Ch. 3)*

MALCOLM'S ROAD BEACH

Few make it out to Malcolm's Road Beach—the only resort here is the exclusive Amanyara—but those who do are rewarded with great snorkeling and diving sites. Just offshore, the wall drops to a depth of more than 7,000 feet. *(Ch. 3)*

PELICAN BEACH

Although not as well known and nowhere near as busy as neighbor Grace Bay Beach, this stretch of white sand and aquamarine water is just as gorgeous. The barrier reef running parallel to the shore means no waves, and there are some great snorkeling spots. *(Ch. 3)*

WEST HARBOUR BLUFF

In addition to stunning cliffs and an open-faced cave, you can spot birds including ospreys, green herons, and the brown pelican. In the water you'll likely see conch, starfish, and stingrays. *(Ch.3)*

GOVERNOR'S BEACH

Known for its rusting shipwreck just offshore, Grand Turk's Governor's Beach separates the cruise center and historic Cockburn Town along the west coast. *(Ch. 5)*

Best Outdoor Activities in the Turks and Caicos Islands

PLAYING A ROUND OF GOLF
The country's only golf course happens to be one of the top-ranked courses in the Caribbean. The challenging course at Provo Golf Club has water on six holes on the front nine and five lake holes on the back nine. *(Ch. 3)*

KITEBOARDING
Adrenaline junkies will love the opportunity to fly across the crystal clear water of the Turks and Caicos Islands. Long Bay Beach along the southern coast of Provo is usually the best spot. Three miles of beach, calm water, few natural or manmade obstacles, and steady wind most of the year make it one of the top kiteboarding spots in the Caribbean. *(Ch. 3)*

KAYAKING AND PADDLEBOARD-ING
Whether you want to explore the clear ocean next to your resort or the mangroves farther afield, you'll see abundant wildlife and get in some exercise via paddleboard or kayak. *(Ch. 3, 4, 5, 6)*

SCUBA DIVING
Home to the third largest barrier reef in the world, the Turks and Caicos has some phenomenal diving. Ship and plane wrecks abound, and in Grand Turk a wall that plunges down more than 7,000 feet is just off shore. *(Ch. 3, 4, 5, 6)*

BIRD-WATCHING
Even the Turks and Caicos' busiest island, Providenciales, is still undeveloped enough to be a haven for migratory and nesting birds. But for really great birding, head to Grand Turk's Salinas, home to ospreys, herons, brown pelicans, and yes, flamingos. *(Ch. 3, 5)*

Whale-Watching

PLAYING WITH A POTCAKE

Visitors line up at Salt Mills Plaza for an opportunity to take a potcake—a formerly stray local puppy—for a walk along the beach. *(Ch. 3)*

WHALE-WATCHING

Every winter from January through mid-April, pods of whales make their way quite close to shore along Grand Turk, South Caicos, and particularly Salt Cay. With an experienced guide there's a good chance you'll see some, and if the conditions are right you may even get to hop in the water with them too. *(Ch. 6)*

CAVING

If you need a break from sun and sand, head to Middle Caicos to see its famous limestone Conch Bar Caves. You'll spot magnificent stalactites and stalagmites as well as bats. *(Ch. 4)*

FISHING

Turks and Caicos is a great spot for deep-sea, bottom fishing, bonefishing, and reef fishing. At some small island restaurants, you can bring in your catch and the chef will clean and cook it up for your dinner. *(Ch. 3, 4, 5, 6)*

HORSEBACK RIDING

Saddle up and ride a horse through bushy trails to the stunning Long Bay Beach on the southern side of Provo. You'll ride your horse into the shallow water, giving you both a welcome break from the Turks and Caicos sunshine. *(Ch. 3)*

Top Hotels for Families in the Turks and Caicos Islands

SANDS AT GRACE BAY
At this Provo resort, you have three pools to choose from, including one with a cascading waterfall and grottoes, complimentary bikes, and a spa that includes packages for kids, too. *(Ch. 3)*

THE SOMERSET ON GRACE BAY
Check infinity pool, spa, and luxurious suites off your resort bucket list at The Somerset, and rest assured kids will also be in excellent care. And, everyone can enjoy the weekly movie night on the lawn. *(Ch. 3)*

GRACE BAY CLUB
Sea views, multiple restaurants, a good location on Providenciales...there are many reasons to love Grace Bay Club. But there's one good reason any type of traveler can be happy here: there are two pools; one is designated adults-only and the other is for families. *(Ch. 3)*

BEACHES TURKS & CAICOS
This all-inclusive was specifically designed with kids in mind, so it's no wonder this property tops the charts for family-friendly hotels in the Caribbean. Not only is Beaches Turks & Caicos situated on a prime spot of Grace Bay Beach, but this sprawling resort boasts a 45,000-square-foot water park—the only thing like it in the country—as well as ten pools and four whirlpools. With 21 on-site restaurants and a never-ending array of activities, there's something for everyone. Did we mention that it's located on the best beach on Providenciales? *(Ch. 3)*

THE PALMS
Enjoying the sunshine on Grace Bay Beach draws visitors to this luxurious hotel—but The Palms also happens to be great for kids. There's a clubhouse for games and activities galore. *(Ch. 3)*

THE ALEXANDRA RESORT
This all-inclusive resort has an incredible spot on Grace Bay, a massive pool, lots of included water sports, and kids 12 and younger stay and eat for free. *(Ch. 3)*

EAST BAY RESORT, SOUTH CAICOS
Located on an incredible beach that goes on for miles, East Bay Resort has a lovely pool and a staff that feel like old friends. It's the kind of place where you can disconnect from technology and reconnect with nature. *(Ch. 4).*

SEVEN STARS
One of the best hotels on Provo whether you have kids in tow or not, this luxurious resort is right on Grace Bay Beach. Washers and dryers in the suites make it easy to manage with a family on a longer stay, and they have a water toy that can't be beat—an ocean trampoline. *(Ch. 3)*

PARROT CAY BY COMO
If you make it to Parrot Cay, the place to stay is COMO Parrot Cay, an upscale resort that really takes care of their guests—no matter the age. Crafts, nature walks, cooking classes, fishing lessons, yoga are just a few of the activities on offer. *(Ch. 4)*

Geography, Flora, and Fauna

The landscape in the Turks and Caicos is relatively flat. In fact, the highest point of land is Flamingo Hill on uninhabited East Caicos at 157 feet. It is also quite dry; the chain experiences the least amount of rainfall of any island nation in the Caribbean region. The beautiful beaches that encircle the islands are made up of coral stone, crushed and ground into sand as soft as powder as it makes its way over the reef into the quieter, more protected waters. Its pearly white appearance creates a stunning contrast to the indescribable hues of the water.

BIRDS

French Cay is a bird-watcher's dream, protected as a national park. Here you can see dozens of white-cheeked pintail, reddish egrets, and ospreys. Ospreys can be seen on all the islands, but their nests are easier to see at Three Mary Cays on North Caicos or at Splitting Rock on Provo. Bright pink flamingos can be spotted on some islands, especially at Flamingo Pond on North Caicos, the pond on West Caicos, and at Provo's only golf course. The country's national bird, the Brown Pelican, can be spotted along the shore on most islands.

FLORA

The official national plant is the Turk's head cactus, so named because of its shape. The best place to see fields of them is on Ambergris Cay. Silver palms grow naturally in the scrub, adding a tropical flair to beaches such as Half Moon Bay, but the trees are most numerous on West Caicos. North Caicos is considered the "garden" island, as it receives the most rainfall of the islands and is greener as a result. The cays all have small limestone cliffs that have formed from years of ocean waves.

OTHER FAUNA

Huge blue land crabs come out in the spring after rains. You're more likely to spot one on the sparsely populated islands of North and Middle Caicos, although they can be seen on Provo, too. The queen conchs that thrive in the flats between Provo and Little Water Cay are an important part of the islands' economies. The Turks and Caicos have the largest population of conch in the world, and conch is the most important food on these islands. Conch diving and deep-sea fishing both require fishing permits. The most important indigenous species of the Turks and Caicos is the rock iguana found at Little Water Cay, also known as Iguana Island.

What's New

Big developments are underway on Providenciales. Traditionally, there was a four-story limit for building height on the island, but that limit is no more. The rule was changed to allow Seven Stars to put up a seven-story resort, and now the Ritz Carlton Residences developers, the Desarollos Hotel Group, got the go-ahead to build a 60-suite property that will tower over everything else on the island. The Ritz Carlton will dwarf the Seven Stars next door at 12 stories. Feelings about the construction are decidedly mixed among residents. Many are concerned that this will set a precedent that will drastically change the look and feel of Providenciales moving forward.

Whatever direction the island development takes, tourism is booming in Turks and Caicos. More than 140 flights arrive at the Providenciales International Airport weekly, and more than 25 percent of the visitors arriving in the country are staying at least a week. The high-end destination is attracting big spenders: at least 20 percent of the 430,000 annual visitors spend as much as $1,000 a day while in the islands.

Although the tourist economy has finally turned around, hurricanes have hindered development and forced government to spend on repairing infrastructure rather than growing it. Focus was placed on getting Providenciales back up and running following the back-to-back hits by Hurricanes Irma and Maria in 2017, and now, slowly, the other islands are starting to get some much-needed attention and TLC.

Salt Cay has been slated for a multimillion dollar Six Senses Luxury resort, but the project, which could set Salt Cay back on track, has been delayed for myriad reasons since talk got started seriously nearly a decade ago. As of this writing, the government still hasn't given this project the green light.

There has been talk that Beaches Resort was going to close up shop on Providenciales. An ongoing legal dispute over taxes between the resort and government prompted a series of announcements signaling the end. In June 2019, the resort's management issued a statement advising that the threat of closure had been rescinded and the family-friendly resort would continue to operate.

Grace Bay Beach is also expected to see a $100 million–plus five-star, seven-story branded resort next to the Coral Gardens resort.

Kids and Families

Most family-friendly activities are on Provo, but the rest of the islands—especially Grand Turk—provide plenty of other options.

ACCOMMODATIONS

Many of the accommodations on Provo and the rest of the Turks and Caicos are in condo-style resorts or private rental villas. These are ideal for families because they offer more space, laundry facilities, and full kitchens for cooking meals. Babysitters can also be arranged to look after young ones while parents enjoy evenings out.

IN PROVO

Coral Gardens is great for off-the-beach snorkeling; kids can see colorful fish in waist-deep water. Those eight years of age or older can try Snuba, a surface-supplied diving experience. Without getting wet, little ones may experience the underwater world by climbing on board the *Undersea Explorer,* a semisubmarine that is even regularly visited by a resident mermaid! On dry land The Bight's **public playground** has swing sets and slides, along with bathrooms. There are **banana boat rides and parasailing, minigolf,** and horseback riding. But a sure thing for families is to contact SURFside Ocean Academy, an outdoor adventure company and licensed school specializing in kids' camps, eco-adventures, and water sports.

Big Blue Unlimited is the most comprehensive water-sports and ecotour outfit in the Turks and Caicos Islands, specializing in stand-up paddleboarding, kayaking, kiteboarding, snorkel tours, diving, and more.

OUTER ISLANDS

On Middle Caicos families can visit one of the largest limestone cave systems in the Caribbean, with its several species of resident bats. **Mudjin Harbour** and Dragon Cay Resort offer hiking trails along the cliffs that are part of the Crossing Place Trail. Within the trail system is a hidden staircase leading to a "secret" beach.

North Caicos has the best plantation ruins to be explored. Wades Green still has remains of the main house, slave quarters, gardens, and rock walls, as well as old cauldrons.

The **Turks and Caicos National Museum can be found on Grand Turk. Gibbs Cay** is always a favorite of kids, offering them a chance to play and to hold gentle stingrays on a secluded "Gilligan's Island." Horseback riding is also available on Grand Turk.

Chapter 2

TRAVEL SMART
TURKS & CAICOS

Updated by
Jessica Robertson

★ **CAPITAL**
Cockburn Town, Grand Turk

♀ **POPULATION**
38,000

💬 **LANGUAGE**
English

$ **CURRENCY**
U.S. dollar

☎ **COUNTRY CODE**
649

⚠ **EMERGENCIES**
999 or 911

🚗 **DRIVING**
On the left side

⚡ **ELECTRICITY**
120 volts, 60 Hz (North American–style)

🕓 **TIME**
Eastern Standard Time (same as New York); 3 hours ahead of Los Angeles

🌐 **WEB RESOURCES**
www.visittci.com, www.turksand-caicosTourism.com, www.where-whenhow.com, turksandcaicos-reservations.com

What to Know Before You Visit the Turks and Caicos Islands

Should you tip? How do you get here? Should you exchange money? What side of the road should you drive on? You may have a few questions before you head out on vacation to this Caribbean paradise. We've got answers and a few tips to help you make the most of your visit to the Turks and Caicos Islands. Read on to ensure your island adventure is smooth sailing.

FLY INTO PROVIDENCIALES

All international flights go through Providenciales, so your adventure starts here. You'll have to take a small inter-island flight or a ferry to get to one of the other islands. Several major airlines fly nonstop to Provo from United States cities including Atlanta, Charlotte, Miami, and New York, although carriers and schedules can vary seasonally.

HOP TO THE SMALLER ISLANDS

You can make air connections on InterCaribbean or Caicos Express Airways to four other islands from Provo: Grand Turk, South Caicos, North Caicos, and Salt Cay. There are also several ferries daily between Provo and North Caicos; a causeway connects North Caicos to Middle Caicos. There is a ferry service between Provo and South Caicos two days a week. You can reach Salt Cay by ferry—but only when the weather is good.

THERE'S NO NEED TO EXCHANGE MONEY

The U.S. dollar is the official currency here, making the Turks and Caicos Islands an easy choice for American travelers who don't want to spend time calculating an exchange rate.

DRIVING IS ON THE LEFT

You can get by on Provo without a car, especially if you are staying on Grace Bay, but rentals are relatively inexpensive, ranging from around $50/day and up. On the other islands they hover around $100/day. Gas is expensive, though, and most often must be paid for in cash. And don't forget that driving is on the left, British-style!

PLAN FOR HURRICANE SEASON

The Atlantic hurricane season spans June to November, and the peak season is in September. Look for hotels and resorts that offer storm/hurricane guarantees. Although they rarely allow refunds, most guarantees do let you rebook later if a storm strikes.

IT'S EXPENSIVE, BUT THERE ARE WAYS TO SAVE

Yes, a vacation to the Turks and Caicos can cost a pretty penny. But many resorts offer free nights and extra perks during the off-season. Rates are lower a block or two from the beach.

Be sure to check if the hotel is part of a package deal, rolling airfare and accommodation into one. The website turksandcaicos-reservations.com is a good place to start. Staying in a condo-style accommodation or a villa means you can cook some meals yourself. Note that airlines will accept a cooler of food as long as perishables are frozen and vacuum-sealed; customs will allow it to enter.

TIPPING IS EXPECTED

Check your bill to see if a 10% service charge has been added. If it has, you may supplement it by 5% or even more if service was outstanding. If no service charge has been added, then tip as you would at home, about 15%. Be aware that when a large party dines together, a hefty service fee may be added at the end. The current government tax is 12%, which is mandatory for all diners. Taxi drivers also expect a tip, about 10% of your fare. Excursion and water-sports staff appreciate tips for their efforts as well; use your discretion.

THERE ARE SOME RULES FOR WEDDINGS

The residency requirement is 24 hours, after which you can apply for a marriage license at the registrar's office. You must present a passport, birth certificate, and proof of current marital status. The current fee is $100. Using a local planner will be helpful. Many resorts now have their own in-house service. Or you may try the most experienced local company, Nila Destinations (*www.niladestinations.com*).

ARRANGE TRANSPORTATION IN ADVANCE

Taxis will be at the Provo airport, but it is important to arrange transportation before your arrival in Grand Turk, South Caicos, North Caicos, and Salt Cay; your accommodation will assist you. If you are heading over just for the day, contact your lunch destination and ask them to assist you. Note that taxis are expensive.

VILLAS, CONDOS, RESORTS...TAKE YOUR PICK

Most of the accommodation along Providenciales' Grace Bay is condo-style, with extra space for families and fully equipped kitchens and laundry facilities. However, you will also find a few hotel room–style resorts to choose from. The majority of places to stay on the outer islands are small inns. What you give up in luxury, however, you gain back tenfold in island charm. Another alternative to a resort-style vacation is staying in one of the numerous villas that dot the islands.

Getting Here

The vast majority of visitors to the Turks and Caicos Islands arrive by air on one of several major carriers, landing on Providenciales—more commonly known as Provo—but some come by private plane. Then there are others who come in by boat, either by cruise ship to Grand Turk or by private yacht. No matter, once on land, you'll want to rent a car or take a taxi to get around. The island of Providenciales is relatively flat and has no traffic lights; most places are no farther than 20 minutes apart, and if you are staying in the Grace Bay area, walking or using one of your hotel's loaner bicycles should get you where you need to go. On Grand Turk it's fun to get around by bicycle or scooter; the island is small and the roads are in good condition. On tiny Salt Cay, Parrot Cay, and Pine Cay, the preferred mode of transportation is a golf cart. Conveniently, a ferry service connects Provo to North Caicos and also Provo to South Caicos; the rest of the islands require a boat or plane to reach them, though you can now drive across a causeway to get from North Caicos to Middle Caicos.

✈ Air

The main gateway into the Turks and Caicos Islands is Providenciales International Airport (PLS)—this is where all international flights come into the country. For private planes, Provo Air Center is a full-service FBO (fixed base operator) offering refueling, maintenance, and short-term storage, as well as on-site customs and immigration clearance, a lounge, and concierge services. Even if you're going on to other islands in the chain, you'll have to stop on Provo first, then take another flight onward.

AIRPORTS

All scheduled international flights to Turks and Caicos Islands arrive in Providenciales International Airport (PLS), so this is where you'll go through immigration and customs. Make sure you have all of your paperwork completely filled out, as immigration lines can be slow; in fact, on a busy day you will wait 30 to 40 minutes from the time you disembark to the time you pass through customs.

For those wishing for a little less stress while traveling, Provo's airport offers the VIP Flyers Club. For a fee, you get speedy check-in, priority through security, and a tranquil waiting room with TV, Wi-Fi, and snacks. It's much nicer than contending with the crowds, which on the weekends fill the departure terminal both upstairs and downstairs. The cost is $200 for the first family member and $75 for each additional person; children under two are free. If you wish to simply use the lounge, there is a $50 fee per person, but availability depends on the number of expedited travelers.

AIRPORT TRANSFERS

If you're staying at a hotel or resort on Provo, there will be a representative just outside the arrivals door to greet you; you'll then be put into a taxi for your transfer. A few hotels are allowed to offer their own personalized shuttle service, but most are required to use the regular service; Amanyara and Parrot Cay, because of their locations away from the main hub, offer such a service. Even if you have not made prior arrangements, there are plenty of taxis around to meet each flight. To the main area of Grace Bay Road, expect to pay around $33 per couple one way. You can also have a car rental waiting at the airport; almost all of the rental car companies offer this service. If someone is picking you up, they may wait for you in the nearby small parking lot that charges $1 an hour.

On South Caicos and Grand Turk you should make your transportation arrangements before arrival. On Pine Cay someone will pick you up in a golf cart. On Salt Cay you could walk if need be.

FLIGHTS

Several major airlines fly nonstop to Providenciales from the United States, although carriers and schedules can vary seasonally. You can fly nonstop from Atlanta (Delta), Charlotte (American), Miami (American), New York–JFK (Delta and JetBlue) and Newark–EWR (United). Canadian cities can be accessed via WestJet and Air Canada. There's also a flight from London on British Airways via Antigua.

Several other parts of the Caribbean are connected to Turks and Caicos through interCaribbean Airways. Flights from Nassau can be found on BahamasAir and interCaribbean Airways. Once on Provo, inter-Caribbean and Caicos Express Airways fly to North Caicos, South Caicos, Grand Turk, and Salt Cay.

CHARTER FLIGHTS

Caicos Express can fly you from Provo to anywhere you need to go in the Turks and Caicos (or the Caribbean, for that matter). Although the airline has some scheduled flights, most of their work consists

Getting Here

of charters. Charters can be expensive because you pay per flight, not per passenger. However, if your group is going to a smaller island, or wants to combine your trip with other Caribbean islands, it might be the best way to go.

🚗 Car

You can most definitely get by without renting a car while staying in the Grace Bay area on Provo, but outside of that, you will want one. If this is your first trip, it's wise to plan on renting a car for at least a couple of days for some exploration; then you can decide whether you need it the rest of the week. Taxis can be expensive, with each round-trip equal in cost to a daily car rental, but if you feel uncomfortable driving on the left or if you want to go out and not worry about having too much to drink, then a taxi is the best option. A car is really the only way to go if you want to do a lot of exploring; taxis will not wait for you in isolated areas.

If you travel to North Caicos or Middle Caicos, you almost always have to rent a car, because everything is so spread out. Of course there is the option of a bicycle tour, but if you're on your own, go with a car. On the other islands,

you can get by just walking or taking an occasional taxi.

To rent, you need to have a valid U.S. driver's license, and you need to be 25 or older.

GASOLINE

Gasoline is much more expensive than in the United States. Expect to pay about $3 to $4 more a gallon. There are numerous gas stations around Provo, and many accept cash only.

PARKING

Parking in the Turks and Caicos is easy and free. Grace Bay has numerous public parking lots, so those not staying in the area have easy access. And all the resorts and restaurants offer free parking; even those that are gated have general public areas to park. North and Middle Caicos also have parking areas at all the restaurants and places to stay.

RENTAL CARS

Avis, Budget, Hertz, and Thrifty have offices on Provo, but you might like to support the local businesses by trying agencies such as Grace Bay Car Rentals, Rent a Buggy, Tropical Auto Rentals, and Caicos Wheels, among others.

On Provo small cars start at around $39 per day, and a small SUV averages about $69 to $85 a day. Almost all rental agencies in the Turks and

Caicos will drop off a car at the airport or your hotel. You can then leave it at the airport upon its return. Otherwise, you'll return it to a nearby off-site rental lot and they'll shuttle you over to the airport.

There are several car-rental agencies on Grand Turk. They will meet you at the airport or the cruise-ship terminal, have you sign the paperwork while standing on the sidewalk, and have you on your way in a matter of minutes. There's also the alternative, a golf cart from Nathan's Golf Cart Rental. No matter what your choice may be, call ahead to make arrangements.

Al's Rent-a-Car, Caribbean Cruisin' and Pelican Car Rentals offer service on North Caicos.

ROAD CONDITIONS
Most of Leeward Highway is a smooth, four-lane divided highway complete with roundabouts. However, the paved two-lane roads through the settlements on Providenciales can be quite rough. A high-clearance vehicle is recommended if you want to head to Malcolm's Beach or if you're staying in the Turtle Tail area; those two areas have graded roads, often with many potholes to navigate around. Strangely enough, the less-traveled roads in Grand

Turk and the family islands are, in general, smooth and paved.

RULES OF THE ROAD
Driving here is on the left side of the road, British-style; when pulling out into traffic, remember to look to your right. Give way to anyone already on a roundabout; be cautious even if you're on what appears to be the primary road as some of the roundabouts on Leeward Highway in particular are so small that you may run right through them without even realizing. And take them slowly. The maximum speed is 40 mph (64 kph), 20 mph (30 kph) through settlements. Use extra caution at night, as drinking and driving, though illegal, does happen—some people forget they must follow the rules when they are relaxed and on vacation.

⌂ Ferry
Daily scheduled ferry service between Provo and North Caicos is offered by Caribbean Cruisin', with several departures from Walkin Marina in Leeward. There's also a service between Provo and South Caicos twice a week. In addition, you can reach Salt Cay by ferry, but only when the weather is good; don't count on it! Your best bet is booking a direct flight from Providenciales with

Getting Here

interCaribbean Airways to be sure to get there on a specific date. The private islands within the chain are reached by boat, either a private charter or one that's scheduled through an associated resort.

🚕 Taxi

On Provo, taxi rates are metered and are based on two people traveling together, but each additional person is charged extra. Fares for children are only half price— but always ask first. You may also be charged for more than two bags per person. Unless you have a rental car waiting for you at the airport, you will be taken to your resort by taxi. If you're using a taxi as your primary mode of transportation and you find one you are happy with, get the driver's direct cell number. You will have to call for service later on; taxis don't hang out anywhere except the airport, especially late at night. And remember, drivers are a great source of information about the islands, so be sure to have them fill you in on what's what. It's customary to tip about 10% per ride.

Renting a car is preferable, as there are only a few taxis available on Grand Turk, North Caicos, and South Caicos. If you want to get around Salt Cay, a taxi is really not necessary. Ask your accommodation or tour operator who might be around to greet you, and know that you can cover most of the island on foot.

Before You Go

⊕ Passport

A valid passport is required for all visitors, and everyone must have an ongoing or return ticket. Visas are not necessary for North Americans or EU citizens. Be sure to check with your consulate to see if one is needed for your travel; most visitors transit through the United States, where clearing customs is a necessity.

🛂 Visa

Visas are NOT required for travelers with a passport issued by the United States to a Caribbean nation, nearly all European countries, much of South America, and parts of Asia. Passport-holders from the Middle East, African nations, most of Asia, and parts of Central and South America must apply for a tourist visa.

💉 Immunizations

No specific immunizations or vaccinations are required for visits to the Caribbean islands, but children should be up-to-date on their routine immunizations (DTaP, MMR, influenza, chicken pox, and polio).

📅 When to Go

Peak season in the Turks and Caicos runs from American Thanksgiving through mid-April, when prices average 20% to 50% higher than in the summer. July and August are becoming more and more popular.

The off-season in Providenciales is getting shorter and shorter—those places that do still opt to shut down do so for a month only (usually September), and Grand Turk's business follows the cruise ship schedules so they open year-round.

CLIMATE

Daytime temperatures in the Turks and Caicos Islands range from 75°F to 85°F year-round, except during the hottest months of August and September, when temperatures jump into the 90s and above. Evening temperatures can sometimes dip to 50°F. The islands are among the driest in the Caribbean region, with an average of 350 days of sunshine. Water temperatures range from the high 70s in the winter to the low 80s in the summer. Hurricane season runs from June through November, but very few storms pass through until late August.

Essentials

🌐 Customs and Duties

Customs in the Turks and Caicos is straightforward and simple. On the flight you will receive two forms. The first is your customs declaration, one per family. The second form is a Turks & Caicos Embarkation and Disembarkation Form. Both forms should be filled out completely before you disembark to avoid delays. If you are 17 years of age or older, you are allowed to bring in free of import duty one liter of spirits or two liters of wine; either 200 cigarettes or 100 cigarillos or 50 cigars or 250 grams of smoking tobacco; and 50 grams of perfume or 0.25 liters of eau de toilette. If you have $10,000 or more in cash, you must declare it.

The immigration entrance lines can be long, especially when several planes arrive in quick succession.

🍴 Dining

Turks and Caicos has almost every kind of restaurant you might wish for, especially on Provo. From small beach shacks to gorgeous upscale dining rooms and everything in between, this destination is a gastronomical delight. There are cafés and delis, international restaurants, and some of the best chefs in the Caribbean; what you won't find is fast food or restaurant chains. Typically, the restaurants offer wide choices, so even vegetarians and picky eaters will find something appealing on most menus. If a restaurant does not have a children's menu, the chef will usually be willing to make something to suit your kids, so don't be afraid to ask. Restaurants cater primarily to American tastes (especially on American holidays). Dinner usually starts a little later than Americans are used to; most restaurants are full by 8. Most restaurants are upscale and expensive, though you will also find a few slightly less expensive, more casual options. A typical meal averages $80 to $120 per couple without a bottle of wine, much more if you add that in.

Unless otherwise noted, restaurants listed are open daily for lunch and dinner.

TURKS AND CAICOS CUISINE

The most typical foods on these islands come from the sea. Grouper and snapper are usually the catch of the day, often grilled with jerk spices. But be sure to ask whether the fish is fresh caught or brought in. In season, spiny lobster is brought in daily—as long as the seas aren't too rough—and used in many ways, in addition to the more familiar Thermidor and broiled. One favorite food in the Turks and Caicos is conch; it even has its own festival in November, with recipe and tasting competitions. Conch is made every way imaginable, including the typical cracked conch and conch fritters. Macaroni and cheese, fried plantain, and peas 'n' rice are common side dishes, especially in spots that serve local food. Coleslaw here even has a Caribbean twist, often including pineapple or mango. For a typical island breakfast, order boiled fish with grits.

PAYING

Most major credit cards (Visa, Discover, and Master-Card—Diner's Club less so) are accepted in almost all restaurants. American Express is accepted in far fewer establishments. It's smart to bring more than one type of credit card with you just in case. Call your credit-card company to see if they charge an additional foreign transaction fee; most add 2.5%, even though all transactions in the TCI are in U.S. dollars. If a place takes cash only, it's noted on the review.

RESERVATIONS AND DRESS

We mention reservations only when they are essential (there's no other way you'll ever get a table) or when they are not accepted. We mention dress only when men are required to wear a jacket or a jacket and tie, which is currently not the case anywhere in the country. Although you don't need fancy dresses or even long pants at most places, you will look out of place in a T-shirt and tennis shoes.

WINES, BEER, AND SPIRITS

You can expect to pay more than you would at home. Imported U.S. beer is particularly expensive; a case of Bud Light or Miller Light can run $65 to $75. For beer lovers, it's always fun to try something new: the brewery for Turks Head, which is a heavier-tasting beer than its American counterparts, offers tours. In addition, some other Caribbean brands are available in local stores, including Kalik from the Bahamas and Jamaica's Red Stripe. Of the rums, Caicos Rum is made for the Turks and Caicos and bottled here. Turks and Caicos' Bambarra Rum is a bargain compared with other rums. Remember that although you can always buy alcohol at a bar, it's against the law to purchase it from a store on Sunday.

Essentials

➕ Health and Safety

Turks and Caicos is a safe and healthy destination. The tap water may not be the best tasting, but it is safe to drink. Food-safety standards are high, and you rarely hear of upset stomachs or outbreaks of food poisoning. If you're feeling unwell, there are very good hospitals on both Provo and Grand Turk, as well as private health care clinics. Grace Bay Beach is usually clean and clear of any pests. There are no poisonous snakes in the Turks and Caicos, or any other animals that may be dangerous. Be sure not to go off the beaten path when exploring around the islands, however, as there are two trees in particular that act like poison ivy; they are difficult to identify, so it is best to stay out of the bush. In the water, be careful not to touch the coral, as a particular variety will burn your skin upon contact. You also must watch out for the lionfish; they are beautiful but very dangerous.

OVER-THE-COUNTER REMEDIES

Most of the supplies are similar to those in the United Kingdom, United States, and Canada. You can find all the major brands that you are used to readily available around Provo, though prices are higher than at home. Over-the-counter drugs can be found at pharmacies and supermarkets, and even at small convenience stores. If you plan to travel beyond Provo, however, you may wish to stock up on necessities. Supplies may be slimmer on the less developed islands. Sunscreen is especially expensive in the Grace Bay area; it's more reasonably priced at the IGA supermarket. If you need bug spray, get something with at least 25% DEET; off-brand spray is readily available. If you forget to buy it and find yourself at dusk with no-see-ums biting, ask your servers at the restaurant; there's a good chance they'll have a bottle on hand.

🛏 Lodging

Accommodations in the Turks and Caicos are not inexpensive, and though there's a wide range of price options, your accommodations will most likely be your greatest expense. If you've prepared for this, you'll find this to be one of the most fabulous vacations you've ever taken. Most resort-style lodgings are made up of individually owned condos placed in the hotel's rental pool when the owners are not in residence. Alternatively, there are a few hotels without all the bells and whistles and no kitchens. There are also two all-inclusive resorts on Provo: the family-oriented Beaches and the adults-only Club Med. The outer islands have more basic accommodations, albeit with a lot more island flair. Providenciales also has an incredible array of private villas to choose from. This is an excellent option for a family, as they offer privacy, added room, and usually work out on the less expensive end. Take a look at VRBO and HomeAway to see the selection.

If your accommodations don't include baby equipment or you need additional baby items, contact Happy Na and have it delivered.

APARTMENT AND HOUSE RENTALS

Villa and condo rentals are quite common in the Turks and Caicos; in fact, they make up the majority of accommodations. On Provo, many of the villas are ultra-luxurious getaways and have prices to match. On the smaller islands, villas are basic and comfortable and tend to be more economical alternatives. Private apartment rentals can save you money but tend to be more residential, with fewer services. On any of the islands they are easy to book, and management companies will send a representative to meet you at

the airport as well as assist you as a concierge might.

HOTELS

Hotels and resorts in Turks and Caicos run the gamut from small inns with basic accommodations to full-service, private-island resorts. There are a few classy boutique hotels on Provo, but no large chain hotels. Parrot Cay and the Meridian Club on Pine Cay are private-island resorts with all the pampering and privileges you'd expect with the high prices. Amanyara is in a category all its own, offering the greatest degree of seclusion and privacy, with a price tag at the top end of the scale.

💲 Money

Prices quoted are in U.S. dollars, which is the official currency in the islands.

Major credit cards and traveler's checks are accepted at many establishments. Bring small-denomination bills to the less populated islands—but bring enough cash to hold you over; many of the smaller islands deal in cash only and have no ATMs. Some islands don't even have banks, so get some cash while on Provo if heading elsewhere.

Prices *throughout this guide* are given for adults. Reduced

Essentials

rates are almost always available for children, students, and senior citizens.

ATMS AND BANKS

On Provo there are ATMs at all bank branches (Scotiabank and First Caribbean), at the airport, at Graceway IGA Supermarket, Ports of Call shopping center, and at Graceway Gourmet IGA. There are also Scotiabank and First Caribbean branches on Grand Turk.

🔲 Packing

Most accommodations in Provo have washers and dryers in the units, so pack light. You can wash your clothes conveniently at your whim and dry swimsuits before repacking. If your resort doesn't offer laundry facilities or a laundry service, you'll find a dry cleaner/laundry facility next to Beaches on the Lower Bight Road. There is also a dry cleaner in the complex just south of Graceway Gourmet IGA, as well as one on the extension of Leeward Highway.

If you travel with a carry-on, remember that airlines allow only 3-ounce bottles of liquids. Don't worry: it's not too expensive to buy sunscreen at the Graceway IGA supermarket. There's really not a huge bug problem in the Turks and Caicos, but sometimes after a rain or at dusk you might get a bite or two, so you will end up needing to bring or buy some repellent.

Almost all the resorts and villas have hair dryers and give you shampoo, conditioner, and a small box of laundry detergent. Check ahead to be certain. "Bring half the clothes and twice the money"—words to live by.

💲 Taxes

The departure tax is included in the cost of your airline ticket, so you don't need to worry about having additional cash ready at the airport. Restaurants and hotels add a 12% government tax. Hotels also typically add 10% to 15% for service.

On the Calendar

January: The Winter Wahoo Fishing Tournament is held at Turtle Cove.

February: The annual Valentine's Day Cup sailing race is held at Bamberra Beach on Middle Caicos.

March: Paddy's Pub Crawl is always held on St. Patrick's Day. The Fishing Fools Wahoo open tournament is held in late March, as is The Wine Cellar's Annual Golf and Fishing Tournament. The Rake n' Scrape festival held on North Caicos is fantastic for music lovers.

April: The Easter Monday Kite Flying Competition is held on Providenciales the day after Easter.

May: The South Caicos Regatta is held during the last weekend in May. Cinco de Mayo is celebrated along the docks of Turtle Cove on May 5.

June: On Provo, there is often a Battle of the Bands in Turtle Cove Marina, and the Middle Caicos Crab Fest is held at the end of the month. The Fools Regatta takes place in Grace Bay; kids compete aboard the smaller Picos or Hobie Cats, and adults race in different classes aboard their own personal vessels. Games and food invite the whole community down for some great beach fun, perfect for the whole family. (Visit ⊕ *www.tcisailing. com* or the Provo Sailing Club on Facebook.)

July: The annual Windvibes Kiteboarding Tournament is held in July. Both the Caicos Classic IGFA Billfish Release Tournament and the Heineken Game Fishing Tournament take place in July on Provo.

September: September is a quiet month when residents get their children back into school.

October: Annual Halloween parties abound around the islands for both kids and adults.

November: Many restaurants participate in Provo's annual Gourmet Safari in November. The annual Turks and Caicos Conch Festival is held on the last Saturday of November, offering live bands, a conch recipe competition, and activities for the kids. It's a Provo event that is not to be missed if you are on the island (⊕ *www.conchfestival.com* ☎ *649/241–9950*).

December: The Maskanoo Street party and parade is held on Boxing Day (December 26) on Grace Bay Road in Provo. This is a must-see celebration, along with the Junkanoo New Year's Eve street party hosting live bands, parades, and fireworks.

Great Itineraries

Three Days in Turks and Caicos

DAY ONE

Fly into Providenciales, where most of the tourists end up at least on their first visit to the Turks and Caicos. This casual, sleepy island that still manages to deliver high-end service will be your home base for the weekend. By the time you get checked in to your resort or villa, you'll be more than ready to sink your toes in the powder white sand and take a dip in the brilliant blue ocean you spotted as you were flying in.

Rent a car and explore the island. Taxis are pricey, and depending on where you are staying and how much you want to see and do, you'll want a car. It's not hard to navigate your way around the island. Signs are lacking, but stop anywhere and someone will point you in the right direction. Just remember to stay on the left!

Pick up a picnic lunch from the IGA deli or stop in along the way at any local restaurant that catches your eye. Most beaches on Provo have public access and even free parking, so feel free to visit as many as you want. Explore the Cheshire Hall plantation ruins. Dating back to the 1700s, what remains of this limestone structure provides valuable insight into this small country's history and is also a great spot for naturalists interested in the local flora and fauna. Then make your way across to Chalk Sound for one of the most breathtaking views you've ever seen. If you have time, rent a kayak for an hour from Neptune Villas and explore the sound.

Coming back, go to Malcolm's Beach at Northwest Point Grace Bay Beach. Chances are you'll be staying in that area somewhere. Sundowners on the beach are the order of the day—just about every beach-front restaurant, resort and bar offers a spectacular view of the ocean. There are well over a hundred restaurants on Provo and with only a few nights, you'll have to choose wisely to enjoy the best the island has to offer. Coco Bistro is consistently one of the top rated restaurants on the island. You'll need to make reservations well in advance—as soon as you book your flights if it's high season. If you didn't get in, the second best (some would say it should be your first choice) option is to pop in to CocoVan airstream bistro right next door. It's casual, but the food is amazing and reservations aren't necessary.

DAY TWO

If you're here in winter (January through April), plan a day trip to Salt Cay to go whale-watching. A number of outfitters, including the dive shops in Grand Turk, offer this incredible opportunity to see humpback whales up close as they migrate past the islands. If the conditions are right, you might even get the chance to hop in the ocean with them.

Otherwise, take the ferry over to North Caicos, rent a car and explore. You'll want to prearrange your car rental on the Provo side. Caribbean Cruising runs the ferry and also offers car rentals so inquire when you check in. While it's fun to run around, and there are so few roads in North and Middle that you'd have a hard time getting lost, the sites are best appreciated with a guide who can provide the history and culture lesson to go with it.

On a tour, you'll almost always see flamingos in the aptly named Flamingo Pond. Take binoculars as they're quite a distance from the viewpoint. You'll also explore the Kew, an old village that seems to have stopped in time. This is where you'll find Wade's Plantation; call ahead to arrange access and a tour.

Grab lunch at whichever spot is open and close when your stomach starts growling. You really can't go wrong—the food here is fresh and tasty. But if it's the slow season, you may have to stop at more than one spot to find somewhere open. North Caicos still observes the high and low seasons and for six months of the year many places that cater to tourists are shuttered up.

Next, head for the causeway that connects North and Middle Caicos. If it's open, stop in at the bright-colored Roadside Caboose just before you cross over to Middle for a cool tour of the garden and another opportunity to step back in time. Dragon Cay Resort is one of the first (and only) places to get a cool drink and lunch if you're still hungry. It also offers one of the most spectacular views in the entire country— looking down on Mudjin Harbour with its majestic cliffs and beautiful beach.

If you're not traveling with a guide you'll want to arrange in advance for a guide to take you on a tour of the Conch Bar Caves. Be sure to leave enough time to get back to catch the final ferry. Whether you did Salt Cay whale-watching or North and Middle Caicos, you'll be back in time for a quick shower and an early dinner. Drive into Blue Hills for a very local dinner at Da Conch

Great Itineraries

Shack. Stick your toes in the sand and catch another glorious Turks & Caicos sunset.

DAY THREE

Get up early to stroll along the never-ending Grace Bay Beach, enjoying a sunrise view and early morning ocean dip. You'll work up an appetite, so head out for brunch at Bay Bistro, where you'll find great value and more ocean views to pair with a mimosa.

A tropical island vacation wouldn't be complete without a spa treatment. Many resorts have in-house spas, but Spa Tropique is consistently good and has a number of locations around town for added convenience. They'll even come to your hotel room or villa. After you've been pampered, make a quick dash into the main hub of Grace Bay to do some shopping. Find a spot to park your car, and you can easily walk to all of the different plazas, where more and more shops offering locally made wares are popping up on Provo. FOTTAC has a great selection, as does Art Provo; both are in the Regent Village. There are also a few small craft markets, much of them offering T-shirts and other trinkets as well as metal art brought in from Haiti.

Plan enough time to visit Five Cays before your flight out. Bugaloo's and Omar's Beach Hut both offer a final taste of yummy island food, a locally brewed beer, and an opportunity to sink your feet in the sand until the final moment you have to head to the airport to catch your flight back home.

Contacts

Air

AIRPORT INFORMATION Pine Cay Airport (PIC). ☎ 649/941–7011 *Meridian Club.* **Providenciales International Airport (PLS).** ✉ *Airport Rd., Airport* ☎ 649/946–4420. **South Caicos Airport** *(XSC).* ☎ 649/946–4999. **Turks & Caicos Islands Airport Authority.** ✉ *Providenciales International Airport (PLS), Airport Rd., Airport* ☎ 649/946–4420 *general inquiries* ⊕ *www.tciairports.com.* **VIP Flyers Club.** ✉ *Providenciales International Airport, Airport Rd., Airport* ☎ 649/946–4000, 866/587–6168 ⊕ *www.vipflyersclub.com.*

AIRLINE CONTACTS Bahamas Air. ✉ *Providenciales International Airport, Airport Rd., Airport* ☎ 800/222–4262 *U.S. toll-free* ⊕ *bahamasair.com.* **Caicos Express Airways.** ✉ *Southern Shores Plaza, Leeward Hwy., Downtown* ☎ 649/941–5730 ⊕ *caicosexpress.com.* **inter-Caribbean Airways.** ✉ *Airport Rd., Airport* ☎ 649/946–4999 ⊕ *intercaribbean.com.*

Car

CAR RENTAL CONTACTS ON PROVIDENCIALES Avis. ☎ 649/946–4705 *airport location,* 649/941–7557 *Grace Bay location* ⊕ *www.avis.tc.* **Budget.** ✉ *Butterfield*

Square, Downtown ⊹ *Downtown on your left just before Airport Rd.* ☎ 649/946–4079 ⊕ *www.budget.com.* **Caicos Wheels.** ✉ *Ports of Call Plaza, Grace Bay Rd., Grace Bay* ☎ 954/363–1119 *US Vonage,* 649/946–8302 *local number* ⊕ *www.caicoswheels.com.* **Grace Bay Car Rentals.** ✉ *Grace Bay Plaza, Grace Bay Rd., Grace Bay* ⊹ *Next door to Bella Luna* ☎ 649/941–8500 *main hotline,* 649/946–4404 ⊕ *www.gracebaycarrentals.com.* **Paradise Scooter and Auto.** ✉ *Grace Bay Plaza, Grace Bay Rd., Grace Bay* ☎ 649/333–3333 ⊕ *www.paradisescooters.tc.* **Rent a Buggy.** ✉ *1081 Leeward Hwy., Right next door to Mac Motors, which is right next door to Central Plaza, Downtown* ☎ 649/946–4158 *landline* ⊕ *www.rentabuggy.tc.* **Scooter Bob's.** ⊹ *Located right after the Marina entrance, next door to Turtle Cove Inn* ☎ 649/946–4684 ⊕ *www.scooterbobstci.com.* **Thrifty Car Rental.** ✉ *Providenciales International Airport, Airport Rd.* ☎ 649/946–4475 ⊕ *www.lac.thrifty.com.* **Tropical Auto Rentals.** ✉ *Tropicana Plaza, Leeward Hwy., Grace Bay* ⊹ *At the junction of Leeward Hwy. and Sand Castle Dr.* ☎ 649/946–5300 ⊕ *www.tropicalautorental.com.*

Contacts

CAR RENTAL CONTACTS ON GRAND TURK Island Autos.
☎ *649/232–0933 mobile.*
Nathan's Golf Cart Rental. ✉ *Outside cruise-terminal gates, Grand Turk Cruise Terminal* ☎ *649/231–4856 mobile.* **Tony's Car Rental.** ✉ *Outside cruise-terminal gates, Grand Turk Cruise Terminal* ☎ *649/231–1806 main line* ⊕ *www.tonyscarrental.com.*

CAR RENTAL CONTACTS ON NORTH CAICOS Al's Rent-A-Car.
✉ *Ferry dock, Sandy Point* ☎ *649/241–1276* ⊕ *www.alsrentacar.com/.* **Pelican Car Rentals.** ☎ *649/245–9449 Donna* ⊕ *www.pelicanrentalstci.com.*

🕛 Ferry
CONTACTS Caribbean Cruisin'. ✉ *Walkin' Marina, Heaving Down Rock, Leeward Hwy. E, Leeward* ☎ *649/946–5406, 649/231–4191* ⊕ *caribbeancruisin.tc.* **Salt Cay Community Ferry.** ⚓ *Departs from Deane's Dock* ☎ *649/241–1009.*

🛏 Lodging
CONTACTS HomeAway. ⊕ *www.homeaway.com.* **Turks and Caicos Reservations.** ☎ *649/432–1708, 877/774–5486* ⊕ *www.turksandcaicosreservations.tc.* **Vacation Rentals by Owner (VRBO).** ⊕ *www.VRBO.com.*

📍 Visitor Information
TURKS AND CAICOS ISLANDS INFORMATION TCI Tourism. ☎ *649/946–4970, 800/241–0824* ⊕ *www.TurksandCaicosTourism.com.* **Turks & Caicos Islands Tourist Board, Providenciales.** ✉ *Regent House, Ventura Dr., Grace Bay* ☎ *649/946–4970* ⊕ *www.turksandcaicostourism.com.* **Turks & Caicos Islands Tourist Board, Grand Turk.** ✉ *Front St., Grand Turk Cruise Terminal* ☎ *649/946–2321* ⊕ *www.turksandcaicostourism.com.*

Chapter 3

PROVIDENCIALES

Updated by
Jessica Robertson

◉ Sights   🍴 Restaurants   🛏 Hotels   🛍 Shopping   🍸 Nightlife

★★★★★   ★★★★★   ★★★★★   ★★★★☆   ★★★★☆

WELCOME TO PROVIDENCIALES

TOP REASONS TO GO

★ **Grace Bay Beach.** This beach is the Turks and Caicos' biggest draw. The soft, powder-white sand with crystal-clear seas seems to go on for as far as the eye can see.

★ **Snorkel, Scuba, and Snuba.** The world's third-largest reef system here makes for an underwater dream. Beginners and experts alike can snorkel right off the shoreline on the Bight Reef.

★ **Fine Dining.** Although the food is incredible across the island, what really stands out is the variety of settings. A top choice is the ever-busy Coco Bistro.

★ **Water Sports.** On Grace Bay you can parasail, ride a banana boat, sail a Hobie Cat, take out a kayak or paddleboard, or learn to windsurf. Long Bay Beach is the newest hot spot for kite surfers.

★ **The Perfect Night Out.** At sunset, have a drink anywhere along Grace Bay Beach, whether at one of the many seaside bars or restaurants or with a bottle you have uncorked in your very own private condo.

1 Grace Bay. Stunning beach and Provo's top attraction.

2 The Bight. Known for snorkeling and its fish fry.

3 Turtle Cove. The end of the Bight is home to excursion companies.

4 Leeward. Upscale residential neighborhood with private villas.

5 Long Bay. Ride horseback on the beach here.

6 Venetian Road. Path that leads to Turtle Tail beaches.

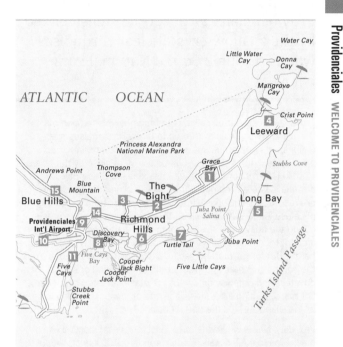

7 Turtle Tail. Quiet area with pretty vacation villas.

8 Discovery Bay. Land across the bay that's good for hiking.

9 Downtown. Commercial area with a cool brewery.

10 Airport. On your way from downtown, stop at local restaurants.

11 Five Cays. Home to the famous Bugaloo's beach shack.

12 Chalk Sound. The national park will take your breath away.

13 West Harbour. Explore small caves on the beach.

14 Blue Mountain. Secluded area with villas and ocean views.

15 Blue Hills. Personality of the island with beach shacks and restaurants.

16 Northwest Point. Great spot for scuba diving and wild beaches.

Passengers typically become silent when their plane starts its descent into the Providenciales airport (PLS), mesmerized by the shallow, crystal-clear, turquoise waters of Chalk Sound National Park below.

Provo, as most visitors call it, is the most developed part of the island chain. Most of the modern resorts, exquisite spas, water-sports operators, shops, business plazas, restaurants, bars, cafés, and its only golf course are on or close by the prized, 12-mile (18-km) north shore with its exquisite Grace Bay. Despite of the ever-increasing number of taller and grander condominium resorts, it's still possible to find deserted stretches on this priceless, sugar-soft shoreline. When residents begin to groan during the busy season, exclaiming how many people are bustling around, tourists exclaim, "You've got to be kidding. There's no one here!" But for guaranteed seclusion, one can head off to explore the southern shores and western tip of the island or set sail for a private island getaway on one of the many deserted cays nearby. For many, renting a private villa in one of the less-developed areas of the island creates the perfect balance.

Providenciales is where the majority of tourists are headed when they come to the Turks and Caicos Islands, or TCI. In fact, regardless of which other island you may be going to, you'll stop here first, as Provo has this country's main international airport, taking in all scheduled international flights. However, with all its modern amenities and unsurpassed beauty there comes a fairly high price tag attached. This is not the island for the budget-conscious traveler to visit; accommodations and dining here are expensive. Provo is definitely an upscale destination. And with this designation, you won't be hassled by beach vendors, and you won't be surrounded by poverty. This is a place to de-stress and unwind in the loveliest of ways.

Of course, for those with a passion for experiencing the real side of Turks and Caicos, Providenciales is conveniently connected to its family islands through a superb ferry service or several small plane flights a day. There are also myriad boat charters that can get you off the island and back again—in a flash. You can head out in the morning and be back to enjoy dinner in one of the many fabulous restaurants islandwide, followed by the comforts of your five-star hotel. No roughing it unless you wish to, and the sky's the limit. Enjoy!

Planning

Getting Here and Around

AIR TRAVEL

All international flights arrive in Providenciales (PLS); from here there are regularly scheduled flights to Grand Turk, Salt Cay, and South Caicos. Charter flights can also get you into North Caicos. Both interCaribbean and Caicos Express Airways offer regularly scheduled flights and a private charter service.

There is a very comfortable VIP lounge at the airport through VIP Flyers Club. The cost is $50/person for use of the lounge; expedited travelers take precedence, so availability is pending. For departing guests, expedited services include priority security screening and check-in, and the use of their tranquil 40-person lounge overlooking the runway until flight time. This extends your vacation time, reducing all stress associated with the din of regular departure procedures. Upon arriving in Provo, staff members organize private transfers, get travelers and luggage to their private licensed car service in record time, and offer assistance through immigration and customs. The cost is $200 for the first person in a group and $75 for each additional person. During high season, this service should be booked as far in advance as possible, as there is limited availability.

CONTACTS interCaribbean Airways. ⊠ *Old Private Airport, Old Airport Rd., Airport* ✢ *Behind Kishco on Airport Rd. (giant yellow building)* ☎ *649/946–4999 reservations, 649/946–3759 customer service, 888/957–3223 toll-free from USA* ⊕ *www.intercaribbean. com.* **Caicos Express Airways.** ⊠ *Southern Shores, Leeward Hwy., Downtown* ✢ *Across from Grace Bay Auto, just past the Do It Centre as you travel to the airport* ☎ *649/941–5730 main office, 305/677–3116 U.S. number, 649/946–8131 International Airport, 649/946–2178 Grand Turk Airport* ⊕ *www.caicosexpress.com.* **VIP Flyers Club.** ☎ *888/226-0042 Toll free from USA reservations line* ⊕ *www.vipflyersclub.com.*

AIRPORT TRANSFERS

Taxis are available after all arriving international flights. Few resorts are permitted to provide their own shuttle service, but most visitors are met at the airport by a representative of their resort or villa and then connected with a regular taxi service. Many guests choose to rent a car; rental companies will have your rental waiting for you at the airport. Cabs are expensive, making car rentals an attractive alternative for those expecting to visit a variety of restaurants during their stay or do any exploration around the island.

A word of caution: the roads on Provo can be dangerous to navigate. Many tourists do not have experience driving on the left. Drinking and driving, though highly discouraged, does happen—some people forget they must follow the rules when they are relaxed and on vacation. Therefore, when driving on Provo—especially during busy season—be sure to take care. Look both ways before entering any roadway. Take a deep breath and enter roundabouts very carefully. Wear seat belts at all times, and be sure to ask your rental agency if there is coverage on your vehicle. There is not always liability insurance, as is mandatory in North America, and it's not included with your credit card.

BOAT AND FERRY TRAVEL
Ferries leave from Provo to North Caicos several times a day, and from there you can rent a car to explore Middle Caicos, though all these arrangements should be made in advance—especially during peak season to avoid disappointment. Caribbean Cruisin' also runs a ferry between Provo and South Caicos twice a week; the trip can be daunting for those a little queasy on the water, because the current can be rough. Ferry transfers between Grand Turk and Salt Cay can be iffy because of weather and water conditions, but there are other shared opportunities if you ask around. If you do wish to try the community ferry service, know that you may have to contact one of the restaurants or a dive operation to track the operator down.

CONTACTS Caribbean Cruisin'. ⊠ *Walkin' Marina, Heaving Down Rock, Leeward Hwy. E, Leeward* ☎ *649/946–5406, 649/231–4191* ⊕ *caribbeancruisin.tc.* **Salt Cay Community Ferry.** ⊹ *Departs from Deane's Dock* ☎ *649/241–1009.*

CAR TRAVEL
It is possible to stay on Providenciales for a week without renting a car if you are willing to rely on very expensive taxis, a bicycle, or your own two feet to get around. There are certainly many wonderful restaurants and shops within walking distance in the Grace Bay area, but for those staying away from the main hub, that is just not the case. Also, tour operators will do pickups only in the Grace Bay area. Therefore, it's advisable to plan to rent a car for at least a few days so that you'll have the flexibility to explore independently and be able to access restaurants and services that may be farther afield. Driving is on the left—British-style!

Sights

Although you may be quite content to enjoy the beaches and top-notch amenities of Provo's resorts, there are certainly plenty of activities beyond the resorts. Provo is a great starting point for island-hopping tours by sea or by air, as well as fishing and diving trips. Resurfaced roads make for easy travel.

Beaches

Everyone comes for Grace Bay, with its miles of clean, powdery sand and the contrasting hues of unimaginably turquoise water set against the deep blues over the reef, but you should not overlook Provo's other beaches, each with its own unique allure. Although some beaches require effort to reach, they will definitely be worth the trek. On the rare chance that chop arises on Grace Bay, you can always head to the other side of Provo for calm and shallower waters. An additional bonus? There are no vendors on any of the beaches to interrupt your relaxation.

Restaurants

Dining options on Provo are numerous. Without a doubt, there must be close to a hundred restaurants on the island, each with its individual ambience and style of food. As the Caribbean has attracted travelers from around the globe since the time of Christopher Columbus, these influences come through in the foods of the region. Today you will experience a hint of Moroccan, Thai, Spanish, and Indian flavors, to name but a few.

There's everything from small beach shacks with the freshest seafood right off the boats to elegant restaurants with extensive wine lists. Most of the restaurants that cater to tourists offer numerous choices, with a little bit of everything on the menu. Don't like seafood? Have chicken or beef. Don't like spice? Ask for the tamer version. Vegetarian? Need kid-friendly food? Feel free to ask for something that's not on the menu; most of the island's chefs will try to accommodate requests. Some restaurants will also set up a table on the beach surrounded by tiki torches for that special occasion. Restaurants on Provo are generally upscale and expensive; you will find no fast-food chains here. As an option, there are excellent caterers on the island, too. The sky's the limit. Invite one, such as Kissing Fish Catering, to pack you a picnic lunch, prepare a pig roast on the beach, or come in to prepare an exquisite dinner in your private villa.

The best local food on the island is conch, which you will find everywhere prepared in many different ways. You may find it as ceviche, as ceviche in a salad, as deep-fried conch fingers, in spicy conch fritters, or as the base in a hearty conch chowder. It is also often found as part of fresh seafood specials, with colorful presentation and a tangy dose of spice.

Some restaurants do close during the slow season, with dates fluctuating yearly—usually from late August through late October. On the rare rainy day—or an unusually hot day—there are even a few indoor restaurants, complete with air-conditioning, as noted in the individual reviews.

Pick up a free copy of *WhereWhenHow's Dining Guide*, which you can find all over the island—or check out their website; it contains menus, website addresses, and pictures of all the restaurants.

What It Costs

$	$$	$$$	$$$$
RESTAURANTS			
under $12	$12–$20	$21–$30	over $30

Prices in the restaurant reviews are the average cost of a main course at dinner or, if dinner is not served, at lunch; taxes and service charges are generally included.

Hotels

Providenciales has become an incredibly popular destination for a reason. No matter the budget, all accommodation meets what North Americans and Europeans consider acceptable standards. You will find the majority of hotels and resorts to be within the greater Grace Bay area, with a few in outlying areas taking advantage of their seclusion or unique beauty. Almost all are impeccably maintained; they are clean and comfortable, with up-to-date, modern conveniences such as air-conditioning, cable TV, and Wi-Fi. Because Provo is relatively new to the tourism business by Caribbean standards, most accommodations are just a few years old. The majority of them are individually owned condos placed in a rental pool and treated as part of a resort. You get the best of both worlds in these condo resorts: consistency in style and standard of accommodation, and shared amenities that would not otherwise be possible, such as glamorous pools, spas, full gyms, and restaurant services. At the moment there are few hotel chains represented, but you will find the all-inclusive Club Med and Beaches resorts.

Most resorts on Provo are composed of privately owned condos that are placed into the resort's rental pool when the owners are not present. Unlike at chain hotels and resorts, you cannot request a particular building, floor, or room unless you are a repeat visitor. If you fall in love with the condo, you can probably purchase it or one that's similar. There are no taxes in Turks and Caicos except for a onetime stamp-duty tax—no property tax and no rental tax—which makes owning your own piece of paradise even more tempting.

Hotel reviews have been shortened. For full information, visit Fodors.com.

What It Costs			
$	$$	$$$	$$$$
HOTELS			
under $150	$150–$250	$250–$350	over $350

Hotel prices are per night for a double room in high season, excluding taxes, service charges, and meal plans (except at all-inclusives).

Private Villas

Provo is one of the better islands in the Caribbean for renting a private villa; there is a plethora to choose from that offer a clean, comfortable home away from home. Villas are scattered across the island, so you can choose whether you want to be close to activity or have peace and quiet. Rentals range from romantic one-bedroom cottages to fantastic multibedroom mansions on private stretches of beach—and everything in between. If you do stay in a villa, then it's most likely that you'll need to rent a car. Only a few are within proximity of restaurants. Some are in quiet residential neighborhoods, such as Leeward, where the homes may be on a canal, a couple of blocks from the beach. Several villas are in quiet Turtle Tail, quite centrally located and overlooking the beauty of the Caicos Banks. Many of those around Sapodilla Bay, Taylor Bay, and Chalk Sound have gorgeous views in all directions. A villa can offer a more budget-friendly vacation if you split the costs with other couples or families.

RENTAL AGENTS
Coldwell Banker TCI
Several agents at Coldwell Banker will assist you in selecting a property island-wide. ⊠ *Caicos Cafe Plaza, Grace Bay Rd.* ☎ *649/946–4969* ⊕ *www.coldwellbankertci.com.*

Engel & Volkers

Engel & Volkers offers modest to magnificent condos and villas throughout Providenciales. ⊠ *229 Grace Bay Rd., Grace Bay* ☏ *649/946–4379* ⊕ *www.turksandcaicos.evfinehomes.com.*

Seafeathers

Based in Providenciales, this locally owned and operated business specializes in Turtle Tail villa rentals. ⊠ *Turtle Tail* ☏ *649/941–5703* ⊕ *www.seafeathers.com.*

T.C. Safari

Based in Florida, T.C. Safari offers reservation services for numerous properties around Provo. ☏ *649/941–5043 local number with answering service, 904/491–1415 in U.S.* ⊕ *www.tcsafari.com.*

TC Villas

TC Villas has representatives to assist you in your villa selection whether you're looking for something cozy for two or six bedrooms to sleep a crowd. ☏ *787/378–8410, 877/467–4858 toll-free* ⊕ *www.TCVillas.com.*

Turks and Caicos Reservations

They call themselves a "mini-Expedia" and are the official booking service on island. The staff can recommend a large inventory of resorts and select villas to those wishing to visit the islands. Everyone who books through the company receives travel rewards that go toward dinner vouchers, car rentals, or excursions, making repeat bookings an advantage. They will work hard to get you the best deal, book your flights, and act as concierge, and when there are storms or delays, they will help find emergency accommodations. ☏ *649/941–8988, 877/774–5486* ⊕ *turksandcaicosreservations.com.*

CONCIERGE SERVICES

After 5 Island Concierge

SPECIALTY STORES | Sometimes you just need help before or during your trip. After 5 Island Concierge can do anything to ease your vacation worries, from grocery delivery and meal reservations to organizing private wine tastings and sorting out bulk wine delivery for that extra-special party or event. They will also help you arrange for a personal chef or catering service so that meals are not a concern during your stay. Virtually any service you can think of can be arranged through this company. ☏ *649/232–3483* ⊕ *www.islandconciergetc.com.*

Shopping

Provo is not really a shopping destination, and you won't find bargains here. However, there is enough upscale shopping to keep your wallet busy, from tropical clothes and jewelry to art prints and accessories. The shopping complexes in the Grace Bay area continue to expand, and the major resorts have small boutiques with signature items, so don't forget to check them out.

There are several main shopping areas in the Grace Bay area: **Saltmills**, **Le Vele**, and **Regent Village,** as well as **Ports of Call** Shopping Village. There are also two cultural centers, one between Ocean Club and Club Med next to Ricki's, and the other across the street from Beaches' easternmost entrance. Handwoven straw baskets and hats, polished conch-shell crafts, paintings, wood carvings, model sailboats, handmade dolls, and metalwork are crafts native to the islands and nearby Haiti. The natural surroundings have inspired local and international artists to paint, sculpt, print, craft, and photograph; most of their creations are on sale in Providenciales.

Provo is an amazing destination if you are looking forward to pampering yourself while on vacation. The spas here offer treatments with all the bells and whistles, and most get good word of mouth. Most of Provo's high-end resorts have spas, with access for those not staying on the property. There are also several independent spas to choose from, and for those staying in one of the many villas, there are services that also come to you.

Nightlife

Although Provo is not known for its nightlife, there are some live bands and bars. Popular singers such as Brentford Handfield, Just, Corey Forbes, and Quinton Dean are island boys who perform at numerous restaurants and barbecue bonfires. Be sure to ask if any ripsaw bands—aka rake 'n' scrape—are playing while you're on island; this is one of the quintessential local music types that is found more often on the family islands.

The best late-night action can be found at the two main casinos, where everyone ends the night. If you want to see a show and dance until late, Club Med offers a night pass, which includes drinks. You'll also find a couple of songsters at the Amanyara in the evening if you have decided to treat yourself to a very special night out.

The long stretch of Grace Bay Beach is home to some of Provo's best resorts and restaurants.

Most restaurants and bars have happy hour every night. Check out Pelican Bay; they have a 50% off all drinks special from 5 to 7 every night of the week. It's a local's choice. You can take in the fish fry on Thursday night at the far end of Grace Bay, followed by some karaoke at Danny Buoys. Somewhere on the Beach is perfect for a Friday if you want to stay on the water; they have a local band play until late. On the upper end of the scale, locals enjoy a mellower evening at the Deck in Seven Stars, as well as Infiniti Bar at Grace Bay Club. If you have dined a bit later than you might have expected, you can grab a late-night drink at the Sand-Box, right across the street from Saltmills Plaza, or head on a bit of a road trip to Club 809. This is a Dominican bar just past Walkin Marine Supplies on the road heading out to Blue Hills; they have a pool table outside as well as dominoes, and a DJ with dancing on the inside. Chance Casino is downstairs.

Keep abreast of events and specials by checking **WhereWhenHow** (⊕ www.wherewhenhow.com).

Full-Moon Parties. Full moons are reputed to make people a little crazy, so full-moon parties can be a lot of fun! Bay Bistro organizes a pig roast with tropical fare such as pineapple coleslaw alongside a bonfire several times a year when the moon is high. Give them a call to see if the month when you're visiting is one of the lucky ones. The evening is a great hit with all ages, even the kids, who can roast marshmallows and make s'mores while running crazy in the moonlight.

Providenciales in One Day

If you are en route to one of the family islands, or have booked a stay along Grace Bay and not imagined to venture off the resort, perhaps you should consider renting a car to explore Provo for just a day. If you are not staying on the island, be sure to take a quick detour through Grace Bay, checking out the beach for future visits and perhaps a couple of the boutique shops. Coming down the island, history buffs might stop at Cheshire Hall. Here are the remnants of an old plantation within walking distance off Leeward Highway. From there, carry on to Chalk Sound; it is definitely an island must-see. The water here is shallow and bright with small islands dotted throughout the middle; the sight truly takes your breath away. While you are out there, be sure to stop at Las Brisas at Neptune Villas. The location offers stunning views of the sound, and it's a perfect spot for lunch and a refreshment. If you are willing and able, you can take one of their rental kayaks for an hour—or longer. But if you are looking for a beach by this time, then Sapodilla and Taylor bays are just a little way beyond; the waters are shallow for hundreds of feet, making them a child's dream. Backtrack to downtown and take a ride to Malcolm's Beach out at Northwest Point, and then finish your day off in Blue Hills, where colorful buildings are the setting for a game of "slamming" dominoes and a few local restaurants serve up wonderful Caribbean cuisine, all on the beach with unobstructed views of the sun as it sets.

Grace Bay

The "hub" of the island is the stunning Grace Bay Beach, a graceful curve of soft sand along Provo's north shore. Between it and the Lower Bight Road, which runs parallel to the beach, are many shops, restaurants, and resorts, the majority of what is to be found on the island. There are sidewalks and streetlights, cafés and coffee shops, restaurants, spas, tour operators, and a variety of specialty stores. This area is where the majority of tourists stay, especially for their first visit to the island.

 Beaches

★ Grace Bay
BEACH—SIGHT | The world-famous sweeping stretch of ivory-white, powder-soft sand on Provo's north shore is simply breathtaking.

Protected within the Princess Alexandra National Park, it's home to migrating starfish, as well as many schools of tiny fishes. The majority of Provo's beachfront resorts are along this shore, and it's the primary reason Turks and Caicos is a world-class destination. **Amenities:** food and drink; parking (free); water sports. **Best for:** sunset; swimming; walking. ⊠ *Grace Bay Rd., along the north shore, Grace Bay.*

🍴 Restaurants

★ Bay Bistro
$$$$ | **ECLECTIC** | **FAMILY** | You simply can't eat any closer to the beach than here at Bay Bistro, directly on Grace Bay Beach. You have the option of dining on a covered deck, on an open-air patio, or with your feet in the sand, surrounded by palm trees with the sound of lapping waves. **Known for:** dining right on the beach; weekend brunch; great food and even better views. ⑤ *Average main: $33* ⊠ *Sibonné Beach Hotel, Princess Dr., Next door to the Somerset, Grace Bay* ☎ *649/946–5396 main line* ⊕ *www.baybistrorestaurant.com.*

Bella Luna Ristorante
$$$ | **ITALIAN** | For wonderfully traditional Italian food, this restaurant uses fresh heirloom tomatoes and herbs from the garden that surrounds the dining area. The restaurant has two distinct experiences: wood-fired pizza on the ground level and a full menu serving authentic Italian dishes upstairs in what many call the tree house. **Known for:** homemade pasta; red and white pizzas; ingredients grown in on-site garden. ⑤ *Average main: $30* ⊠ *The Glass House, Grace Bay Rd., Grace Bay* ☎ *649/946–5214* ⊕ *www.bellaluna.tc* ⊗ *Closed Sun. No lunch.*

Big Al's Island Grill
$$ | **BURGER** | After a few days of local staples and upscale eateries, you may find yourself searching for a great burger. You will find a huge selection of burgers in this '50s-era-designed diner, including the Pretzel Burger, served in a pretzel bun, or the Hawaiian Volcano Island Burger with grilled pineapple, jalapeño, teriyaki glaze, and Jack cheese. **Known for:** extensive burger menu; the Big Al's Slider Challenge; four different styles of fries to choose from. ⑤ *Average main: $15* ⊠ *Salt Mills Plaza, Grace Bay* ☎ *649/941–3797* ⊕ *www.bigalsislandgrill.com.*

★ Cabana Bar & Grille
$$ | **AMERICAN** | This is a great option if you're looking for a quick lunch with a view of beautiful Grace Bay Beach just steps away. The food is simple and good, featuring such basic fare as

hamburgers and wraps. **Known for:** All you can eat and drink Monday night buffet on the beach; loaded Bloody Mary and Bloody Caesar at breakfast; live music three nights a week. $ *Average main: $20* ⊠ *Ocean Club, Grace Bay Rd., Grace Bay* ☎ *649/946–5880* ⊕ *www.oceanclubresorts.com.*

★ Caicos Bakery

$ | **BAKERY** | At this little bakery you will find the perfect coffee, freshly baked croissants or doughnuts, an assortment of fresh bread, French desserts, traditional cakes, and more. Be sure to get there early though, as there's often a line waiting for them to open! **Known for:** coconut rum eclairs; pastries worth jumping out of bed for; inexpensive way to fill up for breakfast or lunch. $ *Average main: $6* ⊠ *Caicos Plaza, Grace Bay* ☎ *649/232–1003* ⊟ *No credit cards* ☽ *Closed Sun.*

★ Caicos Café Bar and Grill

$$$$ | **ECLECTIC** | Here the island dishes come with an Italian twist; everything is fresh and carefully prepared. The bread is baked fresh daily at the bakery next door. **Known for:** handcrafted pasta; oven-warm fresh baked bread; Mediterranean-style seafood casserole. $ *Average main: $32* ⊠ *Caicos Café Plaza, Governor's Rd., Grace Bay* ☎ *649/946–5278* ☽ *Closed Sun.*

★ Coco Bistro

$$$$ | **INTERNATIONAL** | With tables exotically set within a mature palm grove, Coco Bistro is one of the most popular restaurants on Provo. Main courses combine continental dishes with a Caribbean flair, and seafood abounds. **Known for:** dining under the palms; fresh-from-the-sea lobster (when in season); coconut pie to finish off an exquisite meal. $ *Average main: $40* ⊠ *Governor's Rd., Grace Bay* ✛ *Just down from Sunshine Nursery* ☎ *649/946–5369* ⊕ *www.cocobistro.tc* ☽ *Closed Sun.*

★ Cocovan

$$ | **ECLECTIC** | With so many incredible restaurants in Provo, you might wonder how a food truck made it to the top of the pack. Every bite that comes out the kitchen, housed in an authentic 1974 Airstream van, is absolutely delicious. **Known for:** delicious food truck fare; fun outdoor dining; lobster mac and cheese balls (shrimp when it's not lobster season). $ *Average main: $19* ⊠ *Governor's Road, Grace Bay* ✛ *Just down from Sunshine Nursery* ☎ *649/946–5369* ⊕ *www.cocovan.tc* ☽ *Closed Mon.*

Coyaba Restaurant

$$$$ | **ECLECTIC** | Directly behind Grace Bay Club at Caribbean Paradise Inn, this posh little restaurant is in a palm-fringed setting. The nostalgic favorites here are served with tempting, tropical

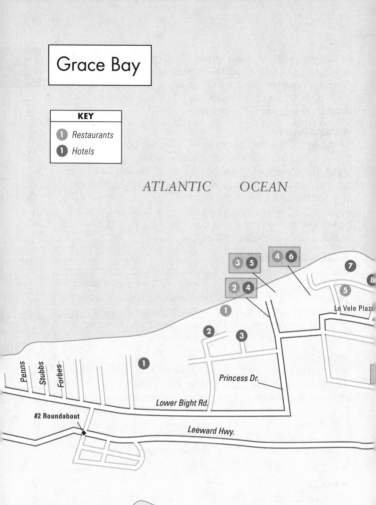

Grace Bay

KEY
- ① *Restaurants*
- ① *Hotels*

ATLANTIC OCEAN

Le Vele Plaza

Penns
Stubbs
Forbes

Princess Dr.

Lower Bight Rd.

#2 Roundabout

Leeward Hwy.

Restaurants

Bay Bistro, **3**
Bella Luna Ristorante, **16**
Big Al's Island Grill, **9**
Cabana Bar & Grille, **32**
Caicos Bakery, **24**
Caicos Café Bar and Grill, **23**
Coco Bistro, **26**
Cocovan, **25**

Coyaba Restaurant, **29**
Crackpot Kitchen, **22**
Danny Buoy's, **10**
The Deck at Seven Stars, **19**
Fairways Bar & Grill, **34**
Rickie's Flamingo Cafe, **31**
Fresh Catch, **11**
Grace's Cottage, **5**

Graceway Juice & Java, **17**
The Grill at Grace Bay Club, **27**
Hemingway's Restaurant, **4**
Infiniti Restaurant & Raw Bar, **28**
Kalooki's, **6**
Le Bouchon du Village, **14**
Lemon2Go, **7**

Opus Wine-Bar-Grill, **33**
Parallel 23, **1**
Pavilion at the Somerset, **2**
Pelican Bay, **30**
Pizza Pizza, **15**
Retreat Kitchen, **21**
Sandbox, **8**
Seven, **20**
The Thai Orchid Restaurant, **13**

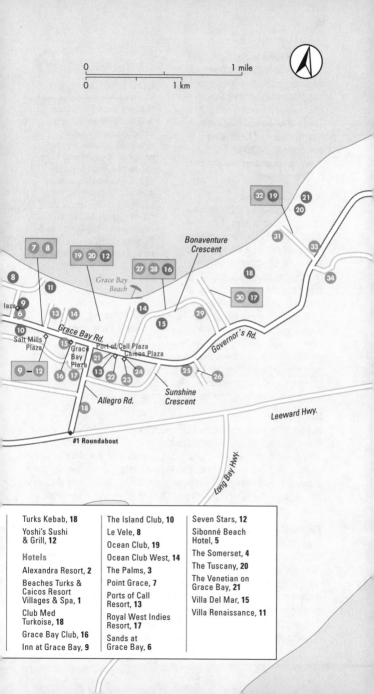

Turks Kebab, **18**

Yoshi's Sushi
& Grill, **12**

Hotels

Alexandra Resort, **2**

Beaches Turks &
Caicos Resort
Villages & Spa, **1**

Club Med
Turkoise, **18**

Grace Bay Club, **16**

Inn at Grace Bay, **9**

The Island Club, **10**

Le Vele, **8**

Ocean Club, **19**

Ocean Club West, **14**

The Palms, **3**

Point Grace, **7**

Ports of Call
Resort, **13**

Royal West Indies
Resort, **17**

Sands at
Grace Bay, **6**

Seven Stars, **12**

Sibonné Beach
Hotel, **5**

The Somerset, **4**

The Tuscany, **20**

The Venetian on
Grace Bay, **21**

Villa Del Mar, **15**

Villa Renaissance, **11**

twists. **Known for:** eclectic menu; delectable desserts; deconstructed beef Wellington. ⑤ *Average main: $48* ✉ *Bonaventure Crescent, Grace Bay* ✛ *Just off Grace Bay Rd west of Club Med entrance* ☎ *649/946–5186* ⊕ *www.coyabarestaurant.com* ♥ *Closed Tues.*

★ **Crackpot Kitchen**

$$$$ | CARIBBEAN | This casual local hot spot is one of the only restaurants in the heart of the Grace Bay tourist area to serve authentic and traditional Turks and Caicos cuisine (beyond the standard cracked conch or conch salad), yet still enjoy

quality service and ambience. From braised oxtail with butter beans to curried goat, you'll find items on this menu that you've never heard of, all infused with life and love from Chef Nik. **Known for:** traditional island food in a tourist-friendly setting; Friday-night happy hour; warm and welcoming service. ⑤ *Average main: $32* ✉ *Port of Call Plaza, upstairs, Grace Bay* ☎ *649/941–3330* ⊕ *www. crackpotkitchen.com* ♥ *Closed Thurs; Sun. lunchtime.*

Danny Buoy's

$$ | IRISH | A true local watering hole, this bar always has a mix of locals and vacationers. There are those who come here for the drinks and entertainment factor, but also to dine on traditional Irish favorites such as fish-and-chips. **Known for:** late night menu; Irish staples; local favorite. ⑤ *Average main: $20* ✉ *Grace Bay Rd., next to the Saltmills, Grace Bay* ☎ *649/946–5921* ⊕ *www.dannybuoys. com.*

The Deck at Seven Stars

$$$ | ECLECTIC | It's hard to think of a more alluring setting than The Deck, perched on the dunes overlooking the ocean at the Seven Stars resort. Tiki torches, fire pits, and awnings lend plenty of chic to this otherwise much more casual sister of the property's more formal restaurant, Seven. **Known for:** Sunday night beach barbecue; incredible setting and sunset views; seared ahi tuna. ⑤ *Average main: $28* ✉ *Seven Stars Resort, Grace Bay Rd., Grace Bay* ☎ *649/339–3777* ⊕ *www.sevenstarsgracebay.com.*

Provo's Thursday Fish Fry

On Thursday night you can enjoy local cuisine from multiple restaurants in one place. Residents and tourists alike gather for the lively atmosphere, great ambience, and chance to see the island's culture expressed in the Junkanoo—a local dancing band extravaganza. The smells from the grills will keep you hungry, so it's a great way to compare who makes the best local dishes. Hole in the Wall and Smokey's are just two of the weekly participants. It's fun for the whole family, and the convenient location means that you don't have to leave the main tourist area to try some of the best local cuisine.

Fairways Bar & Grill

$$ | **ECLECTIC** | Located at the Provo Golf Club, Fairways is open seven days a week for breakfast and lunch. Hot or cold breakfast is offered during the week, while Sunday brunch features such favorites as waffles and eggs Benedict. **Known for:** golf-course views; lively brunch scene; lobster roll (in season). $ *Average main: $20 ⊠ Governor's Rd., Grace Bay ⊹ Opposite Opus upstairs in the Golf Club ☎ 649/946–5833 restaurant, 649/946–5991 pro shop ⊕ www.provogolfclub.com.*

Fresh Catch

$$ | **SEAFOOD** | A small, very casual local restaurant, Fresh Catch serves primarily seafood that is brought in daily straight from the boats. The place is blissfully air-conditioned but offers few other frills; still, it's a great spot to eat like a local with great ambience. **Known for:** fresh fish; shrimp with a local Bambarra rum glaze; local fare. $ *Average main: $12 ⊠ Saltmills Plaza, Grace Bay Rd., Unit 6, Grace Bay ☎ 649/243–3167 ⊘ Closed Sun. No dinner.*

Grace's Cottage

$$$$ | **CARIBBEAN** | This is considered one of the prettiest settings on Provo, and the name says it all. Imagine dining under the stars amidst an English-style garden or at one of the tables artfully set upon the graceful covered verandah skirting the gingerbread cottage. **Known for:** dining under the stars; gourmet Caribbean flavors; chocolate soufflé worth the wait. $ *Average main: $42 ⊠ Point Grace, Off Grace Bay Rd., Grace Bay ⊹ In between the Sands and Bianca Sands resorts ☎ 649/946–5096 ⊕ www.pointgrace.com ⌒ Smart casual attire for dinner.*

Groceries on Provo

If you have traveled throughout the Caribbean, you will have noted that grocery stores are not like they are at home. This is not the case on Provo. Not only is the Graceway IGA a North American–style supermarket—boasting a superb international section and excellent deli—but it rivals many you find across the United States, and is most definitely one of the best in the entire Caribbean. Located mid-island, it is a cab ride from the Grace Bay area. There is also the Graceway Gourmet IGA just down from Seven Stars. In addition, the IGA has opened its third location downtown: \$mart. It is another North American–style supermarket, but offers more to the locals at lower prices.

If you're shopping on a smaller scale, some resorts have small convenience stores for staples such as milk, snacks, and coffee. The best, but by far the most expensive, is the Market at Blue Haven Resort in Leeward.

There is one main stop for alcohol other than in the three main IGA affiliates. The Wine Cellar, otherwise known as Discount Liquors, is on the south side of Leeward Highway between the roundabout at the top of Venetian Road and the roundabout at Suzy Turn.

One last mention is Provo's "red truck." Sitting on the left-hand side of the street as you enter downtown heading toward the airport is a lone red truck curbside. This is where residents pick up fresh fish caught by the little guy so they can avoid paying supermarket prices.

★ Graceway Juice & Java

$ | CAFÉ | If you're looking for a good deal, this might be one of the best kept secrets in Provo. Tucked inside the exit to Graceway Gourmet supermarket, this juice and coffee bar serves blended and pressed juices packed with fresh fruits and vegetables (and, at $7 each, they are a steal). **Known for:** fresh juices; a good cup of coffee; budget-friendly. $ *Average main: $7* ⊠ *Inside Graceway Gourmet, Grace Bay* ✛ *Head toward Leeward Hwy. from the Seven Stars Roundabout; on the right.*

The Grill at Grace Bay Club

$$$ | INTERNATIONAL | The Grill's setting, right on Grace Bay Beach, is simply lovely. Tables are set upon a wooden deck, with the menu more casual than that of Grace Bay Club's Infiniti. **Known for:** family-friendly dining; Tuesday Caribbean beach barbecue; casual setting with upscale service. $ *Average main: $30* ⊠ *Villas*

at Grace Bay Club, Bonaventure Crescent, Grace Bay ☎ 649/946–5050 ⊕ www.gracebayclub.com.

Hemingway's Restaurant

$$$$ | **ECLECTIC** | **FAMILY** | The casual yet gorgeous setting, with a patio and deck offering unobstructed views of Grace Bay, makes this one of the most popular tourist restaurants. At lunch you can't miss the conch, served however you prefer. **Known for:** local seafood; beachside dining on Grace Bay; fish tacos. ⑤ Average main: $36 ⊠ The Sands at Grace Bay, Grace Bay Rd., Grace Bay ☎ 649/941–8408 ⊕ www.hemingwaystci.com.

★ Infiniti Restaurant & Raw Bar

$$$$ | **ECLECTIC** | This chic palapa-style, waterfront, open-air restaurant has the most romantic setting along Grace Bay—some would say the most romantic in all of the Turks and Caicos Islands. Despite its elite clientele and higher prices, the restaurant offers a memorable dining experience minus any formality or attitude; guests are expected to wear resort-elegant attire (men, no sleeveless shirts, please). **Known for:** raw bar; romantic setting; farm- and sea-to-table ingredients. ⑤ Average main: $45 ⊠ Grace Bay Club, Grace Bay Circle Rd., Grace Bay ☎ 649/946–5050 ext. 1 for the restaurant ⊕ www.gracebayresorts.com.

Kalooki's

$$$$ | **CARIBBEAN** | Though the original beachside venue was destroyed by a hurricane in 2017, Kalooki's has relocated to the Vele Plaza on the main strip in Grace Bay. While they may no longer have their old, gritty beachside vibe, they do still offer great island food. **Known for:** good island food; live music Saturday nights; crispy rum and raisin bread pudding. ⑤ Average main: $32 ⊠ Le Vele Plaza, Grace Bay Rd, Grace Bay ☎ 649/331–4188 ⊕ www.kalookisrestaurant.com.

★ Le Bouchon du Village

$$$$ | **FRENCH** | If you close your eyes, the aromas and flavors you will experience at this bistro in Regent Village Plaza may make you think you're sitting in a Parisian bistro. The food is exactly what you would expect, including escargots, foie gras, steak au poivre with frites, duck confit, and charcuterie and cheese boards, as well as superb fresh bread. **Known for:** expat favorite; Parisian staples with island flair; friendly-family service. ⑤ Average main: $34 ⊠ Regent Village, Grace Bay Rd., Grace Bay ☎ 649/946–5234 ۞ Closed Sun.

★ Lemon2Go

$ | **CAFÉ** | Once they discover this little gem, most locals and visitors make a point of starting each day here with a cup of the best coffee on the island. There are a few chairs and tables inside the café, which shares its space with an adorable little florist and gift shop, and more seating outside along the main drag of Grace Bay. **Known for:** the best specialty coffee shop on the island; flower and knickknack shop inside; locally made pastries. ⑤ *Average main: $6* ⊠ *Opposite Saltmills, Grace Bay* ☎ *649/941–4069* ⊕ *www. caicoscafe.com* ◷ *Closed Sun. afternoons.*

Opus Wine-Bar-Grill

$$$$ | **ECLECTIC** | A beautifully landscaped patio makes a quiet, elegant setting, or you may choose to eat in the air-conditioned dining room. You will find a wide range of fish and meat on the menu. **Known for:** vast wine cellar; more than 50 rums to choose from; mouthwatering shrimp bisque. ⑤ *Average main: $32* ⊠ *Ocean Club, Grace Bay Rd., Grace Bay* ☎ *649/946–5885* ⊕ *oceanclubre-sorts.com/our-resorts/dining/opuswinebargrill* ◷ *No lunch. Closed Sun.*

Parallel 23

$$$$ | **CARIBBEAN** | Dining at Parallel 23 is reminiscent of old-world charm. Tall French doors open onto the wide, elevated terrace overlooking a courtyard peppered with uplighted date palms, a fountain adding a quiet tinkle in the background. **Known for:** great spot for a special evening; house-made ice cream and sorbet; impressive wine selection and sommelier to help you with pairings. ⑤ *Average main: $41* ⊠ *Regent Palms Resort, Regent St., Grace Bay* ☎ *649/946–8666* ⊕ *www.regenthotels.com* ◷ *No lunch.*

★ Pavilion at the Somerset

$$$$ | **INTERNATIONAL** | Located at the Somerset Resort, dining may be at one of several tables elegantly set overlooking a formal garden courtyard. Indoors, there is a different vibe altogether—cool and chic with high ceilings. **Known for:** award-winning conch spring rolls; warm crusted Brie; indulgent dessert cocktails. ⑤ *Average main: $35* ⊠ *The Somerset, Princess Dr., Grace Bay* ⊹ *Tucked next to the Regent Palms* ☎ *649/344–0368 hotel front desk* ⊕ *www.paviliontci.com* ◷ *Main restaurant closed Thurs.* ☞ *Island-chic attire at the main restaurant.*

★ Pelican Bay

$$$$ | **INTERNATIONAL** | This beautiful restaurant has French doors that lead to a breezy terrace, with the Royal West Indies pool as a stunning backdrop. Chef Peter Redstone uses local ingredients to create upscale Caribbean dishes, including blackened mahimahi with citrus rice and a deconstructed lobster ravioli during lobster season. **Known for:** Friday night Surf & Turks Carnival featuring local produce and fresh seafood; lobster prepared many different ways; beautiful setting. ⑤ *Average main: $32* ⊠ *Royal West*

Indies Resort, Bonaventure Crescent, Grace Bay ☎ *649/941–2365*
⊕ *www.pelicanbaytci.com.*

Pizza Pizza

$$ | PIZZA | There are days that you just don't want to dress up,
and Pizza Pizza is an economical alternative to dining out. Pick up
a pizza and watch your favorite show, or enjoy it with a glass of
wine on your very own terrace. **Known for:** thin-crust pizzas; one
of the few delivery options on island; reasonably priced. ⑤ *Average main: $20* ⊠ *Grace Bay Plaza, Grace Bay Rd., Grace Bay*
☎ *649/941–8010.*

Retreat Kitchen

$$ | VEGETARIAN | Located next door to the yoga and wellness
studio operated by the same sister team, this vegetarian café and
juice bar has an ever-evolving menu and is a welcome reprieve
from the heavier food offered at most restaurants. Gluten-free
and vegan snacks and light bites are available, including espresso
brownies and turmeric hummus. **Known for:** vegan lunch menu;
healthy cold-pressed juice with fresh ingredients; fun and funky
vibe. ⑤ *Average main: $15* ⊠ *Grace Bay* ☎ *649/432–3485* ⊕ *www.
retreatkitchentc.com* ☉ *Closed Sun.*

Rickie's Flamingo Cafe

$$ | CARIBBEAN | This little local hot spot offers basic local fare right
on the beach beside Ocean Club Resort. It's a great spot to grab a
cold one in the middle of the afternoon or as the sun sets. **Known
for:** grouper prepared seven different ways; chill local hangout;
amazing sunsets. ⑤ *Average main: $20* ⊠ *Cultural Center, Grace
Bay Rd., Grace Bay* ☎ *649/242–7545.*

Sandbox

$$ | ECLECTIC | More a fun bar than a full-fledged restaurant, Sand-
box is good for a light bite while enjoying some music offered up
by a DJ or their impressive vinyl collection. Food is limited and
simple (soups, salads, curries) and changes regularly. **Known for:**
great music; awesome bartenders; simple, light dinner options.
⑤ *Average main: $12* ⊠ *103 Venture House, Grace Bay Road,
Grace Bay* ☎ *649/941–6049* ⊕ *www.turksandcaicosrestaurant.
com* ☉ *Closed Sun.*

Seven

$$$$ | ECLECTIC | Elegant and beautiful, this swanky restaurant at
Seven Stars Resort is one of only a few on island with air-conditioning; there's also a covered patio with attractive outdoor
seating that's ideal on pleasant evenings. Begin your evening with
a beverage on The Deck, and then move over to experience inno-
vative, artfully prepared food. **Known for:** sommelier to assist with

Driving on Provo

Signage for roads on Provo can be hard to come by, but locals use the island's roundabouts as their landmarks. Once you get a feel for those, driving around the island becomes less daunting than it might be at first. The following list gives you an idea of what you're looking for when trying to navigate the island.

1. Rubis. This is at the far end of the divided highway with Seven Stars on the oceanfront.

2. Thomas Stubbs Roundabout. More aptly described as the Beaches Resort turnoff, this one has a sign for the resort front and center in the manicured circle.

3. Felix Morley Roundabout. Leading down Venetian Road to Turtle Tail is another Rubis not far from the main IGA,

with nothing in its center and looking a bit war-torn.

4. Suzy Turn. Don't run through this tiny roundabout across from Napa Auto Parts; this one has a stop sign!

5. Five Cays and Chalk Sound Roundabout. There's no sign for this one, but it's heading down the hill. You will see a giant red gift at Christmastime to mark the spot; it's one of the more traditional wide circles.

6. Fuller Walkin Roundabout. This one is for Blue Hills. It is a bit tricky to navigate and is found at the entrance to downtown.

7. Walter Cox Roundabout. It's an alternative to Five Cays, South Dock Road, and Chalk Sound in one direction; head in the opposite one for the airport.

wine pairings; indoor fine dining, a rarity in Provo; top quality food and service. $ *Average main: $40* ⊠ *Seven Stars Resort, Grace Bay Rd., Grace Bay* ☎ *649/339–3777, 649/941–7777* ⊕ *www. sevenstarsgracebay.com* ☾ *Closed Sun.*

★ **The Thai Orchid Restaurant**

$$ | THAI | Within walking distance of numerous resorts and easier on the wallet than most other nearby restaurants in the heart of Grace Bay, this is a tiny little haunt, tucked neatly away in the Regent Village Plaza. You can dine in a relaxed, air-conditioned dining room or at one of the several tables along the sidewalk. **Known for:** authentic pad thai (unexpected on a small Caribbean island); layers of flavor; casual dine-in option or take-out. $ *Average main: $20* ⊠ *Regent Village Plaza, Grace Bay* ☎ *649/946–4491.*

★ Turks Kebab

$$ | MEDITERRANEAN | A young Turkish man and his wife have set up shop in Alverna's Craft Market, just down from Graceway Gourmet IGA. This is truly authentic and simply awesome; locals often gather for a bite to eat and a beer. **Known for:** cool little dinner shack; street food-style food; outstanding pita doner kebab. $ *Average main: $12* ⊠ *Alverna's Craft Market, Grace Bay* ☎ *649/431–9964* ▭ *No credit cards.*

Yoshi's Sushi & Grill

$$$ | SUSHI | Yoshi's offers excellent sushi in an indoor, air-conditioned setting or open-air on a lovely streetside patio. The menu here is reasonably priced by Provo's standards, but expect a much higher bill than you would find at your average sushi spot near home. **Known for:** sushi with an island twist; lobster rolls in season; nice ambience with leisurely service. $ *Average main: $22* ⊠ *Saltmills Plaza, Grace Bay Rd., Grace Bay* ☎ *649/941–3374* ⊕ *www.yoshissushi.net* ☉ *Closed Sun.*

🛏 Hotels

The vast majority of hotels and resorts on Providenciales are found along its beautiful north shore, between Turtle Cove Marina on the west and Leeward on the east, including world-famous Grace Bay.

Alexandra Resort

$$$$ | ALL-INCLUSIVE | FAMILY | This all-inclusive beachfront resort, on a fine stretch of Grace Bay Beach, offers spacious accommodations and amenities that appeal to families, couples, and corporate travelers alike. **Pros:** kids 12 and under stay and eat free; spectacular stretch of beach just steps away; large pool area. **Cons:** some rooms do not have king beds; service is often on island time; if you have the kids with you, The Beach House sister property is off limits. $ *Rooms from: $700* ⊠ *Princess Dr., Grace Bay* ⊹ *Right next door to the Palms Resort* ☎ *649/946–5807, 800/284–0699 U.S. toll-free* ⊕ *www.alexandraresort.com* ⇄ *90 rooms* ◐ *All-inclusive.*

★ Beaches Turks & Caicos Resort Villages & Spa

$$$$ | RESORT | FAMILY | Designed for families who are eager to spend some time together and reconnect and recharge, Beaches is the largest resort in the Turks and Caicos Islands with much to see and do. **Pros:** great place for families; gorgeous pools; many quality on-site restaurants. **Cons:** with such an extensive all-inclusive plan you miss out on the island's other great restaurants; excursions such as the catamaran trip can get crowded;

per-person rate schedule. $ *Rooms from: $1200* ⊠ *Lower Bight Rd., Grace Bay* ☎ *649/946–8000, 888/232–2437 24-hour assistance* ⊕ *www.beaches.com* ⇌ *758 rooms* ⚲ *All-inclusive.*

Club Med Turkoise

$ | **RESORT** | In contrast to the other, more tranquil Grace Bay resorts, this property has a vibrant party atmosphere with nightly entertainment and even a flying trapeze—it caters to fun-loving singles and couples, as it has a no-child policy. **Pros:** all-inclusive; one of the best bargains to be found on one of the best beaches in the world; adults only. **Cons:** even with some renovations, the rooms are tiny, basic, and dormlike; food is just so-so; summer camp atmosphere. $ *Rooms from: $215* ⊠ *Grace Bay Rd., Grace Bay* ☎ *649/946–5500, 888/932–2582* ⊕ *www.clubmed.com* ⇌ *281 rooms* ⚲ *All-inclusive.*

Grace Bay Club

$$$$ | **RESORT** | **FAMILY** | This stylish resort retains a loyal following because of its helpful, attentive staff and unpretentious elegance. **Pros:** gorgeous pool and restaurant lounge areas with outdoor couches, daybeds, and fire pits; adult-only sections; lots of activities to entertain kids of all ages. **Cons:** must stay in Estates section to use its beautiful pool; expensive; have to travel into town to purchase basic amenities. $ *Rooms from: $800* ⊠ *Bonaventure Crescent, Grace Bay* ⊹ *Off Governor's Rd.* ☎ *649/946–5050, 800/946–5757* ⊕ *www.gracebayresorts.com* ⇌ *82 suites* ⚲ *No meals.*

Inn At Grace Bay

$ | **RENTAL** | This resort in the middle of the hub offers easy access to nearby shops and restaurants, and is within close walking distance of Grace Bay Beach. **Pros:** very economical rates for Provo; great management team with strong track record; close to nightlife so no driving. **Cons:** with everything so convenient you might not venture out to other areas of the island; not on the beach; none of the amenities and activities the resorts offer. $ *Rooms from: $230* ⊠ *382 Grace Bay Rd., Grace Bay* ☎ *649/432–8633* ⊕ *innatgracebay.com* ⇌ *12 suites* ⚲ *No meals.*

The Island Club

$ | **RENTAL** | If you're on a budget, you will find that this small condo complex gives you excellent value. **Pros:** you can't get a better deal on Provo; centrally located so you can walk everywhere; laundry facilities on-site. **Cons:** only a few condos in the complex are in the short-term rental pool, so availability is limited; a block from the beach; queen beds in the master bedroom. $ *Rooms from: $250* ⊠ *Grace Bay Rd., Grace Bay* ⊹ *Next to Saltmills* ☎ *649/946–5866, 844/428–8757* ⊕ *www.islandclubturks.com* ⇌ *24 apartments* ⚲ *No meals.*

Le Vele

$$$$ | **HOTEL** | Modern and chic, this Italian-influenced condo complex with its minimalistic lines reminds one of a Miami South Beach hotel, minus the crowds. **Pros:** great central location; spacious rooms maximize the ocean views; peaceful and quiet. **Cons:** residential feel isn't for everyone; the modern buildings don't blend with other resorts on the beach; pool is set back from beach without much ambience. $ *Rooms from: $800* ⊠ *Grace Bay Rd., Grace Bay* 🕾 *649/941–8800, 888/272–4406* ⊕ *www. leveleresort.com* 🛏 *22 rooms* ⧉ *Breakfast.*

Ocean Club

$$ | **RESORT** | **FAMILY** | Enormous, locally painted pictures of hibiscus make a striking first impression as you enter the reception area at one of the island's most well-established condominium resorts. **Pros:** family-friendly resort with shuttles between the two shared properties; screened balconies and porches allow a respite from incessant air-conditioning; fully equipped kitchens and gas grills make island dining more affordable. **Cons:** if you don't have a rental car, you have to take the shuttle to get closer to the "hub"; the sister properties are a shuttle ride or 20-minute beach walk apart; rooms are starting to show their age. $ *Rooms from: $275* ⊠ *Governor's Rd., Grace Bay* ⊹ *Opposite Provo Golf Club* 🕾 *649/946–5880, 800/457–8787* ⊕ *www.oceanclubresorts.com* ⊗ *Closed Sept.* 🛏 *174 suites* ⧉ *No meals.*

Ocean Club West

$$ | **RESORT** | **FAMILY** | Its central location and large, affordable, comfortable rooms make this resort popular with vacationers. **Pros:** family-friendly resort with shuttles between the two shared properties; situated on a wide section of Grace Bay Beach; central location eases walking to shops and restaurants. **Cons:** condo style means units vary in terms of decor; higher price point than Ocean Club; only rooms in buildings closest to the beach are guaranteed to have fantastic ocean views. $ *Rooms from: $285* ⊠ *Grace Bay Rd., Grace Bay* 🕾 *649/946–5880* ⊕ *oceanclubresorts.com/ocean-club-west-resort/* ⊗ *Closed Sept.* 🛏 *88 suites* ⧉ *No meals.*

★ The Palms

$$$$ | **RESORT** | **FAMILY** | High on luxury, the Palms has consistently scored in the top 100 hotels in the world and is directly in the heart of Grace Bay, right on the waterfront. **Pros:** lively; one of the best spas in the Caribbean; wide range of amenities. **Cons:** in the summer, the sunken pool bar area can get a bit hot when the trade winds die; expensive; island time service doesn't always match high-end expectations. $ *Rooms from: $750* ⊠ *Princess Dr., Grace Bay* ⊹ *Between*

the Alexandra and the Somerset ☎ *649/946–8666, 866/630–5890*
⊕ *www.thepalmstc.com* 🛏 *72 suites* ⦿ *Breakfast.*

Point Grace

$$$$ | RESORT | Keeping history in mind, this resort was built with
a turn-of-the-20th-century British colonial feel; dark mahogany,
granite, marble, and teak create a sense of warmth and comfort
within each of the 33 luxurious one- to four-bedroom suites and
penthouses. **Pros:** relaxing environment; beautiful pool; attentive
service. **Cons:** can be extremely quiet (signs around the pool
remind you); decor is dated; service can be inconsistent. ⑤ *Rooms
from: $630* ⊠ *Grace Bay Rd., Grace Bay* ⚓ *Next door to the
Sands* ☎ *649/946–5097 general number, 888/209–5582 toll-free
reservations, 649/941–7743 reservations* ⊕ *www.pointgrace.com*
🕙 *Closed Sept. through mid-Oct.* 🛏 *27 rooms* ⦿ *No meals.*

Ports of Call Resort

$ | HOTEL | If you don't mind a few minutes' walk or complimen-
tary stretch golf cart shuttle to get to Grace Bay Beach, then the
reasonable room rates are definitely worth it. **Pros:** economical
alternative to beachfront properties; walking distance to main hub;
"attached" to shopping area with restaurants. **Cons:** no restaurants on property; peak season standard rooms require two-night
minimum (though more expensive deluxe rooms do not); not on
the beach. ⑤ *Rooms from: $229* ⊠ *11 Sandcastle Rd., Behind Port
of Call, Grace Bay* ☎ *649/946–8888,* ⊕ *www.portsofcallresort.com*
🛏 *98 suites* ⦿ *Breakfast.*

Royal West Indies Resort

$$$ | RESORT | With a contemporary take on colonial architecture
and the outdoor feel of a botanical garden, this unpretentious
resort on Grace Bay Beach has plenty of garden-view and beachfront studios and suites for moderate self-catering budgets. **Pros:**
great bang for your buck; on one of the longest stretches of Grace
Bay Beach; daily happy hour. **Cons:** Club Med next door can be
noisy; staying in a unit at the back of the resort is no different
from staying at some of the off-the-beach properties because of
the resort configuration; most activities are extra. ⑤ *Rooms from:
$415* ⊠ *Bonaventure Crescent, Off Governor's Rd., Grace Bay*
⚓ *Between Club Med and Grandview* ☎ *649/946–5004, 800/332–
4203* ⊕ *www.royalwestindies.com* 🛏 *115 suites* ⦿ *No meals.*

Sands at Grace Bay

$$$ | RESORT | FAMILY | Spacious gardens and winding pools set the
tone for one of Provo's most popular family-friendly resorts. **Pros:**
one of the best places for families; central to shops and numerous
restaurants; screened-in balconies and porches give an escape
from incessant air-conditioning. **Cons:** avoid courtyard rooms,

Crazy for Conch 👁

"Belongers," otherwise known as islanders, once relied on fishing as the mainstay of their economy—before the arrival of tourism in Turks and Caicos. They truly know the importance of conch, not only as the country's largest export, but also as an integral part of the local diet. Today things have changed ever so slightly; now every part of the conch, from shell to meat, is used. Every restaurant in the Turks and Caicos serves some type of conch, in a sandwich, salad, fritter, soup, or even sushi, and the beauty of its shell has made its way into jewelry design and homewares. The shells may also be purchased in their somewhat natural state, albeit buffed and polished, and taken home as per regulation—two per person. Shells are also crushed and used as exfoliates in a few spas around the islands.

Visitors to the islands may dive for conch as part of a day out on the water, and then enjoy it in a local dish later in the day as part of a beach barbecue. Alternatively, they can find it in any of the local restaurants. Conch can also be found embedded in the walls built around the homes in Salt Cay, not only for a tropical look but also to keep cows and donkeys out of the yard.

which aren't worth the price; restaurant is busy; lots of kids can make poolside rooms less than relaxing. ⑤ *Rooms from: $400* ✉ *Grace Bay Rd., Grace Bay* ☎ *649/941–5199, 877/777–2637* ⊕ *www.thesandstc.com* ⤳ *114 suites* ⑩ *No meals.*

★ Seven Stars

$$$$ | RESORT | FAMILY | Fronting gorgeous Grace Bay Beach, the tallest property on the island also sets a high mark for luxury within its three buildings, a magnificent heated pool, and large in-room bathrooms. **Pros:** Moët champagne shack right next to the beach; walking distance to everything in Grace Bay; lots to keep the kids entertained. **Cons:** some find the giant scale of the resort too big for the rest of the island; higher density than most other resorts; construction on the Ritz Carlton next door is noisy and, when complete, will dwarf the Seven Stars. ⑤ *Rooms from: $747* ✉ *Grace Bay Rd., Grace Bay* ☎ *649/941–7777, 844/332–5315* ⊕ *www.sevenstarsgracebay.com* ⤳ *123 suites* ⑩ *Breakfast.*

Sibonné Beach Hotel

$ | HOTEL | Dwarfed by most of the nearby resorts, the smallest hotel on Grace Bay Beach has snug (by Provo's spacious standards) but pleasant rooms with Bermudan-style balconies and a tiny circular pool that's hardly used because the property is right on the beach. **Pros:** closest property to the beach; the island's best bargain; small and unimposing. **Cons:** pool is small and dated; some rooms have a double bed; lacks amenities offered by most other hotel properties on island. $ *Rooms from: $225* ✉ *Princess Dr., Grace Bay* ✛ *Right next door to the Somerset resort* ☎ *649/946–5547, 888/570–2861* ⊕ *www.sibonne.com* ☉ *Closed Sept.* ⤴ *30 rooms* ⦿ *No meals.*

★ The Somerset

$$$$ | RESORT | This luxury resort has the wow factor, starting with the architecture and ending in your luxuriously appointed suite. **Pros:** the most beautiful architecture on Provo; located in middle, so you can walk to snorkel and to shops; lots of added amenities, including a sunscreen bar. **Cons:** the cheapest rooms are not worth the dollar value—they can get noisy; in-room Wi-Fi can be spotty; included breakfast doesn't live up to five-star expectations. $ *Rooms from: $700* ✉ *Princess Dr., Grace Bay* ✛ *Between the Palms and Sibonné* ☎ *649/339–5900, 888/386–8770* ⊕ *www. thesomerset.com* ⤴ *53 suites* ⦿ *Free Breakfast.*

The Tuscany

$$$$ | RENTAL | FAMILY | This self-catering, quiet, upscale resort is the place for mature, independent travelers to unwind without the need for resort amenities. **Pros:** luxurious; all condos have ocean views; beautiful pool. **Cons:** no restaurant or reception, and it's at the far end of the hub; very expensive for a self-catering resort; can feel like no one else is on the property. $ *Rooms from: $775* ✉ *Governor's Rd., Grace Bay* ✛ *Across from the golf course* ☎ *649/941–4667, 866/359–6466* ⊕ *www.thetuscanyresort.com* ⤴ *30 condos* ⦿ *No meals.*

The Venetian on Grace Bay

$$$$ | RENTAL | This luxury property, focusing on peace-filled privacy, offers magnificent views just minutes from the hub and close to the island's only golf course. **Pros:** away from it all; gorgeous views through the oversize windows; lush landscaping. **Cons:** need transportation to the best restaurants and shops; no restaurant or "reception" on-site; incredibly quiet, almost too much so. $ *Rooms from: $625* ✉ *Grace Bay Rd., Grace Bay* ☎ *866/242–0969, 649/941–3512* ⊕ *www.thevenetiangracebay. com* ⤴ *27 condos* ⦿ *No meals.*

Villa Del Mar

$$$ | HOTEL | Even though it is not directly on Grace Bay Beach, this resort offers some tremendous features for the price. **Pros:** close to some of the best restaurants on the island; within walking distance of Casablanca Casino; a bargain for the luxury. **Cons:** no on-site restaurant; no views from most floors; not directly on the beach. *⑤ Rooms from: $400 ✉ 1 Crescent Dr., Grace Bay* ☎ *649/941–5160, 877/345–4890* ⊕ *www.yourvilladelmar.com* ⇱ *42 units* ❑ *Breakfast.*

Villa Renaissance

$$$$ | **RENTAL** | Short-term rentals are available at Villa Renaissance, and guests love the quiet, residential feel of this luxury property modeled after a Tuscan villa. **Pros:** luxury for less; one of the prettiest courtyards in Provo; peaceful and quiet. **Cons:** not a full-service resort; limited on-property food and beverage options; can be too quiet for some. *⑤ Rooms from: $580 ✉ Ventura Dr., Grace Bay* ⊹ *Between Regent Grand and the Mansions* ☎ *649/941–4358* ⊕ *www.villarenaissanceturksandcaicos.com* ⇱ *32 units* ❑ *No meals.*

👜 Shopping

ARTS AND CRAFTS GALLERIES

★ Anna's and Anna's Too

ART GALLERIES | Anna's sells original artworks, silk-screen paintings, sculptures, and handmade sea-glass jewelry, most made by local artists and artisans. It's a treasure trove of fabulous finds. You won't leave without picking up a little something to take home with you. Her newest edition is Anna's Too, just a couple of doors down. This wonderful shop is filled with fantastic women's wear—all cotton, comfortable, and colorful. Tucked alongside are books and pillows as well as other home decor items. ✉ *Saltmills Plaza, Grace Bay Rd., Grace Bay* ☎ *649/941–8841 Anna's Too, 649/941–8842 Anna's* ⊕ *www.anna.tc* ⊗ *Closed Sun.*

ArtProvo

ART GALLERIES | This gallery features a wide selection of designer wall art, but native crafts, jewelry, handblown glass, candles, and other gift items are also available, including locally made bath products. Mary, the gallery's owner, has lived in TCI for 40 years and has developed relationships with many local artists and artisans. She features creations by the island's own Jill Segal, Alexis, and Dwight Outten. Sandra Knuyt's cigar-smoking female characters are a favorite. ✉ *Regent Village, Regent St., Grace Bay* ⊹ *Turn off Grace Bay Rd. at Caicos Adventures* ☎ *649/941–4545* ⊕ *www.artprovo.tc* ⊗ *Closed Sun.*

Driftwood Studio

ART GALLERIES | You will find fine arts, textiles, photography, and crafts in this small gallery on Provo that prides themselves on bringing local art to their clientele. ✉ *Caicos Cafe Plaza, Grace Bay* ☎ *649/342–3052* ⊕ *driftwoodtci.com.*

Local Souvenirs

What should you bring home after a fabulous vacation in the Turks and Caicos? Here are a few suggestions, some of which are free!

If you're a beachcomber, you might find a sand dollar or conch shells to bring home. But remember, much of the north shore is part of the Princess Alexandra National Park, so you are not allowed to take anything away—enjoy it only while you're there. You'll have to go shelling outside the parks. Of course, you can find wonderfully polished shells at many of the souvenir stops, as well as at the Conch Shack and Bugaloo's.

You'll find locally made ceramics at Art Provo, as well as at Paradise Arts in the Saltmills Plaza.

There are two cultural centers, one between Ocean Club and Club Med in the entrance to Rickie's Flamingo Cafe and the other hidden down a dirt road across the street from Beaches' eastern-most entrance. In addition, there is a crafts market called Alverna's Market on Dolphin Road, just down from Grace-way Gourmet IGA. Here you'll find mostly Haitian metal art and souvenir trinkets. Custom-made pieces can be ordered.

The best free souvenir—besides your phenomenal tan—is a potcake puppy. The puppy you adopt comes with carrier, papers, and all the shots—and will remind you year after year of your terrific vacation. Let's not forget there are local potkittens, too!

Making Waves Art Studio

ART GALLERIES | Alex, the owner and resident artist, paints turquoise scenes, often on wood that doesn't require framing. She is happy to discuss the possibility of transforming your thoughts and emotions about one special spot onto canvas as the perfect souvenir. You'll find artists working on-site—come and meet them in their natural habitats. They don't mind being fed! And bring wine! ⊠ *107 Ocean Club West Plaza, Grace Bay* ☎ *649/242–9588* ⊕ *www.makingwavesart.com* ☉ *Closed Sun.*

CLOTHING

Blue Surf Shop

CLOTHING | This is the only true surf shop on the island. Affiliated with Big Blue Unlimited, they carry gear from such companies as Quicksilver, Billabong, Rip Curl, Roxy, Element, and Dakine. They are also the only ones that carry this country's very own ConchTCI wear. In addition, you will find polarized sunglasses from Oakley, Ray-Ban, SunCloud, and Von Zipper, and GoPro cameras, as they are the only licensed provider. Blue also carries an excellent selection of sandals as well as snorkel gear. ⊠ *Saltmills, Grace Bay* ☎ *649/941–8670.*

Caicos Wear Boutique

CLOTHING | This store is filled with casual resort wear, including Caribbean-print shirts, swimsuits from Brazil, sandals, beach jewelry, and gifts. On the more practical side of things, snorkel gear, inflatable beach toys, and towels might be something you need while visiting the island; you'll find them here. ⊠ *Regent Village, Grace Bay Rd., Grace Bay* ☎ *649/941–3346.*

Hidden Treasures Boutique

CLOTHING | This is the perfect little shop to find an elegant yet casual outfit for warm-weather wear. Hidden Treasures features international brands such as Saint Grace, Goddis, TBags, Yosi Samra, and Vitamin A swimwear. You will also find lightweight lingerie and undergarments, along with a small selection of accessories to complete the ensemble. Call ahead, as their hours are more limited than many other shops in Saltmills. ⊠ *#9 Saltmills Plaza, Grace Bay* ☎ *649/941–7425.*

The Siren & the Pirate

CLOTHING | Immediately inside the Club Med Turkoise main lobby area you'll find this gem of a boutique. In addition to a small selection of bathing suits and resort wear for men and women, you'll find impressive locally made jewelry, photographs, and other souvenir items. ⊠ *Club Med Turkoise, Grace Bay Rd., Grace Bay.*

FOOD

Grocery shopping in Provo is almost as good as at home, with all the American, British, and Canadian brands you crave. Because everything has to be flown in, expect to pay up to 50% more than for similar purchases in the United States. Even many hard-to-find products and special dietary foods can be found on Provo. Shipments come in on Sunday, so Monday is your best food-shopping bet.

Beer is expensive; rum is cheaper. Stores are prohibited by law from selling alcohol on Sunday. Although it's tempting to bring in your own cooler of food, remember that some airlines charge for checked bags, and there is the risk of losing luggage. More than likely, if it's allowed in the States, it's allowed on Provo—meat, fish, and vegetables can be brought in if frozen and vacuum-sealed; always ask your airline if you will be allowed to check a cooler. If you're traveling for more than a week, then you may save enough money by bringing provisions in with you to make it worth your while. But remember, if you're staying on Provo, there will be no problem buying anything you need.

Cuban Crafters Cigars

TOBACCO | This company brings in Cuban tobacco and skillfully assembles a variety of cigars on Providenciales. They do this to bring the product to you at a more economical price. They also have a small selection of spirits to offer. ⊠ *Saltmills, Grace Bay* ☎ *649/946–4600, 649/441–2823.*

FOTTAC

FOOD/CANDY | Flavors of the Turks and Caicos carries such specialties as local Bambarra rum and the spices and sauces that are made with it, plus rum cake, Turk's Head beer, local T-shirts, wineglasses, mugs, and locally made products. ⊠ *Regent Village, Regent St., Grace Bay* ☎ *649/946–4081* ⊕ *www.bambarrarum. com.*

Graceway Gourmet

FOOD/CANDY | The Grace Bay branch of Provo's largest supermarket is likely to have what you're looking for, including a selection of nice wines and beers. It's walkable from many of the resorts, as it's right in the hub. It's especially popular for its prepared foods, which can be taken back and quickly reheated in your condo's kitchen when you don't feel like cooking from scratch or heading out to eat. You will also find it's a good stop for inexpensive beach toys; there's a separate little shop for them just inside the door. ⊠ *Dolphin Ave., Grace Bay* ☎ *649/333–5000* ⊕ *www.gracewaygourmet.com.*

Kissing Fish Catering Co.

FOOD/CANDY | Kissing Fish Catering Co. has the same owners as Bay Bistro. The company will cater events like full-moon bonfires on the beach, weddings, and private parties, including beachside romantic dinners for two. Choose options from pig roasts and ribs to four-course meals with grilled lobster, grouper with mango chutney, or jerk chicken and tasty salads, to name just a few from their extensive menu. If you're staying in a villa or condo with full kitchen, you can hire a personal chef to prepare meals in-house. ⊠ *Sibonné Beach Hotel, Grace Bay Rd., At Bay Bistro, Grace Bay* ☎ *649/941–8917* ⊕ *www.turksandcaicoscatering.com.*

JEWELRY

Jai's

JEWELRY/ACCESSORIES | Jai's is the place to go if you'd like to purchase a piece of luxury jewelry as a reminder of that special vacation. You will find names such as David Yurman, Doves, Gucci, Movado, Cartier, and Rolex, along with less expensive options, including their Pandora collection. If jewelry is not what you're after, they also carry a wide range of fragrances and sunglasses to choose from. With 20 years of experience serving Turks and

Caicos, they know what you're after! You will also find them in the departure lounge at the airport. ⊠ *Regent Village, Regent St., Grace Bay* ☎ *649/941–4324* ⊕ *www.jais.tc.*

★ Rumeurs

CLOTHING | Try not to be in a hurry when you pop into this little gem of a shop as there is so much to take in. Rumeurs has a wide assortment of items under one roof: jewelry, women's clothing, small pieces of art and sculptures, lighting, household items, and furniture—all with an Asian influence. ⊠ *Caicos Cafe Plaza, Grace Bay* ☎ *649/941–5569.*

SOUVENIRS

Caribbean Outpost

CLOTHING | The Outpost, in the Regent Village Plaza, is an enormous souvenir shop, connected directly to the Goldsmith duty-free jewelry shop. You will find such things as T-shirts, hats, beach cover-ups, beach towels and toys, sunscreen, sandals, souvenirs, and so, so much more. This is not a quick stop to get in and out. ⊠ *Regent Village, Grace Bay* ☎ *649/941–5599.*

Mama's Gift Shop

CLOTHING | Mama's is the place for the usual souvenirs and trinkets. She has a great selection of T-shirts and hats, as well as shot glasses and fridge magnets. What's really fun about shopping here is Mama herself; she makes everyone who walks through her door feel like family. ⊠ *Ports of Call Shopping Center, Grace Bay Rd., Grace Bay* ☎ *649/946–5538.*

SPAS

Anani Spa at Grace Bay Club

SPA/BEAUTY | Anani Spa at Grace Bay Club is on the villas side of the complex. There are eight treatment rooms in total, but treatments can also be performed on your terrace if you're staying at the resort, or in the spa tent on the oceanfront. Spa packages are available so that you can enjoy a combination of treatments designed to work together. One of their signature treatments is the Exotic Lime and Ginger Salt Glow; you will emerge refreshed and polished! ⊠ *Villas at Grace Bay Club, Bonaventure Crescent, Grace Bay* ☎ *649/946–5050* ⊕ *www.gracebayresorts.com.*

★ The Palms Resort and Spa

SPA/BEAUTY | Widely considered one of the best spas in the Caribbean, the Palms Spa is an oasis of relaxation. In the main facility you will find a pedicure/manicure space, gym, boutique, and yoga and Pilates pavilion, as well as men's and women's steam rooms and saunas. Outdoors, white tented cabanas grace the edge of a beautiful reflection pool, its waters catching images of towering palms and flowering bougainvillea. However, you don't even have to leave your room; massages may be arranged so that you can enjoy the wonderful sea views right from your very own balcony. Guests are encouraged to indulge in one of the locally inspired signature treatments: a mother-of-pearl body exfoliation incorporating the queen conch shell, or the 90-minute Zareeba herbal cleansing and detox. Rest a while and sip herbal tea or replenish with citrus-infused water before or after your treatment. ✉ *The Palms, Princess Dr., Grace Bay* ☎ *649/946–8666 resort general number, 649/946–8667 direct dial, spa line* ⊕ *www.thepalmstc.com.*

★ Spa Tropique

SPA/BEAUTY | You pick the place, and this spa comes to your hotel room or even your isolated villa. Or, you can go to one of their five locations scattered throughout the Grace Bay area. They offer all the standard treatments as well as a Thai massage that, when combined with the relaxed vibe of the island, will relieve you of any tension you brought with you on vacation. ✉ *Ports of Call, Grace Bay Rd., Grace Bay* ☎ *649/331–2400* ⊕ *www.spatropique.com.*

★ Teona Spa

SPA/BEAUTY | The spa for Bianca Sands, the Renaissance, and the Somerset, Teona also provides a mobile service offering most of their treatments in the comfort of your hotel or villa. Their spaces exude a peace-filled ambience, with every detail carefully thought out. Hush as you enter, and relax while you're there. It is the spa choice for many island residents. Take a peek at the spa specials; there is always a combination package put together for special times of the year. Or try one of the spa parties. What better way to spend time with a young one than a Mommy and Me day? The team also offers wedding packages that include makeup and hair. ✉ *Bianca Sands Resort, Ventura Dr., Grace Bay* ⊹ *Turn off Grace Bay Rd. at the Goldsmiths into Regent Village* ☎ *649/941–5051 main spa, 649/339–5900 Somerset location* ⊕ *www.teonaspa.com.*

★ Thalasso Spa at Point Grace

SPA/BEAUTY | Thalasso Spa at Point Grace offers their services from within three whitewashed open-air cabanas set upon the dunes overlooking Grace Bay. They share the European philosophy of the famous Thalgo Spas of France and combine it with the perfect Caribbean ambience for your enjoyment. Treatments combine elements of the ocean, including sea mud, seaweed, and sea salt, with the properties of seawater to pamper you from head to toe. The setting alone, with the salt air and sea breezes, is worth the visit. This is another favorite with residents. ✉ *Point Grace Resort, Grace Bay Rd., Grace Bay* ☎ *649/946–5097* ⊕ *www.pointgrace.com.*

🍸 Nightlife

Danny Buoy's
BARS/PUBS | A popular Irish pub, Danny Buoy's has lots of slot machines, as well as big-screen TVs. It's a great place to watch sports broadcasts from all over. Different nights feature different nightlife: Tuesday and Thursday are karaoke, Friday is country night with line dancing, and Saturday night has a DJ. It's open until 2 am every night except Sunday when they call it a night at midnight. It's also a great spot to get a late night bite. ⊠ *Grace Bay Rd., Grace Bay* ⊹ *Across from Regent Village* ☎ *649/946–5921* ⊕ *www.dannybuoys.com.*

Casablanca Casino
CASINOS | The Casablanca Casino has brought slots, blackjack, American roulette, poker, and craps to Provo. Because it's open daily until 4 am, you can come late and make it your last stop for the night. There are complimentary drinks while playing, and you can get a free shuttle ride by contacting the casino. ⊠ *Grace Bay Rd., Grace Bay* ☎ *649/941–3737* ⊕ *www.casablanca.tc.*

The Bight

This beach area is popular for off-the-beach snorkeling and an even more popular Thursday night fish fry. The Provo Sailing Club meets most Saturdays at the Bight Park for sailing lessons or family picnics. There is no defining where the Bight starts and Grace Bay ends, so most just assume that it is simply the "quiet end" of Grace Bay.

🏖 Beaches

⭐ Lower Bight Beach
BEACH—SIGHT | Lower Bight Beach blends right into Grace Bay Beach as the western extension of Provo's Princess Alexandra National Park; visitors to the island think the two beaches are one and the same. Unlike its world-famous counterpart, Bight Beach has off-the-beach snorkeling where the fringing reef comes in to touch the shore. The Provo Sailing Club gives lessons most Saturdays for the residents of the island and also holds the Annual Fools Regatta in June, which everyone can enjoy. Both are held at the far western end in what is known as the Children's Park. **Amenities:** food and drink; parking (free). **Best for:** snorkeling; swimming; walking. ⊠ *Lower Bight Rd., The Bight* ⊹ *The Children's Park is at the junction of Pratt's Rd. and Lower Bight Rd.*

🍴 Restaurants

★ Kitchen 218

$$$$ | ECLECTIC | Relatively new on the scene, this restaurant is at the Beach House with the pool as its backdrop, simple and uncomplicated. A unique feature is the Veuve Clicquot champagne bar with a caviar menu. **Known for:** nicest Turks and Caicos Collection restaurant; coconut-herb mahimahi; pick your own lettuce from the garden. ⑤ *Average main: $40* ⊠ *The Beach House, Lower Bight Rd. 218, The Bight* ☎ *649/946–5800* ⊕ *www.beachhousetci.com.*

Somewhere Café and Lounge

$$$ | MEXICAN | Right on Grace Bay Beach overlooking tranquil waters, the Somewhere Café is a pleasant, casual dining option. It's the perfect spot to enjoy midday, as bathing attire is perfectly acceptable, with the incredible Coral Gardens snorkeling only a few steps away. **Known for:** authentic Tex-Mex; great guacamole; live music. ⑤ *Average main: $22* ⊠ *Coral Gardens Resort, Lower Bight Rd., The Bight* ✛ *Right on the beach* ☎ *649/941–8260* ⊕ *www.somewherecafeandlounge.com* ☞ *Menu items may be limited in the off season (Oct.–Nov.) and cafe closes sporadically during this time.*

★ Stelle

$$$$ | CONTEMPORARY | The setting is chic—some would even say swanky—with white fabrics blowing in the wind, diners dressed for clubbing, and tables surrounding a courtyard with views of the lighted pool. It's as if a small piece of South Beach has been transported to the tropics, albeit with an old-world flair. **Known for:** Good but pricey dinner spot; wine pairings no matter what you choose to eat; Thursday night Japanese menu with sake pairings. ⑤ *Average main: $45* ⊠ *Wymara Resort & Villas, Lower Bight Rd., The Bight* ☎ *649/941–7555* ⊕ *www.wymararesortandvillas.com.*

🛏 Hotels

★ Beach House Turks and Caicos

$$$$ | ALL-INCLUSIVE | On the quieter, western end of Grace Bay, this intimate adults-only, all-suites resort has a unique Caribbean air, and its full all-inclusive experience extends to sister properties The Alexandra and Blue Haven. **Pros:** less populated end of the beach, plus one of the widest stretches; all-inclusive access to three hotel properties; adults only means peace and quiet around the pool and on the beach. **Cons:** the pool is small compared to many other properties; no kids allowed; pool and garden view rooms have a bit of a walk to the beach. ⑤ *Rooms from: $1200*

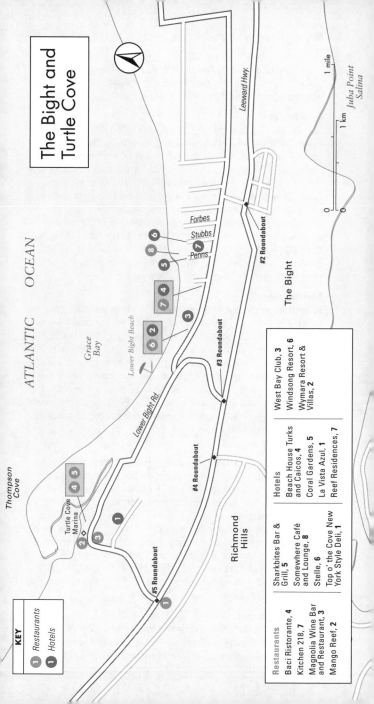

The Bight and Turtle Cove

KEY
- ① Restaurants
- ① Hotels

ATLANTIC OCEAN

Thompson Cove

Grace Bay

Turtle Cove Marina

Lower Bight Beach

Lower Bight Rd.

Forbes
Stubbs
Penns

Leeward Hwy.

Richmond Hills

The Bight

Juba Point Salina

#5 Roundabout
#4 Roundabout
#3 Roundabout
#2 Roundabout

0   1 km   1 mile

Restaurants
Baci Ristorante, **4**
Kitchen 218, **7**
Magnolia Wine Bar and Restaurant, **3**
Mango Reef, **2**
Sharkbites Bar & Grill, **5**
Somewhere Café and Lounge, **8**
Stelle, **6**
Top o' the Cove New York Style Deli, **1**

Hotels
Beach House Turks and Caicos, **4**
Coral Gardens, **5**
La Vista Azul, **1**
Reef Residences, **7**
West Bay Club, **3**
Windsong Resort, **6**
Wymara Resort & Villas, **2**

✉ *218 Lower Bight Rd., The Bight* ✛ *Between West Bay Club and Coral Gardens resorts* ☎ *649/946–5800, 855/946–5800* ⊕ *www.beachhousetci.com* ⇦ *21 suites* ⦿ *All-inclusive.*

Coral Gardens

$$$ | RENTAL | The best off-the-beach snorkeling directly in front of Coral Gardens makes this resort and its large condo units a very popular spot. **Pros:** resort fronts the best off-the-beach snorkeling spot on Provo; spacious rooms all have ocean views; on-site restaurant and bar is one of the liveliest spots on the beach. **Cons:** restaurant can get lively at night so be sure to choose a unit with distance between; car rental recommended to get to the best restaurants and shops on island; confusing management setup. ⑤ *Rooms from: $400* ✉ *Penn's Rd., The Bight* ☎ *649/941–5497 Coral Gardens on Grace Bay, 800/787–9115* ⊕ *www.CoralGardensonGraceBay.com and www.coralgardens.com* ⇦ *25 suites* ⦿ *No meals.*

Reef Residences

$$ | RENTAL | A smaller, more intimate resort set just back off the beach within proximity of some of the best off-the-beach snorkeling, Reef is both economical and convenient. **Pros:** nice pool; spacious rooms; close to a great snorkeling reef. **Cons:** you have to walk through another resort to get to the beach; rental car is recommended to get around; resort structure gets a bit confusing with the overlap with Coral Gardens. ⑤ *Rooms from: $375* ✉ *Stubbs Rd., The Bight* ☎ *649/941–3713, 800/532–8536* ⊕ *www.reefresidence.com* ⇦ *24 suites at Reef Residences, 8 suites at Coral Gardens* ⦿ *No meals.*

West Bay Club

$$$$ | RESORT | A prime location on a pristine stretch of Grace Bay Beach just steps away from the best off-the-beach snorkeling makes this luxury resort a top pick. **Pros:** all suites have a beach view; studios have garden or pool views; amazing luxury for the price; situated on the widest stretch of Grace Bay Beach. **Cons:** you'll need transportation to go shopping and to get to the main hub; spa treatments available only in your room; limited dining options on property or walking distance from the resort. ⑤ *Rooms from: $630* ✉ *242 Lower Bight Rd., The Bight* ☎ *649/946–8550, 855/749–5750* ⊕ *www.thewestbayclub.com* ⊗ *Closed Sept.* ⇦ *46 suites* ⦿ *Free Breakfast.*

★ Windsong Resort

$$$ | RESORT | FAMILY | On a gorgeous beach lined with several appealing resorts, Windsong simply makes you feel at home. **Pros:** pool is unique; huge, gorgeous bathrooms; amazing penthouse rooftop decks. **Cons:** studios have only a refrigerator and microwave; included breakfast is nothing spectacular; not many restaurant options within walking distance. ⑤ *Rooms from: $350* ✉ *Stubbs Rd., The Bight* ⊹ *Between Coral Gardens and Beaches Resort* ☎ *649/946–3766, 800/946–3766 U.S. toll-free* ⊕ *www. windsongresort.com* ➠ *46 rooms* ⧫ *Free Breakfast.*

★ Wymara Resort & Villas

$$$$ | **RESORT** | South Beach Miami meets island time at this gorgeous resort with modern, chic furnishings and minimalistic vibe. **Pros:** service is excellent; luxurious accommodations; gorgeous heated pool and amazing rooms with unprecedented views. **Cons:** need transportation for shops and exploring; high-end luxury comes with a high-end price tag; service not always at luxury resort standards. ⑤ *Rooms from: $600* ✉ *Lower Bight Rd., The Bight* ⊹ *In between the Bight Park and the Beach House* ☎ *649/941–7555, 888/844–5986* ⊕ *www.wymararesortandvillas. com* ➠ *91 rooms* ⧫ *Breakfast.*

Turtle Cove

The Bight Beach eventually blends into the beach around the opening to Turtle Cove. Inland, around the marina that harbors many of the fishing charters and smaller private yachts, is where you will find several excursion companies and fishing charters, as well as a couple of popular restaurants, including Sharkbite and Baci Ristorante.

🍴 Restaurants

Top o' the Cove New York Style Deli

$ | **DELI** | Order a coffee, tea, bagel, deli sandwich, salad, or dessert at this island institution (opened in 1992) on Leeward Highway, just south of Turtle Cove. They also have great pizza, which you can order by the slice or by the box. **Known for:** bagels; hearty breakfast; quality picnic fixin's. ⑤ *Average main: $10* ✉ *Leeward Hwy., Turtle Cove* ☎ *649/946–4694* ⊕ *www.topothecove.com* ⊙ *No dinner.*

★ Baci Ristorante

$$$ | **ITALIAN** | Aromas redolent of the Mediterranean waft from the open kitchen as you enter this local favorite directly on Turtle Cove. Outdoor seating is on a lovely canal-front patio, or you may choose to dine at a table in the open-air, covered restaurant. **Known for:** build your own pizzas; authentic, made-from-scratch Italian desserts; a nice break from the standard American or island fare. ⑤ *Average main: $25* ✉ *Harbour*

Towne, Turtle Cove 🕿 *649/941–3044* ⊕ *www.baci-ristorante. com* 🕓 *Closed Sun. No lunch Sat.*

Magnolia Wine Bar and Restaurant

$$$$ | ECLECTIC | The hands-on owners here, Gianni and Tracey Caporuscio, make success seem simple. Expect well-prepared, uncomplicated dishes. **Known for:** sunset views; European fare with Caribbean flair; fresh tuna seared to perfection. $ *Average main: $38* ✉ *76 Sunburst Rd., Turtle Cove* ⊹ *On the ridge overlooking Turtle Cove, just off Lower Bight Rd. in the old Miramar Hotel* 🕿 *649/941–5108* ⊕ *www.magnoliaprovo.com* 🕓 *Closed Mon.*

★ Mango Reef

$$$ | ECLECTIC | Dine alfresco while watching yachts sail in and out of the Turtle Cove Marina at this restaurant, located well west of the hustle and bustle of Grace Bay. Casual and popular with families, Mango Reef serves standard island and American fare for lunch and dinner, including lots of conch, quesadillas, burgers, and salads. **Known for:** outdoor dining; family-friendly atmosphere; casual island fare. $ *Average main: $23* ✉ *Turtle Cove Marina, Turtle Cove* 🕿 *649/946–8200* ⊕ *www.mangoreef.com.*

Sharkbites Bar & Grill

$$ | AMERICAN | FAMILY | At this casual local favorite, the standard fare includes everything from the local catch of the day, sandwiches, and island specialties to wings or nachos and beer along with other bar snacks. For those French Canadians visiting, they have a great poutine. **Known for:** casual spot for lunch; live music; Friday-night happy hour. $ *Average main: $17* ✉ *Turtle Cove Marina, Bridge Rd., Turtle Cove* 🕿 *649/941–5090.*

🛏 Hotels

La Vista Azul

$ | RENTAL | You can save money by staying slightly away from the beach without giving up comfort or location at these condos overlooking Turtle Cove, which you can rent via Airbnb and VRBO. **Pros:** space and high-end comfort for a fraction of the cost on Grace Bay; views from the rooms are gorgeous; free Wi-Fi. **Cons:** too many stairs (three flights up from lobby to reach the elevators); rental car or taxi needed to get to many of the popular restaurants and sights; parking lot is at elevator level. $ *Rooms from: $175* ✉ *Lower Bight Rd., Turtle Cove* 🕿 *649/946–8522, 866/519–9618* ✉ *reservations@lvaresort.com* ⊕ *www.lavistaazulresorttci.com* ⤴ *23 condos.*

What Is a Potcake?

Potcakes are indigenous dogs of the Bahamas and Turks and Caicos islands. Traditionally, these strays would be fed leftovers from the bottom of the pot, hence the name. Much is being done today to control the stray-dog population. The TCSPCA and Potcake Place are two agencies working to find homes for the puppies. You can do a good deed by adopting one of these gorgeous pups; they will have received all their shots and have all the paperwork required to take them into the United States or Canada. Even if you don't adopt, you can help by volunteering to bring one to its adopted family, found online. Clearing customs in the United States is surprisingly easy when you bring back a potcake! If that's just not possible, be sure to stop by Saltmills and adopt a dog for an hour or two; they will very much appreciate a walk on the beach and a bit of love. For more information on how you can help, check out the website for Potcake Place (⊕ *www. potcakeplace.com*).

🛍 Shopping

LIQUOR

Wine Cellar

TOBACCO | Visit this store for its large selection of duty-free spirits, wine, and beer. The Wine Cellar also carries a range of cigars. ✉ *1025 Leeward Hwy., The Bight* ✛ *East of Suzie Turn* ☎ *649/946–4536* ⊕ *www.winecellar.tc*.

Leeward

An upscale residential area, Leeward is the eastward extension of the island. Yes, it is possible to stroll right off the end of Grace Bay proper and onto the more quiet stretch of Pelican Beach, where you'll find a few quite grand residences and villa rentals. Working your way around the point, you can look across Leeward Channel to Little Water Cay, home of the rock iguana. Stop there, as the shoreline gets rocky and the mangroves soon begin. It is not possible to continue along unless you cut through private property. At the easternmost end of the island are the Heaving Down Rock and Walkin marinas, accessible only by boat and by car. This is where the ferry to North and South Caicos is based.

Half Moon Bay's white sand and turquoise water are minutes from Provo by boat.

Beaches

★ Half Moon Bay

BEACH—SIGHT | This natural ribbon of sand linking two uninhabited cays is only inches above the sparkling turquoise waters. Only minutes from Provo's eastern tip, Half Moon Bay is one of the most gorgeous beaches in the country. There are small limestone cliffs to explore on either end where rock iguanas sun themselves, as well as small, sandy coves. Most of the island's tour companies run excursions here or simply offer a beach drop-off. As an alternative, rent a kayak from Big Blue Collective and venture over independently. **Amenities:** none. **Best for:** solitude; swimming; walking. ⊠ *Between Big Water Cay and Little Water Cay* ⊕ *bigbluecollective.com.*

Pelican Beach

BEACH—SIGHT | Pelican Beach is another gorgeous stretch of beach that blends right into Grace Bay Beach at its eastern extension, also within the protection of the Princess Alexandra National Park. There is little distinction between where one beach ends and the other begins. Because of a cut in the reef, you may find wonderful shells here to enjoy—but remember that you are within the national park, so they must be left behind for others to see long after you have gone home. This end of the bay is slightly quieter than the rest, as there is much less development here. Enjoy. **Amenities:** parking (free). **Best for:** solitude; swimming; walking. ⊠ *Sandpiper Ave., Leeward* ✛ *Travel east along Grace Bay Rd. until you pass the small manned gatehouse.*

At the big circle take your first left, Sandpiper Ave. At the small roundabout, take a left and follow until the road ends, and park. The beach blends with Grace Bay Beach to the left; on the right, walk around to Pelican Beach. Some acknowlege a small stretch in between as Leeward Beach.

 Restaurants

Fire & Ice

$$$ | ECLECTIC | This restaurant is exquisitely set at the Blue Haven Resort & Marina, with Leeward Chanel and red mangroves as its backdrop. Start and end your evening with a drink in one of the waterside hammocks or lovely nooks set along the man-made spit overhanging the channel; the seating is comfortably arranged around a fire table, with glass to block the stronger breezes and cooler winds during the winter months. **Known for:** best dining this end of the island; tableside hibachi do-it-yourself barbecue dinner; fireside nightcaps overlooking the ocean. $ *Average main: $30* ⊠ *Blue Haven Resort, Leeward* 🕾 *649/946–9900* ⊕ *www. bluehavenctci.com* ☉ *Closed Wed.*

Salt

$$ | ECLECTIC | This is the casual counterpart to Fire & Ice, set off to the side from the resort at Blue Haven Marina, again with views of Leeward Channel and the magnificent yachts moored at the docks. It's very simple with a modern edge. **Known for:** casual dining; good spot to head after kayaking or diving at Big Blue next door; outdoor pool table and volleyball. $ *Average main: $20* ⊠ *Blue Haven Marina, Leeward* 🕾 *649/946–9900* ⊕ *www. bluehaventci.com.*

Hotels

The Atrium

$$ | RENTAL | FAMILY | This resort offers modern luxury with upscale furnishings, only a 10-minute walk from the far eastern end of Grace Bay. With resort beach chairs and umbrellas set up on a secluded beachfront, it's a bargain at a fraction of the price compared with staying in the hub. **Pros:** luxury for the money; beachfront setup is isolated with only beach-strollers passing through; great option for extended stay vacations. **Cons:** rental car is necessary for access to all that Provo has to offer—even the closest beach is a 15-minute walk away; studios have only kitchenettes; daily housekeeping costs extra. $ *Rooms from: $279* ⊠ *Governor's Rd., Leeward* 🕾 *649/333–0101, 888/592–7885* ⊕ *www.theatriumresorttci.com* ⌨ *38 suites* ⍾ *No meals.*

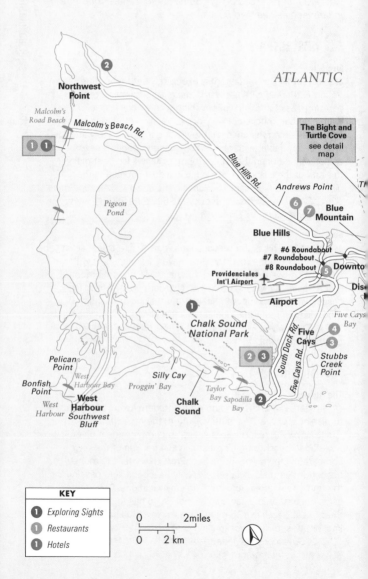

Providenciales

ATLANTIC

Northwest Point

Malcolm's Road Beach

Malcolm's Beach Rd.

Blue Hills Rd.

The Bight and Turtle Cove
see detail map

Andrews Point

Pigeon Pond

Blue Mountain

Blue Hills

#6 Roundabout
#7 Roundabout
#8 Roundabout

Downto

Providenciales Int'l Airport

Airport

Dis

Chalk Sound National Park

Five Cays Bay

Pelican Point

West Harbour Bay

Five Cays

Stubbs Creek Point

Bonfish Point

Silly Cay

Proggin' Bay

Taylor Bay

South Dock Rd.

Five Cays Rd.

West Harbour

West Harbour

Southwest Bluff

Chalk Sound

Sapodilla Bay

KEY

1 Exploring Sights
1 Restaurants
1 Hotels

0   2miles
0   2 km

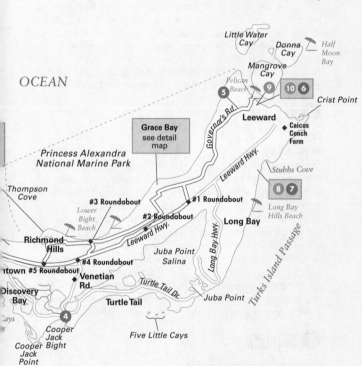

Water Cay

Little Water Cay

Donna Cay

Half Moon Bay

Mangrove Cay

Pelican Beach

5

9

10 **6**

Crist Point

Leeward

Caicos Conch Farm

OCEAN

Grace Bay
see detail map

Princess Alexandra National Marine Park

Leeward Hwy.

Governor's Rd.

Stubbs Cove

8 **7**

Thompson Cove

#3 Roundabout

#1 Roundabout

Long Bay Hills Beach

Lower Bight Beach

#2 Roundabout

Long Bay

Leeward Hwy.

Long Bay Hwy.

Turks Island Passage

Richmond Hills

Juba Point Salina

ntown **#5 Roundabout**

#4 Roundabout

Venetian Rd.

Turtle Tail Dr.

Juba Point

Discovery Bay

Turtle Tail

Cays

4

Cooper Jack Bight

Five Little Cays

Cooper Jack Point

Sights

Chalk Sound National Park, **1**

Sapodilla Hill, **2**

Restaurants

Bugaloo's, **4**

Da Conch Shack, **6**

Fire & Ice, **10**

Homeys, **5**

Las Brisas Restaurant & Bar, **2**

Omar's Beach Hut, **3**

The Restaurant at Amanyara, **1**

Salt, **9**

Shay on the Beach, **7**

Sui-Ren, **8**

Hotels

Amanyara, **1**

The Atrium, **5**

Blue Haven Resort and Marina, **6**

Harbour Club Villas, **4**

Neptune Villas, **3**

Northwest Point Resort, **2**

The Shore Club, **7**

Blue Haven Resort and Marina

$$$$ | RESORT | High on luxury, Blue Haven is the only resort on the far eastern end of the island, overlooking the beauty of au naturel Mangrove Cay and the mega-yachts moored dockside. **Pros:** fabulous amenities; all-inclusive dining at three different hotels; free shuttle day and night to the Beach House and the Alexandra. **Cons:** on a canal, so there is a current; very far away from everything else; beach is very small. ⑤ *Rooms from: $1750* ✉ *Marina Rd., Leeward* ☎ *649/946–9900, 855/832–7667* ⊕ *www.bluehaventci. com* ◷ *Closed Sept.–early Oct.* ⇥ *51 rooms* ✌ *All-inclusive.*

🛍 Shopping

FOOD

★ The Market

CONVENIENCE/GENERAL STORES | The Market prides itself on offering high-end gourmet and organic items, including a wide selection of fresh produce, international items, gourmet coffees and teas, dry goods, wine, beer, and spirits, as well as a range of smoothies and juices. While you're there, check out their café-style deli. You can grab a quick bite to eat and then pick up your shopping while enjoying a wonderful cappuccino. This is much more than convenience for those staying in the Leeward area. It's also the perfect spot for picking up specialty items that you may not find anywhere else on the island and where you can create a lovely picnic to take out on a boat trip leaving from right in front of the Market's door. ✉ *Blue Haven Resort, The Boathouse, Leeward* ☎ *649/946–9900.*

🍸 Nightlife

Blue Haven Resort, The Pool Bar

BARS/PUBS | Servers at the Pool Bar are more than happy to keep the drinks flowing by delivering them to your quiet spot on the water's edge, with Mangrove Cay and the mega-yachts of the marina as a dramatic backdrop. Three gas fireplace seating areas are absolutely wonderful spots from which to enjoy a breezy evening. ✉ *Blue Haven Resort, Leeward Marina, Leeward* ⊹ *Far eastern tip of the island* ☎ *649/946–9900 hotel, front desk* ⊕ *www.bluehaventci.com.*

Long Bay

 Beaches

Long Bay Hills Beach

BEACH—SIGHT | On the southeastern end of the island, visitors will find this a lovely stretch to stroll. It's not much of a place to swim, as the water is shallow and shells litter the floor. This is where you can pick up a conch shell to take home, as it is not part of the country's park system. It's ungroomed, so you'll find many along the shore. Long Bay is also where some will have their dreams of riding horseback fulfilled. The guides with Provo Ponies will also let them swim. Of course, the kitesurfers have also made this their mecca. On any one Saturday, there may be up to a hundred kiters enjoying the shallower waters and warm trade winds to advance their skills and ride their cares away. If you're not a participant, come out and enjoy the show. You can watch world-class boarders daily. It might spark some interest so that you find yourself checking in with one of the several instructors giving lessons out on Long Bay. **Amenities:** parking (free). **Best for:** kitesurfing; walking; windsurfing. ⊠ *Long Bay Rd., Long Bay* ⊹ *On Leeward Highway, continue onto its "extension" as if traveling to Walkin Marina. Watch on the right for the entrance to the Shore Club. Follow this road until you get to the public access point next to their parking lot.*

 Restaurants

★ Sui-Ren

$$$$ | **PERUVIAN** | Dine under the stars (and the palms) at this Peruvian-Japanese fusion hot spot on the southern side of Providenciales. The menu is small, but the delicious offerings are different from anything else you'll find on Provo. **Known for:** unique ceviche menu; Peruvian-Japanese menu is unique on the island; beautiful setting with music and lively bar scene. ⑤ *Average main: $36* ⊠ *Long Bay* ☎ *649/339–8000* ⊕ *www.theshoreclubtc.com.*

🛏 Hotels

★ The Shore Club

$$$$ | **RESORT** | **FAMILY** | One of the newest luxury resorts on Provo is also one of the only options on Long Bay—far away from the crowds along the more popular Grace Bay Beach—and its elegant suites, penthouses, and free-standing villas are spread across nine acres of lush beachfront property. **Pros:** five-star touches;

no other resorts around; luxurious decor and amenities. **Cons:** far away from everything else on Provo; limited meal options nearby; beach is nice, but pales in comparison to Grace Bay Beach. ⑤ *Rooms from: $925* ✉ *Long Bay* ☎ *649/339–8000, 888/808–9488 toll-free from U.S.* 🛏 *106 rooms* ¶⊙¶ *Free Breakfast.*

Venetian Road

Behind the Graceway IGA supermarket on Leeward Highway, this major road leads to the beaches and villas of Turtle Tail. At times it's a great spot to observe several visiting flamingos as they feed in Turtle and Flamingo lakes. This is a lovely road to take an early-morning run, as it is flat and parallels the water, with little traffic. From Leeward Highway to the end is approximately 6 miles (10 km).

Turtle Tail

Look south, out to the ocean behind Graceway IGA, and you'll see homes dotted along a ridgeline. Turtle Tail is the long spit of land that curves around on the south side of the island, and the beauty of the Caicos Banks lies in front of the homes. Although centrally located, it is one of the quietest areas of the island, and the location of many stunning vacation villas.

🛏 Hotels

Harbour Club Villas

$$ | **RENTAL** | **FAMILY** | Although not on the beach, this small complex of villas is by the marina, making it a good base for scuba diving, bonefishing, or that quieter-style vacation. **Pros:** centrally located only a five-minute drive from Grace Bay; great value; great base for divers. **Cons:** need a car to get around the island; have to drive to a beach; not much in the way of amenities. ⑤ *Rooms from: $300* ✉ *36 Turtle Tail Dr., Turtle Cove* ⊹ *Next to South Side Marina* ☎ *649/941–5748, 888/240–0447* ⊕ *www.harbourclubvillas.com* 🛏 *6 villas* ¶⊙¶ *No meals.*

Discovery Bay

The point of land across the bay from Turtle Tail and the south-side marinas is called Discovery Bay, where there is another ridge with several vacation homes. If you drive out to the end, you can hike out and put your nose in the wind. Five small cays just offshore are the perfect contrast to the mesmerizing blues of the Caicos Banks, making this picture-perfect.

🛍 Shopping

BOOKS

Unicorn Bookstore

BOOKS/STATIONERY | FAMILY | This is the place to go to supplement your beach-reading stock or if you're looking for island-specific materials. Unicorn has a wide assortment of books and magazines. There is also a large children's section with crafts, games, and art supplies. If you want to be sure to find your selection there, call ahead, as they will order it in for you. If you're staying in the Grace Bay area, check out their smaller outpost in the Saltmills Plaza. ☒ *Leeward Hwy., in front of Graceway IGA* ☎ *649/941–5458* ⊕ *www.unicornbookstore.com.*

CLOTHING

Undercover

CLOTHING | Just in case your suitcase has gone missing, you'll be able to find a selection of undergarments and nightgowns in Undercover, conveniently located off Leeward Highway in Graceway Plaza. It's really the only place on the island to satisfy those needs. Both men and women will find what they need here. ☒ *Graceway House, Grace Bay* ☎ *649/941–5911.*

FOOD

★ Graceway IGA

CONVENIENCE/GENERAL STORES | With a large fresh-produce section, bakery, gourmet deli, and extensive meat counter, Provo's largest supermarket will have what you're looking for. The most consistently well-stocked store on the island carries known brands from the United Kingdom and North America, as well as a good selection of other international foods, and prepared items such as a great rotisserie chicken and pizza. The IGA also has an excellent selection of wine, beers, and spirits; no alcohol sales on Sundays. Expect prices to be higher than at home. ☒ *Leeward Hwy., The Bight* ⊹ *Halfway down the island on the main highway* ☎ *649/941–5000* ⊕ *www.gracewaysupermarkets.com.*

Quality Supermarket

CONVENIENCE/GENERAL STORES | When the IGA is out of stock, this fairly typical small-town-style grocery store can sometimes fill the gaps. ☒ *Hospital Rd.*

Flamingos on Provo ◉

Have you always wanted to see flamingos in their natural habitat? If so, then the Turks and Caicos is your place. On Provo the best place to see them up close is at the golf course, though to do so you have to play a round of golf. But across the island they are often spotted only a stone's throw away. Behind the IGA supermarket on Leeward Highway is Flamingo Pond, a popular feeding ground; to get there you must drive all the way down Venetian Road out to Turtle Tail. Beware: they're not always there, and the road is very rough. North Caicos has its own Flamingo Pond, with a small deck lookout, but you'll need binoculars to get a good look. And just across the causeway to Middle Caicos you'll stand a good chance of sighting flamingos up close if the weather is favorable.

Downtown

Although there are some businesses concentrated here, downtown is primarily a commercial area near the airport that does not offer much for tourists. Close by, however, are the ruins of an old plantation.

🍴 Restaurants

Homey's

$ | **CARIBBEAN** | This is a must-try, as it has delicious home-style island cooking. They have a wide array of local dishes and something for everyone. **Known for:** Provo's only drive-through; mac and cheese. ⑤ *Average main: $8* ⊠ *Leeward Hwy., Downtown* ☎ *649/941–5758* ▭ *No credit cards.*

👜 Shopping

FOOD

$mart

CONVENIENCE/GENERAL STORES | The IGA has now opened its third location downtown: $mart. It's another North American–style supermarket but offers more to locals at lower prices. You can cut your travel budget considerably by purchasing Essential Everyday brand items, which are usually lower priced than the brand names you know from home. This branch also carries alcoholic

Taxi Fares on Providenciales

Taxi fares are expensive on Provo. Rates are published in a schedule, which is based on distance. Knowing approximate fares in advance may help you decide if you want to rent a car or enjoy the freedom of not having to think. Just remember that all taxi fares are based on two people traveling and include two pieces of luggage each. Extra luggage is an additional charge (golf bags are $5 each), but grocery bags are free. Kids under 12 traveling with an adult are half rate, and if a taxi is left standing at the grocery store or elsewhere, the first 10 minutes may be complimentary—depending on the driver—and after that there will be a 60¢ per minute wait charge. Here are some approximate fares based on two people traveling together from the airport; the fee for each additional person is half the published fare:

Turtle Cove: $16

Discovery Bay (Graceway IGA or South Dock): $20

The Bight (Coral Gardens or Reef Residences): $23

The Bight (Beaches): $27

West Grace Bay (Sibonné, Alexandra, Sands, Somerset, Point Grace, Villa Renaissance, or Saltmills): $28

Mid-Grace Bay (Grace Bay Club, Seven Stars, Graceway Gourmet, Coco Bistro): $33

Grace Bay (Ocean Club West, Caribbean Paradise Inn, Ports of Call): $33

Long Bay: $36

Upper Chalk Sound: $48

East Grace Bay (Ocean Club, Tuscany, Royal West Indies, Club Med): $38

Leeward (Marina): $43

Lower Chalk Sound, Silly Creek: $48

Northwest Point (for Amanyara): $86

beverages. ✉ *Town Centre Mall, Downtown* ☎ *649/946–5525* ⊕ *www.gracewaysupermarkets.com.*

JEWELRY

Royal Jewels

JEWELRY/ACCESSORIES | This chain sells gold and luxury-brand jewelry, designer watches, perfumes, fine leather goods, and cameras—all duty-free. The main store is on Leeward Highway close to downtown, but they do have another location in Saltmills that is more convenient for guests staying in the Grace Bay hub. ✉ *Leeward Hwy., Downtown* ☎ *649/946–4699.*

🏃 Activities

⭐ Turks Head Brewery

GUIDED TOURS | Just about every restaurant and bar serves the local brew, made on island by Turks Head Brewery. They have fun names like I Ain' Ga Lie Lager, Gon Ta Nort Amber Ale, and Down Da Road IPA. The brewery offers daily tours that end with a tasting, so you'll know which one to order at your next stop. ⊠ *52 Universal Dr., Downtown* ☎ *649/941–3637* ⊕ *www.turkshead-brewery.tc.*

Airport

Aside from the airport itself, there's not much to attract tourists. The restaurant in the main check-in area—*Gilley's Cafe*—has an extensive menu serving up local specialties and American fare. They open early for breakfast and stay open until the last scheduled flights are headed out. There is a smaller location inside the main departure lounge, and if you really want something off the main menu they'll cook it, pack it up, and have it sent through security for you. Along the road between downtown and the airport proper you'll find some great little local restaurants, however, and some interesting beauty supply shops and department-like stores. If you are stuck without a suitcase for a few days, this might be the area where you'll find many of your basics at a much reduced cost.

Five Cays

The biggest attraction in this community is the ever-popular Bugaloo's. Go on a Sunday afternoon for some lively fun when the whole island seems to turn up, or enjoy it seven days a week as a spot with lots of local flavor. Five Cays is also home to Provo's fishery. Keep to the left after passing Bugaloo's, and you'll find the spot to purchase fresh conch and lobster—when in season. These are cash transactions only, and note that it is open only for the two hours before sunset when the boats come in, on days when the ocean is calm enough for the boats to go out.

 Restaurants

★ Bugaloo's
$$ | **CARIBBEAN** | Bugaloo's beach shack started the conch craze, and visitors make the trek across the island to have drinks or dine at the one of the fun tables inside two beached boats. Island attitude, with sayings such as "Ain't saying it had to been" and loud music abound. **Known for:** conch and rum punch; Sunday afternoon conch crawl; lively atmosphere. $ *Average main: $15* ⊠ *Five Cays Beach, Downtown* 🕾 *649/941–3863*.

★ Omar's Beach Hut
$$ | **CARIBBEAN** | **FAMILY** | Much more relaxed than Bugaloo's next door, this new beachside bar and restaurant is worth checking out. The fish is as fresh as it gets—they're located immediately next to the dock so they grab the best that's brought in from the sea each afternoon. **Known for:** freshest fish around; jerk pork and chicken; casual spot to chill on the beach. $ *Average main: $15* ⊠ *Just past Bugaloo's, Five Cays Beach, Downtown* 🕾 *649/231–6691* 🕾 *Closed Thurs. evening*.

Chalk Sound

You will first see the beauty of Chalk Sound on approach into Providenciales' airport. At the end of the runway, this protected body of water dotted with wee islands creates your first impression of the Turks and Caicos Islands. You will never lay eyes on anything lovelier.

👁 Sights

★ Chalk Sound National Park
LOCAL INTEREST | As you drive out to the end of South Dock Road, on your right you will catch glimpses of the beautiful Chalk Sound; the water here is luminescent. The best places to stop for pictures are on Chalk Sound Drive. You can enjoy lunch overlooking the park at Las Brisas Restaurant or drive to the very end of the road and take a walk along the shoreline where there are few homes. No matter how many times you see it, it will always manage to take your breath away. ⊠ *Chalk Sound Dr., Chalk Sound*.

Sapodilla Hill
ARCHAEOLOGICAL SITE | **FAMILY** | On this hilltop overlooking the beauty of Sapodilla Bay, you might find what is left of several rock carvings. It is thought that sailors carved the names and dates into the rocks while they watched over their ships from a high

vantage point, perhaps while the hulls were being cleaned or repairs were being made. The details are uncertain, but they have been dated back to the mid-1700s to mid-1800s. You will see replicas displayed at Provo's International Airport. ⊠ *Off South Dock Rd., West of South Dock, Chalk Sound.*

☺ Beaches

Sapodilla Bay

BEACH—SIGHT | One of the best of the many secluded beaches around Provo is this peaceful quarter-mile cove protected by Sapodilla Hill. The soft strand here is lapped by calm waves, while yachts and small boats rock with the gentle motion. During low tide, little sandbar "islands" form—they're great for a beach chair and make the waters easily accessible to young children. **Amenities:** parking (free). **Best for:** sunbathing. ⊠ *End of South Dock Rd., Chalk Sound ⊹ From Leeward Hwy., take Roundabout 6 at the bottom of the Leeward Hwy. hill toward Five Cays. Follow until almost the end, and at the small police station turn right onto Chalk Sound Dr. The road on the left leads to a small parking area that offers public access to the beach.*

Taylor Bay

BEACH—SIGHT | **FAMILY** | Taylor Bay is shallow for hundreds of feet, making it the perfect place for kids; they become giddy at the fact that they can run free through shallow waters without their parents worrying about them. The beach also offers gorgeous views of the villas that hang over the shoreline on one side of the bay with natural coastline on the other. As it has had many amazing reviews over the years, don't expect to have this one all to yourself. There is even the odd tour that pulls up. **Amenities:** none. **Best for:** sunbathing; wading. ⊠ *Sunset Dr., Chalk Sound ⊹ From Leeward Hwy., take the roundabout exit toward Five Cays at the bottom of the Leeward Hwy. hill. Follow the road until almost the end, and at the small police station, take a right onto Chalk Sound Dr. Take a left at Ocean Point Dr., and park next to the tennis courts where there are big boulders blocking a sand path. Follow this path to the beach.*

☻ Restaurants

Las Brisas Restaurant & Bar

$$$ | **ECLECTIC** | **FAMILY** | With exquisite views of Chalk Sound, the setting here is deliriously lovely. The restaurant terrace deck and elevated gazebo offer picture-postcard views of the intensely blue waters of the sound. **Known for:** breathtaking views; great

On a Budget in the TCI

If you would like to visit one of the world's most beautiful beaches but feel you can't afford this expensive destination, there are ways to save money in the Turks and Caicos and still have a wonderful trip. Traveling during nonpeak season, when many resorts offer free nights and extra perks, is one way to save. The discount season coincides with hurricane season, June through November, so consider purchasing travel insurance if you visit then. If you don't mind being a block or two from the beach, you can save even more. And staying in one of the many private villas does not always mean higher prices. In fact, there are lovely little homes dotted all over the island that are more than comfortable, with only a short drive to all that Provo has to offer. You might also look at searching for package deals that combine air, accommodation, and even diving.

Most resort rooms and condos, as well as all private villas, have at least a refrigerator and microwave, so you can stock up at the supermarket and prepare some of your meals "at home." Graceway IGA has an awesome rotisserie chicken and prepared pasta and potato salads. Visit the Graceway Gourmet for an amazing deli that almost doesn't make it worth it to purchase anything that needs preparing. Also, airlines allow you to bring a cooler of food as long as perishables are frozen and vacuum sealed; despite airline charges for checked bags, this strategy could save you some money, especially on meat.

At restaurants, dinner might be more expensive than for the same entrée at lunchtime, so arrive 15 minutes before the switchover and order from the lunch menu. You can pick up pizza or another island takeout meal and have a balcony picnic. There are also several little local haunts throughout Grace Bay as well as along Airport Road that are not nearly as expensive. To be sure, ordering nonalcoholic beverages while out will save a great deal of money.

And of course, many of the best experiences are free: walk the beach, swim in the ocean, snorkel where the reef comes in to touch the shore. The options are endless. A good source for events and specials is ⊕ www.TCIEnews.com.

spot to stop for a drink or lunch while exploring the island; fun tapas menu. $ *Average main: $25* ⊠ *Neptune Villas, Chalk Sound Rd., Chalk Sound* ☎ *649/946–5306* ⊕ *www.neptunevillastci.com* ⊗ *Closed Tues.*

Hotels

Neptune Villas

$$ | RESORT | Although not on the beach, this wonderful complex of villas is the only resort-style accommodation on the magical waters of Chalk Sound National Park, with nearby Sapodilla and Taylor Bays. **Pros:** quiet location on Chalk Sound; great value; fabulous restaurant on-site. **Cons:** a car is highly recommended; have to drive to all other attractions, services, and main beaches; nothing much to do if you want a break from the sun, sand, and sea. ⑤ *Rooms from: $300* ✉ *533, Chalk Sound Rd., Chalk Sound* ☎ *649/331–4328* ⊕ *www.neptunevillastci.com* ⇩ *9 villas.*

West Harbour

Otherwise known as Pirates' Cove, West Harbour offers small caves, Osprey Rock, and rock carvings that all make this an enticing place to explore. On a secluded southwest part of the island, it's a long drive out, and the parking lot has had some break-ins, so be sure to stow your belongings out of sight and lock your car.

Glowworms 👁

If you're here on the third to fifth days after a full moon, you might get to see glowworms. The phenomenon occurs when tiny marine worms mate. You have to time it perfectly to see their dance, as the show lasts only a half hour at most. Magically, the female begins to glow, waiting patiently for a male to notice. If one does, his colors are shown as he dashes in for the "explosion," resulting in what appears like stars twinkling at dusk across the water's surface. The best places to view them from land are along the canals that open onto the Caicos Banks and within the Chalk Sound residential neighborhoods. You can also choose to view them from an excursion boat.

🏖 Beaches

West Harbour Bay

BEACH—SIGHT | This is about as isolated as it gets on Provo. West Bay has long stretches of beaches to walk and possibly not see another person for hours. You might see large red starfish in the water here, or if you walk out to Bonefish Point you may spot small reef sharks and the odd ray hunting in the shallows. Don't leave valuables in your car, as there have been break-ins reported in the past. **Amenities:** none. **Best for:** exploring; solitude; swimming; walking. ✉ *Northwest Point* ✛ *Traveling west on Millennium*

Hwy. past Blue Hills, take the last left before Provo's landfill site. Continue for 5 miles (8 km) along a relatively rough road until you come to the ocean's edge. Walk along the shoreline to get to the caves. Walk right to Bonefish Point.

Blue Mountain

Many gorgeous private villas with ocean views can be found here. The beaches are smaller and more private than those elsewhere on the island, and although it's in a central location, visitors staying here will require transportation to reach the best beaches.

Blue Hills

The "personality" of the island, this area populated with locals is west, beyond Grace Bay and Turtle Cove. The beachfront is lined with quirky beach shacks and colorful restaurants. It's a place to "chill" with water views, but no one ever swims here because there are better areas for hanging out on the sand. The beach-combing is much better than on Grace Bay, however, as there surely isn't anyone raking the sand! This is where you will find Da Conch Shack.

🍴 Restaurants

★ Da Conch Shack
$$ | **CARIBBEAN** | **FAMILY** | An institution on Provo for many years, this brightly colored beach shack is justifiably famous for its conch and seafood. The conch is fished fresh out of the shallows and broiled, spiced, cracked, or fried to absolute perfection. **Known for:** fresh-as-it-gets conch; day and night parties; toes-in-the-sand dining. ⓈAverage main: $18 ⊠ Blue Hills Rd., Blue Hills ✚ Right on the beach and next door to Kalooki's ☎ 649/242–2883, 649/332–8501 mobile ⊕ daconchshack.com.

Shay on the Beach
$$ | **CARIBBEAN** | The menu at this little beachside spot isn't particularly exciting, but they've got all the standard fare—conch, burgers, fish—and an incredible view. The food is tasty and the cocktails are just the thing to cool you off. **Known for:** amazing ocean view; one of the only spots in the Blue Hills area; to-die-for homemade carrot cake. ⓈAverage main: $18 ⊠ Next to Da Conch Shack, Blue Hills ☎ 649/339–7429 ۞ Closed Mon.

Northwest Point

The farthest point northwest on the island, this is a great scuba spot with one secluded resort. The Northwest Point Resort is a long way from everything, but the beaches are amazing—albeit wild—and the Northwest Point Nature Reserve is tucked in behind.

Beaches

Malcolm's Road Beach

BEACH—SIGHT | This is one of the most stunning beaches you'll ever see, but you'll need to tread carefully; the road is a little rough in spots, and there have been reports of break-ins at the parking area. It's best not to keep any valuables in your car or on your person, and never go alone. Bring your own food and drinks because there are no facilities for miles around. **Amenities:** parking (free). **Best for:** solitude; swimming; walking. ☒ *Malcolm's Beach Rd., Northwest Point* ✛ *On Leeward Hwy., take the Fuller Walkin roundabout toward Blue Hills. Keep to the Millennium Hwy. until after it turns into hard-packed sand. Turn left at the intersection where right indicates the route to Wheeland. Follow the road until the end, which takes about 20 mins. Expect a relatively rough, windy, and isolated road.*

🍴 Restaurants

★ The Restaurant at Amanyara

$$$$ | **ECLECTIC** | You'll be in awe as you walk through the stunning grand foyer of Amanyara into the open-air dining pavilion; you can sink into a cozy nook or choose from one of many teak tables scattered under the shade of island mahogany trees or overlooking the lovely reflecting pools. But make sure to begin at the bar, with its high wooden ceiling a feat of engineering; all seating has dramatic sea views across the beauty of the lava rock–lined infinity-edge pool. **Known for:** fresh organic vegetables from their aquaponic garden; best romantic sunset spot on the island; Asian inspired elegance. ⑤ *Average main: $40* ☒ *Amanyara Resort, Malcolm's Road Beach, Northwest Point* ☎ *649/941–8133.*

Hotels

★ Amanyara

$$$$ | RESORT | Amanyara is nestled in nature with the ultimate zenlike atmosphere, and it's *the* place for peace and quiet in a remote setting on a stunning waterfront. **Pros:** fabulous restaurant; unprecedented service; best full-service secluded beach on Provo. **Cons:** isolated; far from restaurants, outside excursion companies, and other beaches; expensive. ⑤ *Rooms from: $1800* ✉ *Northwest Point* ✛ *Off Millennium Hwy.* ☎ *649/941–8133* ⊕ *www.aman.com* ↝ *58 rooms* ⦿ *No meals.*

Northwest Point Resort

$$ | RENTAL | Miles from nowhere, this resort should be your destination if you need complete solitude. **Pros:** good rate for what you get; pool is great; perfect for those wishing total solitude. **Cons:** water at beach access has turtle grass; inconsistent restaurant service so you certainly cannot count on it; far from everything. ⑤ *Rooms from: $300* ✉ *1 Davie Bight Rd., Northwest Point* ☎ *649/941–8961 (office)* ↝ *49 rooms* ⦿ *No meals* ⌲ *3-night min. during peak season.*

Activities

Biking

Most hotels have bicycles available for guests, or you can rent one from an independent company. Within Grace Bay, stick to the sidewalks for safety and be extremely careful when leaving the hub; drivers don't pay much attention to bikes!

★ Caicos Cyclery

BICYCLING | Comfortable beach cruisers are available from Caicos Cyclery from $20 a day, as well as the wider-tired Choppers, mountain bikes, and hybrids. Delivery to a private villa is possible. There's a tandem bike available for rent as well. You can also look forward to a 50% discount with a two-week rental. They offer guided cycling tours of Provo and North & Middle Caicos. ✉ *Saltmills Plaza, Grace Bay Rd., Grace Bay* ✛ *Adjoining Big Al's Island Grill* ☎ *649/941-7544* ⊕ *www.caicoscyclery.com.*

Scooter Bob's

BICYCLING | You can rent beach cruisers at Scooter Bob's for $15 for a 24-hour period, and they offer a very reasonable drop-off service at $15 anywhere on the island if you rent for five days or longer and the rental drops to $12 per day. ⊠ *Turtle Cove Marina, Turtle Cove* ☎ *649/946–4684* ⊕ *www.scooterbobstci.com.*

Boating and Sailing

Provo's calm, reef-protected seas combine with constant easterly trade winds for excellent boating conditions. Several companies offer charters with snorkeling stops, food and beverage service, and sunset vistas. Prices range from $80 per person for group trips (subject to passenger minimums) to $800 or more for private charters.

Beluga Sailboat

BOATING | FAMILY | Beluga offers private charters for two to eight passengers. Captains Tim and Nik know these waters after years of sailing them. This is true sailing, no motors allowed. Staff will pick you up and take you to the marina where the boat is moored, and then ferry you off for a day of magic, exploring the reef and the cays east of Provo. Their specialty is a romantic encounter; all trips begin at $800. ☎ *649/231–0372* ⊕ *www.sailbeluga.com.*

★ Caicos Dream Tours

BOATING | Caicos Dream Tours offers several boating options, including one that has you diving for conch before lunch off a gorgeous beach. You may choose from two different excursions shared with others, starting at $99/person, or charter a private boat for as many as 12 people, beginning at $1,200 for a half day. With 10 boats in their fleet, Dream Tours is able to accommodate a few hundred guests at the same time, so wedding parties and conference groups have the option of enjoying a day out together. Maximum capacity on one boat is 90 including crew. They also offer a bottom-fishing charter for up to 12 people for those die-hard fisherpeople traveling together. Note that Caicos Dream Tours is the only island excursion operator that offers a combo of bottom-fishing and snorkeling on the same charter; this one makes the whole family happy! ⊠ *Alexandra Resort, Princess Dr., Grace Bay* ☎ *649/231–7274* ⊕ *www.caicosdreamtours.com.*

★ Island Vibes

BOATING | FAMILY | Turks and Caicos–born and raised, the owner-operaters of Island Vibes make their excursions stand out. If conditions are right, they'll give you the opportunity to snorkel out over the wall, where the reef drops an amazing 3,000 feet. With a 12-foot curve slide off the roof, a diving board, and spacious bathroom onboard with freshwater showers, these fun excursions add just a little more excitement to your day. Join a group for the half-day snorkel at $100 per person, or throw yourself into their full-day barbecue adventure ($200 per person) that combines an amazing lunch set up under the shade of tall island pines with exploring small cays, snorkeling, conch diving, and beach strolling. There is also the option of a private sunset cruise seven days a week. ⊠ *Turtle Cove Marina, Lower Bight Rd., Turtle Cove* ☎ *649/231– 8423* ⊕ *www.islandvibestours.com* ⊠ *From $100 per person.*

Kenard Cruises

BOATING | These luxury private catamarans are first-class all the way, including a chef who can prepare gourmet meals, a 42-inch TV, air-conditioning, and Bose surround sound. They can be chartered for a half day or full day on a custom itinerary—so you'll feel like a celebrity! ☎ *649/232–3866* ⊕ *www.kenardcruises.com.*

Sail Provo

BOATING | **FAMILY** | Very popular for private charters, Sail Provo also offers scheduled half-day, full-day, sunset, and dedicated snorkeling trips to those who don't mind sharing with other holidaymakers on 52- and 38-foot sailing catamarans. They also head out on starlit evening cruises to share the marine world's glowworm extravaganza: underwater creatures light up the sea's surface not long after sunset a few days after the full moon each month. Check the website to peruse the wide variety of excursions available with beach pickup right in front of your Grace Bay resort. ⊠ *Blue Haven Marina, Marina Rd., Leeward* ⊕ *Far eastern tip of the island* ☎ *649/946–4783 local office* ⊕ *www.sailprovotci.com.*

Silver Deep

BOATING | Silver Deep excursions include several half-day and full-day trip options. Choose from all types of fishing, a dedicated snorkeling adventure, exploration of North and Middle Caicos, and the most popular: a Native Beach Barbecue. Their most unique opportunity is the night-fishing private charter, just in case your days are too busy with naps and enjoying the beach. Other private charters may be arranged starting at $1,200; your itinerary may be personalized to include a multitude of activities, keeping all members in your group happy. ⊠ *Ocean Club West Plaza, Grace Bay Rd., Grace Bay* ⊕ *Right across from Caicos Café Plaza* ☎ *649/946– 5612* ⊕ *www.silverdeep.com* ⊠ *From $99 per person.*

★ Sun Charters

BOATING | **FAMILY** | The *Atabeyra,* operated by Sun Charters, is a 70-foot schooner with a big wide belly. It's the residents' choice for special events, as it is by far the most family-friendly adventure. Kids can run around without too many worries about going overboard, and the boom overhead is strong enough for them to sit and survey the seascape—just as a pirate would have done. Although primarily known as a private charter service, Sun also offers an amazing sunset rum punch party and glowworm excursions as their specialty, with a weekly Sail & Snorkel for individuals to join. Their newest trip is Night with da Stars, when the *Atabeyra* sails out at sunset and then throws anchor in a secluded spot; a night sky app and laser discussion will introduce you to a light-pollution-free night sky. The boat is perfect for larger groups, accommodating up to 50 people. ⊠ *Blue Haven Resort, Marina Rd., Leeward* ⚓ *Operates from the resort's VIP dock in front of Fire and Ice Restaurant* ☎ *649/231–0624* ⊕ *www.suncharters.tc.*

Undersea Explorer

BOATING | For sightseeing below the waves, try the *Undersea Explorer,* a semi-submarine operated by Caicos Tours out of Turtle Cove Marina. It's an ocean adventure that takes you into the underwater world without getting wet. Your one-hour tour of the reef is led by a knowledgeable captain and viewed through large windows below the surface on either side, all in air-conditioned comfort. It's the perfect trip for young and old alike. Your choice: the Mermaid Adventure, which is a theatrical voyage with a "surprise" spotting of Mermaid Bella along the way and a pirate captain making a guest appearance, or the Turtle Reef Adventure, which sticks strictly to the business of exploring the reef as an informative voyage. ⊠ *Turtle Cove Marina, Lower Bight Rd., Turtle Cove* ☎ *649/432–0006* ⊕ *www.caicostours.com* ⌧ *$70* ⊙ *Closed Sun.*

Water Play Provo

WATER SPORTS | Right on the beach, Water Play Provo has kiteboards, windsurfers, stand-up paddleboards, and kayaks. You can take a lesson, join a guided tour, or rent the equipment for multiple days or by the week. The owner, Jill, also conducts swim lessons in private villa pools; she specializes in infant self-rescue, and she's also an open-water swim coach and an American Red Cross swim instructor. ⊠ *Ocean Club (East), Governor's Rd., Grace Bay* ⚓ *Found on the Tuscany side of Ocean Club on Grace Bay Beach* ☎ *649/231–5483* ⊕ *www.waterplayprovo.com.*

Diving and Snorkeling

Scuba diving was the sport that drew visitors initially to the Turks and Caicos Islands in the 1970s; diving here today is considered among the best in the world. The reef and wall drop-offs thrive with bright, unbroken coral formations and lavish numbers of fish and marine life. Mimicking the idyllic climate, waters are warm all year, averaging 76°F to 78°F in winter and 82°F to 84°F in summer. With minimal rainfall and soil runoff, visibility is usually

Giving Back

Want to do some good on your vacation? Here are some worthwhile organizations you can contribute to.

■ **Edward C Gartland Youth Centre.** This nonprofit organization helps empower the youth of TCI, offering a variety of programs outside school hours. ⊕ *ecgyouthcentre.com.*

■ **Potcake Place.** This organization rescues stray puppies from around the islands. You can donate, volunteer to be a courier to take puppies to their forever homes, or "adopt" one for the day. ⊕ *www.potcakeplace.com.*

■ **Provo Children's Home.** This organization takes in orphans and is always in need of some kind of contribution. ⊕ *www.pch.tc.*

■ **TCSPCA.** In addition to rescuing strays, the TCSPCA is also improving the horse and donkey compound on Grand Turk. Donations are appreciated, whether in cash or volunteer time. ⊕ *www.tcspca.tc.*

■ **The TCI National Trust.** The Turks & Caicos National Trust helps with preservation throughout the islands, maintaining historical sites and wildlife park areas. ⊕ *nationaltrust.tc.*

■ **Turks and Caicos Reef Fund.** Helping to improve the awareness and preservation of the nation's reefs, this organization has annual fundraising events. ⊕ *tcreef.org.*

■ **The Turks & Caicos Rotary Club.** They give back in many ways, including island cleanups. ⊕ *rotary.tc.*

good and frequently superb, ranging from 60 feet to more than 150 feet. An extensive system of marine national parks and boat moorings, combined with an eco-conscious mind-set among dive operators, contributes to an uncommonly pristine underwater environment. It is not unusual to spot reef sharks on every dive or to swim with whales during their migratory period between January to April. Turks and Caicos has a wide variety of coral to note.

Off Providenciales, dive sites are primarily along the north shore's barrier reef. Most sites can be reached in anywhere from 10 minutes to 1½ hours. Dive sites feature spur-and-groove coral formations atop a coral-covered slope. Popular stops such as **Aquarium, Pinnacles,** and **Grouper Hole** have large schools of fish, turtles, nurse sharks, and gray reef sharks. From the south side, dive boats go to **French Cay, West Caicos, Southwest Reef,** and **Northwest Point.** Known for typically calm conditions and clear water, the West Caicos Marine National Park is a favorite stop. The area has dramatic walls and marine life, including sharks, eagle rays, and octopus, with large stands of pillar coral and huge barrel sponges.

Dive operators on Provo more regularly visits sites off **Grace Bay** and **Pine Cay** and make the longer journey to **Northwest Point** and **West Caicos,** depending on weather conditions. All major dive companies offer open-water dive and other certifications. You will even find technical diving, including re-breathers and nitrox, available on island. Night diving is also available on the closer dive sites. A two-tank dive will range from $90 to $220. All companies offer gear rental at an additional fee. There are also two live-aboard dive boats available for charter working out of Provo.

Caicos Adventures

SCUBA DIVING | FAMILY | Run by the well-known and friendly Frenchman Fifi Kunz, Caicos Adventures offers daily excursions out of their private marina on the south side of Provo to sites off West Caicos, French Cay, and Southwest Reef. The company runs two dive boats, with groups up to 20 able to dive together. If you are not yet certified, you may enjoy one of their snorkel adventures as an alternative. They also have the *Lady K,* a luxury motorboat, available for private charters operating out of Blue Haven Marina on the eastern tip of the island. It's best to book over the phone. ⊠ *Regent Village, Grace Bay Rd., Grace Bay ⊹ Their private marina is off Venetian Rd. Watch for their sign on the right after you pass between Flamingo Lake and Turtle Lake* ☎ *649/941–3346* ⊕ *www. caicosadventures.com.*

★ Dive Provo

SCUBA DIVING | Dive Provo is a PADI five-star operation that runs daily one- and two-tank dives to popular Grace Bay sites, as well as to West Caicos. In addition, they offer the exciting night dive, as well as their unique three-tank Scuba Safari, where they head out to dive sites farther afield, such as Molasses Reef, Sandbore Channel, and Southwest Reef. This excursion includes one tank of nitrox to make it easier on the diver to spend as much time as possible under the water. Note that this is not offered to junior divers. Dive Provo has a full array of dive courses: Discover Scuba, Open Water Certification, Advanced Open Water, and Nitrox Certification. They also offer snorkeling excursions. Check out their packages including accommodation; it's a great way to save money on your next dive holiday. ⊠ *Ports of Call, Grace Bay Rd., Grace Bay* ☎ *649/946–5040, 800/234–7768* ⊕ *www.diveprovo.com.*

Provo Turtle Divers

SCUBA DIVING | Provo Turtle Divers, with offices at Ocean Club East and Turtle Cove Landing, has been operating dive trips on Provo since the 1970s. The staff is friendly, knowledgeable, and unpretentious. Their boats operate solely out of Southside Marina off Venetian Road. This location makes their boat trips quicker to the less-traveled sites off French Cay, West Caicos, Northwest Point, and Sandbore Channel. Their years of experience make diving with them like spending the day with friends. ⊠ *Turtle Cove Landing, Lower Bight Rd., Turtle Cove* ☎ *649/946–4232, 904/687–0175 Vonage* ⊕ *www.provoturtledivers.com* ⊗ *The shop is closed on Sun. even though the boats still go out.*

★ Snuba Turks & Caicos

SCUBA DIVING | FAMILY | Snuba offers the next-best thing to diving for a noncertified diver; it's a very different experience from snorkeling, but requires no experience. With the Surface Nexus Underwater Breathing Apparatus, you go underwater amongst the coral and schools of fish like a scuba diver, but your air tank stays on a raft at the surface. It's a great way to experience the sport, giving you the opportunity to get a feel for it so that you might decide to take the full course and become certified at a later date. Children must be at least eight years old to participate. Using the catamaran *Snuba Doo,* trips include a two-site day; one location focuses on the snuba experience, and the other offers a chance to do some more adventurous snorkeling out on the less frequently visited reefs off the Grace Bay Barrier Reef. Year-round off-the-beach snuba takes place on the reef right in front of Coral Gardens. Private charters are available for groups of up to 28. And note that the owner, Jodi Taylor, will take a picture of you underwater as a keepsake. ⊠ *Turtle Cove Marina, The Bight* ☎ *649/333–7333* ⊕ *www.snubaturksandcaicos.com.*

Turks & Caicos *Aggressor II*

SCUBA DIVING | The Turks & Caicos *Aggressor II,* a live-aboard dive boat, plies the waters throughout the islands, enjoying numerous pristine dive sites; weekly charters are out of Turtle Cove Marina. The *Aggressor II* has nine air-conditioned staterooms, all with TVs and DVD players, plus communal sundecks, wet bars, and hot tubs to keep you spoiled while on the water. You're met on arrival at the Providenciales International Airport and taken directly to the ship. Rates include up to five dives daily, plus all meals and beverages, including local beers and wine. ☎ *800/348–2628* ⊕ *www. aggressor.com.*

Fishing

The fertile waters around Turks and Caicos are great for angling—anything from bottom and reef fishing (most likely to produce plenty of bites and a large catch) to bonefishing and deep-sea fishing (among the finest in the Caribbean). Several tournaments annually attract anglers from across the islands and around the world—with a significant number of Americans on the roster—who compete to catch the biggest Atlantic blue marlin, tuna, or wahoo. For any fishing activity, you are required to purchase a $15 visitor's fishing license; operators generally furnish all equipment, drinks, and snacks. Prices start at around $800 for a half day and go up from there, depending on the length of trip and size of boat. Outside of the following list of deep-sea operators, *see Boating and Sailing above* for operators who may take you out reef-, bottom-, and bonefishing.

Bite Me Fishing Charters

FISHING | For deep-sea sportfishing, Captain Fineline does not require anyone to have previous experience, just a desire to get out on the water and enjoy the day. Having spent his entire life fishing the waters of TCI, there isn't any local captain with more experience, or more passion for his sport. ⊠ *Turtle Cove* ☎ *649/231–0366* ⊕ *www.turks-caicos-fishing.com.*

Grand Slam Fishing Charters

FISHING | For deep-sea fishing trips in search of marlin, sailfish, wahoo, and tuna, look up this company. Grand Slam operates three boats: a 45-foot Hatteras, a 42-foot Pursuit, and a 252 Mako Center Console. ⊠ *Turtle Cove Marina, Turtle Cove* ☎ *649/231–4420* ⊕ *www.gsfishing.com.*

Panoply Sportfishing & Charters

FISHING | *Panoply,* owned and operated by residents of TCI for more than 25 years, is a 46-foot Bertram Sport Fisherman that charters deep-sea fishing trips, boasting a soft interior and state-of-the-art electronics. ⊠ *Blue Haven Marina, Slip A19, Leeward* ☎ *649/432–3566* ⊕ *www.panoply.tc.*

★ Silver Deep

FISHING | FAMILY | Silver Deep has been operating out of Provo for more than 30 years. In the fishing department, they offer the full range: deep-sea, bone, fly, night, and bottom fishing. Families can choose to participate in a private excursion where fishing, beach time, and snorkeling can all be included to keep every member content. With a large fleet of boats, there is the perfect fit for all occasions—no matter the charter request or the water conditions on any given day. ⊠ *Ocean Club West Plaza, Governor's Rd., Grace Bay* ⊹ *Opposite Caicos Café Plaza* ☎ *649/232–5612* ⊕ *www.silverdeep.com.*

Provo Golf Club is one of the Caribbean's top 18-hole courses.

Fitness

Retreat Yoga & Wellness Studio
AEROBICS/YOGA | This is a studio for physical, mental, and spiritual development through the practice of yoga, tai chi, and holistic nutrition. Laura and Lindsay also offer nutrition consultations and wellness workshops. Their Retreat Kitchen next door is a vegetarian cafe and juice bar. ⊠ *Ports of Call, upper floor, Grace Bay* ☎ *649/432–2485* ⊕ *www.retreattc.com.*

Golf

Golfing in the Caribbean can be quite an experience. The Provo Golf and Country Club has one of the finest layouts in the islands. Along with its smallish greens, the course is well manicured. If you forget your clubs, don't worry; you can rent a set that will accommodate your game. After a challenging round be sure to grab a drink or quick bite in the clubhouse that overlooks the 18th green. Usually, flamingos are spotted at the fifth green. Bring your "A" game, as this is truly a shot-maker's course.

★ Provo Golf Club
GOLF | Among the Caribbean's top courses, the 18 holes here (par 72) are a combination of lush greens and fairways, rugged limestone outcroppings, and freshwater lakes. Rack rates are $195 for 18 holes, however the avid golfer can save through their twilight specials, a multi-round pass, or a biweekly or monthly pass. The

club also offers two hard-court, flood-lit tennis courts, which are among the island's best. Nonmembers can play until 5 pm for $20/hour/adult or $15/hour/junior (reservation required), with racket rentals available. Inquire at the pro shop about tennis lessons. ✉ *Governor's Rd., Grace Bay* ☎ *649/946–5991, 877/218–9124* ⊕ *www.provogolfclub.com* 💲 *$185 for 18 holes, $95 for 9 holes with shared cart* ⅄ *18 holes, 6705 yards, par 72.*

Horseback Riding

Provo Ponies

HORSEBACK RIDING | FAMILY | Provo Ponies offers morning and afternoon rides along quiet dirt roads, through short brush trails, and then out onto the beauty of Long Bay Beach, where you and your horse may take a dip in the shallow waters of the Caicos Banks before heading back to the stable. Horses are matched according to your riding ability, with no rider under seven and no double riding allowed. Reservations are required, and there is a 240-pound weight limit and only seven horses that can carry riders who weigh more than 150 pounds. Pickup at your Grace Bay hotel or villa can be arranged for an additional $10 per person, which is great for those who've decided not to hire a rental car. It's closed on Sundays to give the horses their well-deserved rest and Saturday afternoon rides are available by special request only. ✉ *Dolphin Rd., Long Bay* ✛ *Take Leeward Hwy. east to Long Bay Hills Rd. Turn left onto Lignumvitae and left again onto Dolphin La.* ☎ *649/946–5252, 649/241–6350* ⊕ *www.provoponies.com* 💲 *$110 for 60-min ride, $130 for 90-min ride; additional fee for a private ride* ⊗ *Closed Sun.*

Paddleboarding

Stand-up paddleboarding is one of the fastest-growing sports in the Caribbean. Check out the following option if you wish to partake while on Provo:

Neptune Villas

BOATING | You can rent paddleboards and kayaks at Neptune Villas to explore the magical waters of Chalk Sound National Park. On-site is also a superb restaurant overlooking the sound, Las Brisas, so you can enjoy a nice lunch after your independent excursion. ✉ *Neptune Villas, Chalk Sound Rd., Chalk Sound* ☎ *649/331–4328* ⊕ *www.neptunevillasci.*

Parasailing

Captain Marvin's Watersports

HANG GLIDING/PARAGLIDING/PARASAILING | A 15-minute parasail-
ing flight over Grace Bay is offered for just $85 (single) or $170
(tandem) from Captain Marvin's Watersports, which includes
hotel pickup in the cost of your flight—within the Grace Bay area.
This is not just for thrill-seekers, as the views from as high up as
450 feet give you a good understanding of how the Caicos cays
are slung across the water between Provo and North Caicos. It
also gives you spectacular views of the barrier reef that are truly
unforgettable. You can also take a nonflyer along for the boat ride
at $25. ⊠ *Grace Bay* ☎ *649/231–0643* ⊕ *www.captainmarvinswa-
tersports.com/.*

SkyPilot Parasail

WATER SPORTS | You'll know you've spotted their sails when you see
the bright orange one flying overhead, a large smiley face front
and center. Here's another bird's-eye view that simply can't be
beat, but you're not so high that you miss out on the larger marine
life passing far below in the crystal-clear waters of Grace Bay.
⊠ *Grace Bay* ☎ *649/333–3000* ⊕ *www.skypilotparasail.com.*

Tennis

You can rent tennis equipment at the Provo Golf and Country Club
and play on the two lighted courts, which are among the island's
best.

Graceway Sports Centre

RACQUET SPORTS | A full sports center with other activities available,
Graceway has four tennis courts to which visitors have access
for $20/hour per court. Each court is equipped for cool, more
refreshing night play, with hours from 9 am to 8 pm. There's an
additional light fee if you play after dark. A tennis pro is on-site if
you would like to take advantage of your vacation time for a lesson
or two. You will find the center right behind the main Graceway
IGA Supermarket. ⊠ *Grace Bay* ☎ *649/442–6348* ⊕ *www.grace-
waysports.com.*

Provo Golf and Country Club

TENNIS | You can rent tennis equipment at Provo Golf and Country
Club and play on the two recently refurbished hard-surface, lighted courts, which are among the island's best. Nonmembers can
play until 5 pm for $20 per hour. Rackets can be rented for $5 per
hour. Court times are from 7:30 am until 8:30 pm; reservations

are required. ✉ *Governor's Rd., Grace Bay* ☎ *649/946–5991,*
877/218–9124 Toll Free ⊕ *www.provogolfclub.com.*

Tours

★ Big Blue Collective

BICYCLING | **FAMILY** | This ecotour operator got its start offering dive
excursions in 1997, but has since widened its scope considerably.
Big Blue has several educational kayak ecotours to choose from,
as well as the very popular stand-up paddleboard (SUP) safari
tours as an alternative, though they don't cover quite as much
territory as the kayak tours. Big Blue also has outposts on Middle,
North, and South Caicos, with an extensive network of guides,
bikes, kayaks, and boats, so they are able to offer a number of
interactive ecotourism excursions for those wishing to learn
more about what Turks and Caicos has to offer. Private charters
up to a maximum of 12 passengers may incorporate a snorkeling
adventure to the reef off the outer islands or on the Caicos Banks
near French Cay and West Caicos. They are also the only operator
offering excursions to the pristine coral reefs surrounding South
Caicos. As their latest foray, they are now also recognized for their
outstanding kiteboarding and kitesurfing instruction, downwind-
ers, and kite safaris. The Cabrinha Kite and Board gear is used
for both instruction and rentals. ✉ *Leeward Marina, Marina Rd.,
Leeward* ☎ *649/946–5034* ⊕ *www.bigbluecollective.com.*

Froggie's Ultimate Tours

FOUR-WHEELING | From this location in Blue Hills, adventurous indi-
viduals may head off into the more rugged end of Providenciales
on their very own ATV. Small groups are led along winding roads,
on tracks cut through the brush, and down pristine natural beaches on the northwest end of the island to discover a side of Provo
you could not otherwise get to know—all while having loads of
fun. There's a small eatery where you "saddle up" and can grab a
bite before or after your adventure, or pick up a cold drink to enjoy
along the way. Note that you must be 18 years of age with a valid
form of identification to rent the ATV, but only 12 years old to ride.
✉ *Wheeland end of Blue Hills Rd., Blue Hills* ☎ *649/231-0595,
231–0595* ⊕ *froggiesatv.com.*

Paradise Scooters

GUIDED TOURS | New Vespa tours have arrived on Provo, where
riders are guided throughout various island neighborhoods with
stops along the way at Blue Hills, Sapodilla Bay, and Chalk Sound;
a full lunch at Bugaloo's in Five Cays is included. Tours cost $146.
The company also rents scooters starting at $30/day for a single

rider, as well as hybrid electric bicycles. ⊠ *Grace Bay Plaza, Grace Bay Rd., Grace Bay* ☎ *649/333–3333* ⊕ *www.paradisescooters.tc.*

Waterskiing and Wakeboarding

Nautique Sports

WATER SPORTS | Nautique Sports offers a water-sports dream: a range of activities from wakeboarding to waterskiing, wakesurfing, barefoot waterskiing, slalom waterskiing, wakeskating, tubing, and snorkeling. What better place to learn than on the calm, crystal-clear waters of Providenciales. A great company for beginners, Nautique offers private instruction and will have you skiing in no time. Experts can even try barefoot skiing—in the summer months. ⊠ *Near Blue Haven Marina, Leeward* ☎ *649/431–7544, 649/431–7544* ⊕ *www.nautiquesports.com.*

Windsurfing

Although the water appears calm, the breezes always blow along Provo's northern shore. Most resorts will provide Windsurfers. If you're on Grace Bay Beach, stay inside the white buoys; boats can pass by beyond them. Nautique Sports also rents kitesurfing equipment *(see Waterskiing, above).*

★ SURFside Ocean Academy

BEACHES | **FAMILY** | SURFside is the only scuba outfit in TCI to offer mobile scuba services and will bring the lesson to *you*! Why leave your private villa when you can have the adventure brought to your pool and oceanfront? SURFside also offers PADI's Discover Scuba Diver Program, their most popular scuba course, for individuals who are not yet certified but would like to try scuba diving, for ages 10 and up. In addition to scuba, the company provides custom charter cruises for smaller groups (maximum of eight passengers) on a private 20-foot *Edgewater*. The boat includes a tow arch for wakeboarders and water-skiers and stops for a custom barbecue lunch at the more remote and uninhabited islands like French Cay and West Caicos. You can also spend the day on the beach with provided chairs, umbrellas, and even coolers. SURFside is also well known for their stand-up paddleboard (SUP) experiences, and offers a variety of classes and tours, as well as an hour-long PaddleFit Fitness boot camp–style class and SUP "yoga on the water." ⊠ *Grace Bay Club, Grace Bay* ☎ *649/231–5437* ⊕ *www.surfsideoceanacademy.com.*

TC Kiteboarding

FLYING/SKYDIVING/SOARING | **FAMILY** | This is a small and friendly kiteboarding company that offers lessons from beginner through advanced, as well as providing kite rentals and repairs. You can find their office by heading out to Long Bay Beach, right next door to the Shore Club; they are under the black flag with a large white TCK emblazoned on it... unless they're out on the water. All TCK's gear is by Slingshot. This company is definitely teen-friendly. ⊠ *Long Bay Beach (next door to the Shore Club), Long Bay* ☎ *649/442–2423* ⊕ *www.tckiteboarding.com.*

WaterPlay Provo

KAYAKING | Windsurfers find the calm, turquoise water of Grace Bay ideal. WaterPlay Provo offers lessons and rents all the gear you need to explore the island via kayak, windsurf board, Hobie Cat, stand-up paddleboard, or kitesurf. They also offer SUP yoga classes and an eco-kayak or SUP tour into the mangroves. ⊠ *Long Bay Beach and Grace Bay, Grace Bay* ☎ *649/231–5483* ⊕ *www. waterplaytci.com.*

Chapter 4

THE CAICOS AND THE CAYS

Updated by
Jessica Robertson

⊙ **Sights**   🍴 **Restaurants**   🛏 **Hotels**   🛍 **Shopping**   🍸 **Nightlife**
★★★★☆   ★★★☆☆   ★★★☆☆   ★★☆☆☆   ★★☆☆☆

WELCOME TO
THE CAICOS AND THE CAYS

TOP REASONS
TO GO

★ **Day excursions.** All of Provo's excursion companies offer trips to the cays, where you can snorkel the reef, check out the iguanas at Little Water Cay, and dive for conch all in one afternoon. On a full-day excursion you can go as far as Middle Caicos, where you can hike trails and explore caves.

★ **Parrot Cay.** Live like a rock star, if only for a day. Reservations are mandatory, but if you can get here for lunch, it's oh-so worth it for access to the gorgeous beach, pool, and one of the best spas in the world.

★ **Pine Cay.** Everything here is rustic and charming, laid-back and relaxing, and the beach is one of the best. Call the Meridian Club to organize a boat transfer and head over for lunch.

★ **Slowing Down.** When you visit the North, Middle, and South Caicos, it'll make Provo seem fast-paced by comparison. Nothing happens fast here, and that's just the way the locals (and those who visit) like it.

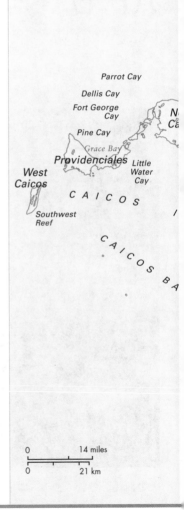

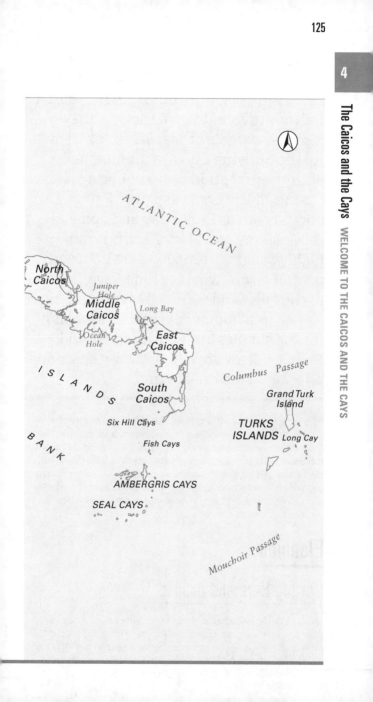

Turks and Caicos consists of more than forty islands, eight of which are inhabited. Few visitors venture out from the tourist hub of Provo, but when they do, they discover a whole other side to the islands. All the outlying cays are uninhabited with the exception of two, offering much for the adventurous explorer. Parrot Cay, once known as Pirate Cay and home to Anne Bonny and Mary Reid, is now a highly sought-after 1,000-acre luxurious private resort, whereas Pine Cay is home to the quiet and secluded Meridian Club as well as a number of residents looking for the simpler life. South, North, and Middle Caicos are laid-back and charming, offering a step back in time.

All the cays have something unique to offer, whether that be observing iguanas, hiking through bird sanctuaries, or sitting on a quiet beach watching whales go by. With the fringing reef keeping the waves at bay, there is also great snorkeling. And then there's the beauty of East Caicos, uninhabited by humans, and populated by donkeys and flamingos. The highest point of land in the Turks and Caicos is on East Caicos, where there are cave systems and endless beaches to comb.

Planning

Getting Here and Around

Many of the uninhabited cays can be explored on day trips out of Provo. Boat excursion companies offer small-group trips to several of them, and you can also charter your own trip. Although the smaller islands between Provo and North Caicos can be reached only by boat from Provo, there is a regularly scheduled ferry service between Provo and North Caicos; from there you can drive across a causeway to Middle Caicos, which takes only about 30 minutes from the ferry landing by car. South Caicos can also be reached by ferry, albeit a long and often bumpy ride, so many choose one of several daily flights offered by interCaribbean Airways.

Hotels

Accommodations throughout the Caicos islands are generally simple yet comfortable. There are small basic hotels and a few privately owned villas scattered throughout, offering clean lodgings with air-conditioning and some even have satellite TV. At the other end of the spectrum is Pine Cay's Meridian Club, like a luxury camp with a clubby atmosphere. And then there's Parrot Cay, one of the finest resorts in the world. The Sailrock Resort, high on a ridge in South Caicos, provides luxury in a remote setting.

Hotel reviews have been shortened. For full information, visit Fodors.com.

Restaurants

The outer islands don't offer much in the way of independent restaurants, and each island has only a handful of places to eat. Menus are often based on what was caught that day, which equates to wonderfully fresh fish, conch, and lobster dishes. It is always a good idea to call ahead. In fact, it is highly recommended that day-trippers take a small picnic with them, just in case the chef has decided to take the day off or everyone's at church. Sunday is the day most restaurants in North, Middle, and South Caicos give everyone the day off, so be sure to plan ahead. If you're staying at the Meridian Club on Pine Cay, meals are included in your room rate. Parrot Cay has two elegant and upscale restaurants. Both Parrot Cay and the Meridian Club are private resorts, but with advance reservations it's possible for nonguests to dine at both places. The excursion is very expensive, but many travelers find that it's worth it for the chance to visit.

Planning Your Time

The smaller cays are all accessible only by boat, whether as part of an excursion or by private charter. A few may be reached by kayak for the more adventurous; check with Big Blue Unlimited,

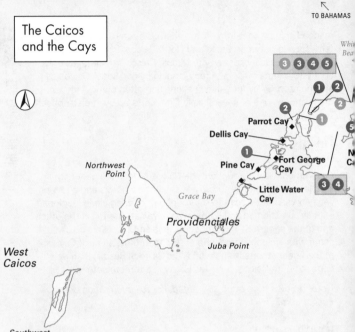

The Caicos and the Cays

TO BAHAMAS

Whit
Bea

Parrot Cay
Dellis Cay
Fort George Cay
Pine Cay
Little Water Cay

Northwest
Point

Grace Bay

Providenciales

Juba Point

West
Caicos

Southwest
Reef

C A

N
C

Sights
Boiling Hole, **7**
Cockburn Harbour, **8**
Conch Bar Caves, **6**
Cottage Pond, **1**
Flamingo Pond, **5**
Kew, **4**
Three Mary Cays, **2**
Wades Green, **3**

Restaurants
Aquatic Restaurant & Bar, **6**
Asia's Takeout, **14**
Barracuda Beach Bar, **3**
Blu, **17**

The Cove Restaurant + Beach Bar, **12**
Dolphin Grill at the Ocean and Beach Resort, **16**
Frank's Cafe, **8**
Great House Restaurant, **13**
Green Island Café, **1**
Last Chance Bar and Grill, **9**
Miss B's, **5**
Mudjin Bar and Grill, **11**
My Dee's Restaurant, Bar & Grill, **7**
ReadyMoney Roadside Caboose, **10**
Silver Palm Bistro, **4**
Silver Palm Restaurant, **2**

Sunset Cafe Bar & Grill, **15**

Hotels
Caicos Beach Condos, **3**
Dragon Cay Resort, **6**
East Bay Resort, **9**
Hollywood Beach Suites, **4**
The Meridian Club, Turks & Caicos, **1**
Parrot Cay Resort, **2**
Pelican Beach Hotel, **5**
Sailrock, **7**
South Caicos Ocean & Beach Resort, **8**

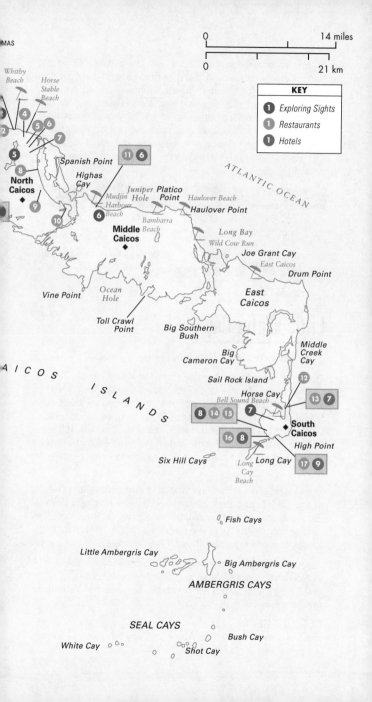

as their kayak rentals are closest to the cays between Provo and North. Both Parrot Cay and Meridian Club have private transportation from Provo for their own guests, whereas day-trippers must incur the transportation over at a cost. North Caicos and South Caicos are accessible by the very reliable ferry service offered by Caribbean Cruisin' operating out of Provo. Middle Caicos is connected to North Caicos by a causeway, so both of these islands can be visited in a single day, as can South Caicos if you're traveling by plane.

What It Costs in U.S. Dollars			
$	$$	$$$	$$$$
RESTAURANTS			
under $12	$12–$20	$21–$30	over $30
HOTELS			
under $275	$275–$375	$376–$475	over $475

Little Water Cay

5 minutes by boat from Walkin or Leeward Marina.

This small, uninhabited cay is a protected area under the Turks & Caicos National Trust, and it's just a stone's throw away from Providenciales' Walkin and Leeward marinas. The trip over takes only 5 minutes from the Leeward end of the island, and an excursion boat out of Grace Bay takes 5 to 15 minutes. On these 150 acres are two trails, red mangroves, and an abundance of native plants. Boardwalks protect the ground, and interpretive signs explain the habitat.

The small island—known to many as Iguana Island—is home to about 2,000 rare, endangered rock iguanas. Although often described as shy, these creatures are actually quite curious. They waddle right up to you, as if posing for a picture. Please do not feed or touch the iguanas. They are wild animals.

Several water-sports operators from Provo and North Caicos include a stop on the island as a part of a snorkel or sailing excursion. There's a $5 permit fee to visit the cay, and the proceeds go toward conservation in the islands.

GETTING HERE
The only way to reach Little Water Cay is by organized excursion or private boat (including kayak).

Little Water Cay is known as Iguana Island and is home to the rare rock iguana.

Pine Cay

15 to 20 minutes by boat from Provo.

Pine Cay's 2½-mile-long (4-km-long) beach is among the most beautiful in the archipelago. The 800-acre private island, which is in the string of small cays between Provo and North Caicos, is home to a secluded resort and almost 40 private residences. The beach alone is reason to stay here.

Nonguests of the Meridian Club can make reservations for lunch, and boat transfer can be arranged for an extra cost. Plan to spend the day enjoying the stunning beach, and be sure to ask what's on the day's menu since it changes daily. Saturday and Wednesday nights are buffet-style. Saturday is also Jump-Up night, where the resort puts out their largest speakers and encourages everyone to "jump up and dance the night away!" On Wednesday, a quieter option, the kitchen staff pitches in to produce their favorite meals, making it the perfect time to try some local dishes.

GETTING HERE

The only way to reach Pine Cay is by private boat or on the Meridian Club's private service. Ask the resort to explain your transfer options, because the cost varies, depending on whether you take advantage of a shared boat or decide to organize a private trip (small boats cost $170 each way, larger boats cost $250 each way and up). You must make reservations, so don't count on making same-day arrangements.

🛏 Hotels

⭐ The Meridian Club, Turks & Caicos

$$$$ | **RESORT** | On one of the most beautiful beaches in Turks and Caicos, the Meridian Club is the place to de-stress. **Pros:** one of the finest beaches in the Caribbean; rates include some of the best food served in TCI, as well as snorkeling trips; perfect place to completely unwind. **Cons:** no TVs or phones, so you are truly unplugged here; expensive to get back to Provo for shopping or other Provo-based excursions or activities; the simplicity comes at a cost. ⑤ *Rooms from: $1095* ✉ *North Shore* ☎ *649/946–7758, 888/286–7993* ⊕ *www.meridianclub.com* ☉ *Closed Aug.–Oct.* 🛏 *28 rooms* ⑩ *All meals.*

Fort George Cay

15 to 20 minutes by boat from Leeward Marina.

An uninhabited cay and a protected national park, Fort George Cay was once a fortified island that protected the surrounding waters from pirates. Some of the 18th-century cannons that were put in place on the island are now underwater and can be viewed by snorkelers. The beach itself is stunning, a photographer's delight: the curved shoreline creates swirls of different shades of turquoise in the water; at low tide sandbars appear, and the blue-and-green water looks even brighter. This is a great spot to search for sand dollars, so bring a cookie tin to carry them back home in. You can collect only white sand dollars; gray or dark ones are alive and illegal to take. Most of the excursion companies make stops here on their full-day trips, so ask if the island is on an itinerary that you may plan to take.

GETTING HERE

The only way to reach Fort George Cay is by organized excursion or private boat.

Dellis Cay

20 minutes by boat from Leeward Marina.

This stunning small island, the second-to-last cay in the string of small islands between Providenciales and North Caicos, has a gorgeous sandy beach and decent snorkeling; it's also a good place to search for sand dollars. It's uninhabited but looks ominous with its partially built Mandarin Oriental resort, which was abandoned when the economy tanked; the shells of buildings can be seen for miles. It's really not worth the stop.

GETTING HERE
The only way to reach Dellis Cay is by private boat.

Parrot Cay

20 minutes by boat from Provo.

The last in the string of small islands between Provo and North Caicos is Parrot Cay, once a hideout for pirate Calico Jack Rackham and his lady cohorts Mary Read and Anne Bonny. The 1,000-acre cay, between Fort George Cay and North Caicos, is now the site of an ultra-exclusive hideaway resort. Originally called Pirate Cay (because of the Spanish galleon treasures believed to be buried somewhere on the island), the name was changed to Parrot Cay when the resort was built, to rid itself of the somewhat negative connotations.

Non-hotel guests may dine at the resort. Reservations are mandatory and may not be available during the busy periods, but if you go, it will be a memorable experience. While there, you may want to join one of their classes, enjoy one of the many amazing treatments at their world-class spa, or take a dip in the infinity pool.

GETTING HERE
There are three options for reaching Parrot Cay: charter a private boat, join the resort's service ferry operated from their private dock on Providenciales, or take the public ferry ($25 each way) to North Caicos and then catch the complimentary staff shuttle between North and Parrot Cay. A $100 day pass (which includes the boat transfer over) is necessary for all day guests, in addition to any services you might use. The availability of day passes depends on the resort's occupancy and cannot be confirmed more than a day in advance.

 Hotels

★ Parrot Cay Resort
$$$$ | RESORT | This private paradise, on its own island, pairs tranquility with service ranked at the top in Turks and Caicos. **Pros:** impeccable service; gorgeous, secluded beach; spa is considered one of the best in the world. **Cons:** only two restaurants to choose from island-wide; excursions are expensive; you are away from everything else to see and do in Turks and Caicos. ⑤ *Rooms from:*

Parrot Cay Resort is on its own private island.

$795 ✛ *Northeastern tip of Parrot Cay* ☏ *649/946–7788, 866/388–0036* ⊕ *www.parrotcay.com* ⌁ *113 rooms* ❤◎❤ *Breakfast.*

🛍 Shopping

★ Como Shambhala at Parrot Cay

SPA/BEAUTY | Asian holistic treatments, yoga with the world's leading teachers in a stunning pavilion, and a signature health-conscious cuisine are all part of the program here. In fact, visiting masters from "off island" are featured throughout the year. The infinity pool, Pilates studio, steam room, sauna, and outdoor Jacuzzi make you feel complete. If you're staying on Provo, you can call for reservations, but you have to pay for a day pass to Parrot Cay. Some consider this to be one of the finest spas in the world. ✉ *Parrot Cay Resort* ☏ *649/946–7788* ⊕ *www.comohotels. com/en/parrotcay/wellness.*

North Caicos

Thanks to abundant rainfall, this 41-square-mile (106-square-km) island is the lushest in the Turks and Caicos chain. With an estimated population of only 1,500, the expansive island allows you to get away from it all. Bird lovers can see a large flock of resident flamingos here, anglers can find shallow creeks full of bonefish, and history buffs can visit the ruins of a loyalist plantation. Although there's little traffic, almost all the roads are paved, so bicycling can be an excellent way to sightsee. Even though it's a quiet place, you can find a few small eateries around the island offering local specialties, often served with homegrown okra or corn. The beaches are au naturel, littered with seaweed and pine needles and whatever else the winds and tides bring—perfect for the beachcomber. Nevertheless, some of these secluded strands are breathtaking.

North Caicos definitely moves at a much slower pace, especially in comparison with shiny Provo. Accommodations are clean but fairly basic, and locals are consistently friendly.

GETTING HERE

You can reach North Caicos from Provo on the ferry from Walkin Marina in Leeward. There are several daily trips, with the earliest leaving at 6:30 am (8:30 on Sunday) and the last returning at 5:30 pm (4:30 on Sunday); the trip takes only 30 minutes. Once you get there, you can arrange for a driver for the day (an expensive option) or rent a car. Remember that a causeway connects North to Middle Caicos, making it a great day trip from Provo. If you miss the last ferry back to Provo you have two choices: book what's bound to be a pricey private charter, or give "Big Josh" of Big Josh Bar & Grill a call to see if one of his three basic hotel rooms nearby is available ☎ 649/241–1890.

CONTACTS Caribbean Cruisin'. ⊠ Walkin Marina, Heaving Down Rock, Leeward ☎ 649/946–5406 ⊕ www.tciferry.com.

◉ Sights

Cottage Pond

LOCAL INTEREST | A short distance from the North Caicos ferry terminal and en route to where the flamingos rest is Cottage Pond. Watch on the right side of the road, as the sign can be hidden in the foliage. The roadway deteriorates the closer you get, so just park and walk the rest of the way. At the end you'll find this lovely, quiet freshwater pond where slaves would come to wash clothes. Today, there's always an assortment of ducks swimming, with ferns as their backdrop. Local lore has it that the pond has no bottom and a mermaid was once spotted swimming there. ⊠ Sandy Point ⊹ Just east of the ferry terminal.

★ Flamingo Pond

LOCAL INTEREST | The pond is home to approximately 2,000 resident flamingos. These spectacular pink birds come and go during the day, so if you miss them on your drive down the island, be sure to double-check at the end of the day. Bring binoculars to get a better look; they feed quite a ways out, and you're not allowed to hike closer. ⊠ *Whitby Hwy., Whitby* ⊕ *South of Whitby, east of Kew.*

★ Kew

ARCHAEOLOGICAL SITE | This settlement includes a small school and a number of churches, as well as tropical fruit trees that produce limes, papayas, and the more exotic custard apples. Nearby are the well-preserved ruins—old cauldrons, main house structure, and other outbuildings—of Wade's Green Plantation. The fully intact ruins of a historic Baptist church sits roadside just past the modern Church of God of Prophecy as you enter the village. Kew's heartbeat is still present, and visiting will give you a better understanding of the daily life of the islanders before development; it's wonderful to see the more traditional lifestyle coexisting with the present day. Contact the National Trust to make special arrangements to view the plantation. It is usually open weekdays 9:30 to 11:30 and 2:30 to 4 pm. ⊠ *Kew* ☎ *649/232–6284 National Trust* ⊕ *tcnationaltrust.org* 🎫 *$10, which includes a 30-minute tour* ⊙ *Closed weekends.*

Three Mary Cays

ISLAND | Three small rocky cays within swimming distance of Whitby Beach give you some of the best secluded snorkeling in all of the Turks and Caicos. You will often find ospreys nesting there, too. This is a wildlife protection area, so don't feed the fish, touch any of the corals, or disturb the birds. ⊕ *Off Whitby Beach.*

★ Wades Green

ARCHAEOLOGICAL SITE | FAMILY | You wander down the shaded laneway, bordered by walls made from the rocks once found in the fields of this cotton plantation established by Loyalist Wade Stubbs in 1789. The walls of the great house still stand, albeit with foliage now growing on the inside. Giant iron cauldrons, once used to prepare meals for the slaves, rest in the yard. There are also partial remains of the kitchen, the overseer's house, slave quarters, and several storage buildings. A lookout tower provides views for miles. TCI National Trust offers visits and 30-minute tours on weekdays 9:30 to 11:30 and 2:30 to 4:00. ⊠ *Kew* ☎ *649/232–6284 TCI National Trust* ⊕ *tcnationaltrust.org* 🎫 *$10.*

⊕ Beaches

The beaches of North Caicos are superb for shallow snorkeling and sunset strolls, and the waters offshore have excellent scuba diving.

Horse Stable Beach

BEACH—SIGHT | Horse Stable Beach is the main beach for annual events and beach parties for the resident population of North Caicos. Get-togethers spring up occasionally at the North Caicos Community Centre that sits along the beach, making you quite lucky if you happen to be around for one; visitors are always welcome. Stop by if you're a beachcomber, as you'll find shells and sun-bleached coral as well as many other items washed in from the sea off of passing ships. Of course the sand is soft and the stroll a delight. **Amenities:** none. **Best for:** solitude; walking.

Whitby Beach

BEACH—SIGHT | Whitby Beach usually has a gentle tide, and its thin strip of sand is bordered by palmetto palms and taller trees, which provide a bit of shade. As the beach is in its natural state, you may enjoy a bit of beachcombing as you stroll; you'll find small shells, sun-bleached coral, and other ocean castoffs. There are also some coral heads just offshore for those who wish to don a mask and fins. During the high season you can break up your visit with a nice lunch at Silver Palm Restaurant, which is right behind Caicos Beach Condominiums. **Amenities:** food and drink. **Best for:** snorkeling; solitude; walking. ⊠ *Whitby*.

🍴 Restaurants

Visiting North Caicos is all about exploring the more laid-back style of the Turks and Caicos Islands. Expect just that when dining, too. You'll find many little restaurants roadside; all of them are worth the experience, serving up local fare in a variety of ways. Chefs are often your hosts or hostesses, so be patient, as every meal is part of the adventure.

It's important to note that restaurants do not stay open late and that if the day is slow, they might just close up early. And be forewarned: on Sunday many locals spend much of the day at church, and most of the little restaurants will be closed.

Aquatic Restaurant & Bar

$$ | CARIBBEAN | What Aquatic lacks in ambience, they make up for in the food. Fresh fish fried, steamed, or grilled and burgers and cracked conch are always on the menu. **Known for:** fresh fish cooked many ways; late-night bar scene; open year-round. ⑤ *Average main: $12* ⊠ *Whitby* ☎ *649/241–2398, 649/231–0005* ⊗ *Closed Sun.*

Barracuda Beach Bar

$$ | CARIBBEAN | Though it's just a shack on the beach with a view, this is the epitome of what a Caribbean beach bar should be. Your

North Caicos in a Day

From Provo a wonderful ferry service runs out of Walkin Marina in Leeward; it's comfortable, efficient, and timely, taking only about 30 minutes each way. Not only does it get you to North, but it's also a great way to have a quick overview of all the cays that lie between Provo and North, with views of some of the homes of the rich and famous along the shores of secluded Parrot Cay.

Visitors to North can hire a driver ($300 per day for group of four), go with a tour company such as Big Blue Unlimited, or prearrange a car rental. There are several rental companies that can arrange to have a car waiting for you at the Sandy Point ferry dock. If you miss the last ferry back, a private charter is the only alternative, at a high cost. Avoid Sunday, as many places including most restaurants and variety stores, are closed.

An afternoon drive around the island is well worth it for those who wish to know the real side to this country. Near the settlement of Kew you'll find the ruins of Wade's Green Plantation *(See North Caicos Sights)*. If you want to see the plantation, you need to make arrangements with the TCI National Trust in advance; otherwise, the entrance will be chained. These are the country's best ruins, so it's worth making the call.

A visit is not complete without a quick stop at Flamingo Pond, which is home to the country's largest resident flock.

Close by is Cottage Pond, a historical site connected to plantation days but also a nice refuge for those wishing to visit a watery habitat quite different from what you find throughout the islands; a variety of birds make this their home.

You can also stop and visit several beaches, snorkel at Three Mary Cays, and watch for the Caicos crows cawing in the trees overhead. Note that many of the feathery-looking coniferous trees growing around North are the Caicos pine (otherwise known as the Caribbean pine), the country's national tree. And do stop at one of the little roadside bars or eateries to grab a cold drink and a bite to eat. The food is basic but tasty, and it hits the spot after a few hours of exploring. You can call ahead to most of the smaller spots from the ferry and place your order. It will be ready by the time you make your way there. Don't be shy! If you're lucky, you will arrive when a couple of the local gentlemen are just beginning their heated rally of dominoes.

feet are in the sand, and your table is an old wooden cable spool. **Known for:** melt-in-your-mouth cracked conch; storytime with Clifford; quintessential island beach bar vibes. $ *Average main: $12* ✉ *Pelican Beach Hotel* ☎ *649/243–4794* ▭ *No credit cards* ⊘ *Closed Aug.–Sept.*

Frank's Cafe

$$ | **CARIBBEAN** | There's a wooden sign on the roadside, but none on the restaurant—just look for the bright orange house at the top of the steep, rocky driveway. It's the only spot in Bottle Creek for traditional home-cooked island food, including fish fingers, conch prepared every which way, and a few non-seafood dishes, too. **Known for:** good local food; monthly fish fry; air-conditioned break from the heat. $ *Average main: $12* ✉ *Bottle Creek* ☎ *649/243–6839* ⊘ *Closed Sun; call ahead for Sat. hours* ▭ *No credit cards.*

Green Island Café

$$ | **CARIBBEAN** | Located at the Sandy Point Marina, this café offers something for everyone, including cracked conch and fresh fish, as well as burgers and sandwiches. It's a great little place to grab a bite to eat before you head out to explore the islands or before catching the ferry back to Provo. **Known for:** cracked conch; great takeout; umbrella-covered tables. $ *Average main: $12* ✉ *Sandy Point Marina, Sandy Point Rd.* ☎ *649/247–6173* ▭ *No credit cards* ⊘ *Closed Sun.*

★ Last Chance Bar and Grill

$$$$ | **ECLECTIC** | Now serving dinner only, this delightful restaurant housed inside a lovingly restored 1930s home is a regular stop for locals and visitors alike. The food is delicious, but get there early enough to enjoy the views of Bottle Creek; the colors of the water are unlike anything you've ever seen. **Known for:** great view; homemade desserts using fruit grown on the property; the area's best option for a home-cooked dinner. $ *Average main: $36* ✉ *Bottle Creek* ☎ *649/232–4141* ▭ *No credit cards* ⊘ *Closed May 15–Nov. 15.*

★ Miss B's

$$ | **CARIBBEAN** | Miss B is the cook, the bartender, the hostess, and even leads karaoke sessions when there's a crowd, and she still makes the time to chat with every guest. The menu is simple, but the food is good and includes fresh fish and conch, juicy burgers, and jerk chicken. **Known for:** Wednesday afternoon fish fry; delightful owner who welcomes you with a smile and a chat; homemade ice cream and desserts. $ *Average main: $14* ✉ *Whitby* ☎ *649/946–7727, 649/241–3939* ⊘ *Closed Sun.*

My Dee's Restaurant, Bar & Grill

$$ | **CARIBBEAN** | Friday night's barbecue ribs are reason enough to stop by this small restaurant, serving traditional island fare for breakfast, lunch, and dinner. Sit inside the air-conditioned dining room for a welcome break from the heat, or grab a picnic table under the trees outside. **Known for:** lively spot on a Friday night with best ribs around; seafood pizza; fresh snapper, grilled or fried. $ *Average main: $15* ✉ *My Dee's Plaza, Whitby* ☎ *649/946–7059, 649/245–1239* ▭ *No credit cards.*

★ ReadyMoney Roadside Caboose

$$ | **CARIBBEAN** | It's amazing to see the variety and quality of food that Miss Curalena churns out of her 8x12-foot kitchen at this brightly colored shack, with its picnic tables and umbrellas, just before you hit the causeway to Middle Caicos. In addition to local breakfast and lunch specials, this is the place to get fresh squeezed juices. **Known for:** fresh squeezed juices using fruits grown on site; delicious island recipes; local owner Miss Curalena, who will tell you all about the area. $ *Average main: $12* ✉ *Whitby* ☾ *Closed weekends* ▭ *No credit cards.*

Silver Palm Bistro

$$ | **CARIBBEAN** | You can get island food for lunch and dinner at this little spot, but nothing beats their homemade ice cream. You never know what flavors you'll find in the freezer, but the most popular are the rum raisin and the toasted coconut. **Known for:** homemade ice cream made with local fruits; delicious island cooking; pizza if you give them advance notice. $ *Average main: $15* ✉ *Horse Stable Rd., Whitby* ✛ *In the same building as the island's police station* ☎ *649/241–6340* ⊕ *www.northcaicos-everything.com* ▭ *No credit cards.*

★ Silver Palm Restaurant

$$$ | **ECLECTIC** | Located just behind the Caicos Beach Condos in the settlement of Whitby, the Silver Palm serves great food in a setting more refined than any other in North Caicos. If you're day-tripping from Provo, start with breakfast here, or call ahead to order a picnic lunch to take with you as you explore. **Known for:** homemade bread; friendly and welcoming owners; fancier food than you'd expect to find in such a remote spot. $ *Average main: $28* ✉ *Whitby* ☎ *649/241–6340* ⊕ *www.northcaicos-everything.com* ▭ *No credit cards* ☾ *Closed mid-June–mid-Nov.*

Hotels

Caicos Beach Condos

$ | RENTAL | On Whitby Beach, this horseshoe-shaped, two-story, older hotel offers amazing ocean views in comfortably furnished apartments, at quite reasonable rates. **Pros:** on a lovely secluded beach; excellent restaurant right next door; full kitchens make dining easier. **Cons:** you need a car to get anywhere on North Caicos; property is aged and could use some TLC; only some units have been updated, therefore accommodation is inconsistent. ⑤ *Rooms from: $200* ⊠ *Whitby* ☎ *649/946–7113* ⊕ *Check VRBO to rent* ⊗ *Closed June 15–Nov. 15* ⟿ *10 rooms* ⦿ *No meals.*

★ Hollywood Beach Suites

$$ | RENTAL | With 7 miles (11 km) of secluded beach and few others to share it with, this property can only be described as simple and relaxing. **Pros:** secluded and tranquil; updated furnishings; daily light housekeeping. **Cons:** might feel a little too secluded; no good food store to grab something you need or forgot; you've really got to be happy doing nothing much or entertaining yourself. ⑤ *Rooms from: $375* ⊠ *Hollywood Beach Dr., Whitby* ☎ *649/231– 1020, 855/217–8796* ⊕ *www.hollywoodbeachsuites.com* ⟿ *4 suites* ⦿ *No meals.*

Pelican Beach Hotel

$ | HOTEL | North Caicos islanders Susan and Clifford Gardiner built this small, palmetto-fringed hotel in the 1980s on this quiet and almost deserted beach in Whitby. **Pros:** the beach is right outside your room; the owners make you instantly feel at home; perfect spot to get away from it all. **Cons:** property is tired; location may be too remote and sleepy for some people; beach is au naturel—a positive for many. ⑤ *Rooms from: $150* ⊠ *Whitby* ☎ *649/946– 7112* ⊕ *www.pelicanbeach.tc* ⊗ *Closed Aug.–Sept.* ⟿ *6 rooms* ⦿ *Some meals* ⟿ *Stay may include breakfast plan.*

⚽ Activities

BIKING

★ Big Blue Unlimited

BICYCLING | Join the kayak ecoadventure that takes you through protected Bottle Creek and East Bay Cay National Park on North Caicos. Or, if you want to go at your own pace, try a self-guided kayak tour, as their rentals are available on North Caicos. On a land-based tour, visit the Flamingo Pond Nature Reserve, explore Conch Bar Caves, and visit a local artisan workshop. You can also bike North Caicos; the 15-mile (24-km) group excursion takes you through Kew town, past the ruins of Wades Green, and to a

250-foot-deep blue hole; the trip ends with lunch and a chance to take a cooling dip. There are also trips to South Caicos to see the Bermudian-style architecture, flamingos, expansive salt flats, and the older part of town. Divers can book private charters, weather depending. ⊠ *Pinta La., Leeward* ☎ *649/946–5034, 649/231–6455* ⊕ *bigblueunlimited.com.*

★ Caribbean Cruisin'

ADVENTURE TOURS | This outfitter runs the daily ferry between Provo and North Caicos, rents cars so you can get around North and Middle Caicos, and offers a variety of tours by land, by boat, or even by Jet Ski. On the Seaside Scavenger Hunt you'll dive for queen conch, and they'll turn it into your lunch. It's best to book in advance, as some tours require minimum numbers. Their main office and reservation desk is based at the Walkin Marina in Providenciales, but representatives are on-site at the marina in North Caicos whenever a ferry is due to arrive or depart. ⊠ *Leeward* ☎ *649/946–5406* ⊕ *www.caribbeancruisin.tc.*

★ North Caicos Outfitters

SELF-GUIDED | Bottle Creek is stunning when you see it from high above on land. It's even more incredible to explore by kayak. Long-time resident Howard Gibbs will rent you a kayak and point you in the right direction or take you out on guided bonefishing expeditions. ⊠ *Last Chance Bar & Grill, Bottle Creek* ☎ *649/232–4141.*

🍸 Nightlife

Big Josh Bar & Grill

BARS/PUBS | You can't miss this colorfully painted establishment—it's the first stop on the main road leading to and from the marina. A restaurant is planned, but for now it's a great place to grab a cocktail or cold beer. Sit indoors where there's shade and a cool breeze, or perch on the wall at the outside bar. With $3 beers at happy hour, this might just be the best deal in all of the Turks and Caicos islands. This is also where you can find a reasonably priced, very basic room if you miss the last ferry. They're open from 10 am to 11 pm. ⊠ *Whitby* ☎ *649/241–1890.*

👜 Shopping

★ Caicos Tea Company

LOCAL SPECIALTIES | Long ago, islanders used to cure all ailments with local bush teas. Donna, the owner of this micro-tea manufacturer, is determined to keep that culture alive with her special blends. Try a cup of the Caicos Sunshine Tea, a blend of citrus, fever grass (lemongrass), and mint that is said to relieve just about everything. If she's around, Donna will gladly give you a tour and share the history of Turks and Caicos bush tea culture with you. On Provo, you can purchase the teas in FOTTAC and Art Provo. ⊠ Airport Rd., Whitby ☎ 649/245–9449 ⊕ www.caicosteacompany.com.

★ Middle Caicos Co-Op

CRAFTS | Support local artisans by stopping into this little spot, where you can purchase handmade straw baskets, placemats, and floor mats. Their huge handwoven beach bags are perfect for toting beach towels and snorkel gear. They also sell local art and beach rope bracelets woven from fishing nets that have washed ashore. They have another location in Middle Caicos near the Conch Bar Caves. ⊠ My Dee's Plaza, King's Rd., Whitby ☾ Closed Sat.–Mon.

Nique's Food Mart

CONVENIENCE/GENERAL STORES | This tiny grocery store has dry goods as well as some fresh vegetables, frozen meats, and even tubs of ice cream. ⊠ My Dee's Plaza, King's Rd., Whitby ☎ 649/946-7761.

Middle Caicos

At 48 square miles (124 square km) and with fewer than 300 residents, this is the largest yet least developed of the inhabited Caicos islands. The landscape is unique in that a limestone ridge runs to about 125 feet above sea level, creating dramatic cliffs on the northwest shoreline; a quick glance down the waterfront from Mudjin Harbour is reminiscent of the south coast of England. There is also the largest cave system in the Lucayan Archipelago on Middle Caicos. Rambling trails along the coast are an easy hike; the Crossing Place Trail, maintained by the TCI National Trust, follows the path used by early settlers to connect the islands. Inland are quiet settlements with friendly residents.

The best time to visit is mid-November through mid-April. The rest of the year most of the hotels and many of the restaurants that cater primarily to tourists are closed. That said, you can pack a small cooler with all you'll need for the day and take the ferry over. Cars can be rented throughout the year, and the beaches and other natural sights of interest never close.

North Caicos and Middle Caicos are linked by a causeway, so it's possible to take a ferry from Provo to North Caicos, rent a car, and explore both North Caicos and Middle Caicos in a single day if you get an early start.

GETTING HERE

You can reach Middle Caicos by car (over the causeway that connects it to North Caicos), by private boat, or by organized tour.

Sights

★ Conch Bar Caves

CAVE | FAMILY | These limestone caves make up one of the largest cave systems in the Caribbean, with good examples of stalactites and stalagmites, as well as small—and slightly eerie—underground bodies of water. Archaeologists have discovered Lucayan artifacts in the caves and the surrounding area; these natives to the island would have used the caves to weather the storm season. Currently, the caves are inhabited by five species of bats—some of which are endangered and bring scientists here annually to study them—but they don't bother visitors. Half-hour tours are available through TCI's National Trust. Guides provide flashlights and a sense of humor. It's best to wear sturdy shoes, as the ground is rocky and damp in places. If you don't have much time, Indian Cave is a smaller version that's worth exploring. Watch for the sign on your left after leaving the causeway. It's only a few steps off the road, parallel with Dragon Cay Resort. ⊠ *Conch Bar* ✛ *Main cave system is just outside Conch Bar; Indian Cave is near Dragon Cay Resort on main highway.* ☎ *649/941–5710 TCI National Trust, local direct dial* ⊕ *tcnationaltrust.org/Conch-Bar-Caves* ⊠ *$20* ⊗ *Closed weekends* ☞ *Must arrange through TCI National Trust.*

⊕ Beaches

Middle Caicos is blessed with two particularly stunning beaches, Mudjin Harbour and Bambarra Beach, as well as the untamed stretches of Haulover Beach and Wild Cow Run, both on the very far northeast part of the island.

Bambarra Beach

BEACH—SIGHT | As with all Middle Caicos beaches, Bambarra seems to stretch on forever, shaded by casuarina trees and littered with refuse from the sea. Visiting Bambarra Beach means no amenities, but enjoying a picnic lunch here provides a lifetime memory. Water is shallow, with coral heads nearby so that snorkeling is possible. Stroll on the beach or out to a nearby cay. Watch for rays and juvenile sharks as they patrol the shoreline. Probably the only time you will see others here is when a community gathering takes place; each Valentine's Day, Bambarra Beach hosts the Middle Caicos Model Sailboat Race, which features hand-carved boats painted in bright colors as well as local music and a number of food and beverage stalls. **Amenities:** none. **Best for:** solitude; walking.

Haulover Beach

BEACH—SIGHT | Don't be put off by the overgrown roundabout, because if you carry on to the left you'll find yourself at a wide swooping bay. There are miles to stroll, trees for shade, and only the odd photographer to meet along the way. The water is crystal clear and shallow, and the entire bay is a protected haven. This is where the boats would moor, bringing goods in to the nearby plantation and taking out what they wished to sell. If you cross over the rise where the unfinished home sits, you will find an unprotected coastline, a beachcomber's delight. As an aside, you will pass Haulover Plantation on the drive out. There's a wonderful little path that winds through the indigenous underbrush bordered by low rock walls that will lead you to the ruins. The walk out and back takes about 30 minutes. **Amenities:** none. **Best for:** solitude; walking. ⊹ *Head toward Lorimers; take the road to your left just before the settlements and follow that parallel to the water on your right.*

★ Mudjin Harbour Beach

BEACH—SIGHT | You can hike the trails on the cliffs overlooking Mudjin Harbour and then dip down a hidden staircase to your own private cove if you're looking for total privacy. The main beach, accessible from Dragon Cay Resort, is the beginning of miles that you can stroll. The point of land that joins it to Dragon Cay at low tide is often littered with sea glass. Little tidal pools between the cay and beach also provide endless entertainment when the wave action is minimal. But as this is Mudjin Harbour, a bit of bodysurfing can be had, because a break in the reef allows larger waves to make it to shore. Kids love it, and it's relatively safe, as there is little rip on most days. Just remember that there's no lifeguard on duty. Shade can be found in the giant, cavelike overhang at the base of the path down to the water, perfect for getting out of the sun. Of course, there's always the possibility of spending a bit of time in the spectacularly placed restaurant overlooking the harbor; great food, drinks, and viewing are provided. **Amenities:** food and drink. **Best for:** swimming; walking. ⊠ *Mudjin Harbour.*

Wild Cow Run

BEACH—SIGHT | If you're feeling adventurous and want to explore an amazing strand, check out Wild Cow Run. It's at the end of the island, and you're likely to have the beach, as well as the views of the channel and Joe Grant's Cay, all to yourself. Numerous sandbars form at low tide, and beachcombing is at its best; you'll

probably stumble upon the hull of a boat or two that lost its battle against Mother Nature. **Amenities:** none. **Best for:** solitude; walking. ✛ *Far northeastern end of the island.*

🍴 Restaurants

★ Mudjin Bar and Grill

$$$$ | **CARIBBEAN** | The view alone from the outside deck overlooking the dramatically stunning Mudjin Harbour makes a meal here worthwhile. The food is great, with its presentation as beautiful as the setting. ⑤ *Average main: $38 ⊠ Dragon Cay Resort, Mudjin Harbour* 🕿 *649/246–4472, 649/231–4472* ☺ *Closed Sun. Dinner by reservation only.*

🛏 Hotels

★ Dragon Cay Resort

$$ | **HOTEL** | At this property, dramatic cliffs skirt one of the most beautiful beaches in the Turks and Caicos, while turquoise-roofed cottages dot the hillside, all with outstanding views of the coastline and reef beyond. **Pros:** breathtaking views of Mudjin Harbour from the rooms; lack of development makes you feel like you're away from it all; hiking, kayaking, and beaching for adventure enthusiasts. **Cons:** need a car to explore; may be too isolated for some; three-night minimum. ⑤ *Rooms from: $350 ⊠ Mudjin Harbour* ✛ *Just after crossing the causeway on your left* 🕿 *586/354–3664* ⊕ *www.dragoncayresort.com* 🛏 *7 rooms* ⑩ *No meals.*

🏃 Activities

ISLAND TOURS

Belmont Car Rental and Tours

GUIDED TOURS | Local guide Charles "Mac" Handfield will take you up and down North and Middle Caicos on a guided land-based tour or rent you a car and give you all the information you need to explore on your own. His Discovery Tour starts at your hotel on Provo. His associates pick you up, take you to the ferry dock, and bring you back where you started at the end of the day. All transfers, site entrance fees, and even lunch are included. It's $230 per person for this small-group exploration tour. ⊠ *Bottle Creek* 🕿 *649/247–7880, 649/247–1543.*

★ Cardinal Arthur

BIRD WATCHING | Although exploring Middle Caicos on your own can be fun, a guided tour with Cardinal can illuminate the island's secret spots, from caves to where flamingos flock. He has lived

A Day in Middle Caicos

After picking up your car from the ferry dock in North Caicos, head for the causeway to Middle Caicos. As a general guideline, the trip from the ferry to Bambarra Beach can take up to 60 minutes, with only a brief stop along the way. Once you're over the causeway, it's fairly straightforward; there is only one main road the length of Middle Caicos. You'll see the turquoise roofs of Dragon Cay Resort on the hilltops almost immediately on your left. Either turn in for the pleasure of visiting Mudjin Harbour and an amazing restaurant or bypass the entrance to save it for later and watch for the Indian Cave sign on your left for your brief visit there. It is a lovely photographic location, with vines climbing up through sinkhole entries. Continue along the highway until you come to the sharp turn to the left into Conch Bar. If you go straight, you find yourself on the road to the Conch Bar Caves. If you forgot to make arrangements, you can try stopping in to see if there are any guides present to make a viewing. Again, this cave system is well worth the visit. Conch Bar is a small settlement with a couple of turns, but all roads eventually lead back to the main highway. Be sure to stop

in at the Middle Caicos Co-Op to buy some native straw work. Just beyond, you'll find a much less traveled road. This is passable by car, and makes for a lovely, slow drive along the coastline. Not far after that "trail" winds its way to meet the road, there will be a wide sweep in the otherwise straight road. Keep your eyes open for the knee-high "Bambarra Beach" sign just after the bend. The beach has several tiki huts built for community gatherings, as well as very tall coastal trees that offer shade. At low tide you can walk out to a small cay for something to do. Follow the sandy laneway until you see the beach ahead. Bring bug spray and refreshments; there are no shops or restaurants nearby. Back to the main hard-topped road, farther along is the wee settlement of Bambarra; if you blink, you'll miss it. Continue along and visit Lorimers; try to pick out the home on the left with fishing buoys and other paraphernalia hanging in the trees. The turn just before Lorimers takes you out to Haulover Plantation, Haulover Beach, and Wild Cow Run. It's a very, very full day if you plan to take it all in, and don't forget how long it takes to make it back to the ferry terminal!

The Middle Caicos are home to the Conch Bar Caves, where you can spot stalactites and stalagmites.

on Middle Caicos all his life, so his stories go way back, and his local knowledge of the flora and fauna satiates the appetite of budding naturalists. He is able to tell you the history of every nook and cranny of both Middle and North, as well as drop you off on hidden beaches—some accessible only by skiff. He can arrange almost anything and also runs a taxi service—the only one on the island! ⊠ *Conch Bar* ☎ *649/241–0730.*

🛍 Shopping

Middle Caicos Co-Op Production Studio and Sales Outlet

CRAFTS | Developed in an effort to encourage the traditional heritage and culture of the Turks and Caicos Islands, interpretive displays of island crafts are on view. You can watch basket weaving and engage in a Q&A with one of the artisans. A variety of woven baskets and bags are on sale, as well as homemade dolls, paintings, and conch jewelry and key chains. ⊠ *Conch Bar* ☎ *649/946–6132.*

South Caicos

This 8½-square-mile (21-square-km) island with a population of only 1,200 was once an important salt producer; today it's the heart of the country's fishing industry. You'll find long, white beaches; jagged bluffs; and quiet backwater bays. Life here is slow-paced and simple. Driving around the island, you'll pass through its largest settlement, Cockburn Harbour.

Multiple hurricanes over the past decade have left many of the island's buildings in ruins. With not much of a population and fewer tourists than the other islands, restoring South Caicos hasn't been a top priority for the government. Look past the rubble to see the beauty that remains of a time gone by. Hundreds of donkeys roam the island, a throwback to the days of salt processing when they played an integral role in the industry.

The major draw for South Caicos is its excellent diving and snorkeling on the pristine wall, which drops dramatically from 50 to 6,000 feet just off the south and east coastline facing Grand Turk; there's an average visibility of 100 feet. It is a treat enjoyed by only a few. The only dive operator on the island is based at the East Bay Resort where they have their own boats and equipment rental. The alternative is to explore one of the nearby cays or lie on one of the many lovely beaches as well as partake in a day or two of fishing.

GETTING HERE

There are two ways to reach South Caicos. InterCaribbean Airways offers daily flights, conveniently timed so that a day trip with time to explore the island is possible. The alternative is with TCI Ferry Service. They run a ferry between Provo and South on Friday and Sunday.

AIRLINE CONTACTS interCaribbean Airways. ⊠ *Old Private Airport, Old Airport Rd., Airport* ⊹ *Behind Kishco on Airport Rd. (giant yellow building)* ☎ *649/946–4999 reservations, 649/946–3759 customer service, 888/957–3223 toll-free from USA* ⊕ *www. intercaribbean.com.*

◉ Sights

Along the Caicos Bank side of the island, there are fine white-sand beaches; spiny lobster and queen conch are found here and are harvested for export by local processing plants. The bonefishing in its shallow waters is also considered some of the best in the West Indies, as is its renowned game fishing. Long stretches of more windswept beaches on the eastern shoreline have excellent snorkeling just offshore where one can see stands of elkhorn and staghorn coral. In addition, several small cays nearby offer total seclusion and wonderful beachcombing. The south coast has superb scuba diving and snorkeling along the reef and wall. The main settlement on the island is called Cockburn Harbour, which hosts the South Caicos Regatta each May. This is one of the islands easily explored by bicycle.

Boiling Hole

HISTORIC SITE | Abandoned *salinas* (natural salt pans) make up the center of this island, the largest receiving its water directly from an underground cave system that is connected directly to the ocean through this "boiling" hole. Don't expect anything too dramatic, other than a sense of what the industry once was. Multiple hurricanes have clogged the connection to the ocean.

Cockburn Harbour

FESTIVAL | The best natural harbor in the Caicos chain hosts the Big South Regatta each May. It began as a sailing regatta where all the families with traditional Caicos sloops would come over from Middle and North to race, but sloops are now being replaced by conch boats hosting 85-hp motors for a rip-roaring race. ⊠ *Cockburn Harbour*.

Beaches

Bell Sound

BEACH—SIGHT | The beaches of Bell Sound on the Caicos Bank side of South Caicos will take your breath away; lagoonlike waters are warm and shallow, perfect for lollygagging. Expect the beach to be au naturel. **Amenities:** none. **Best for:** walking.

East Caicos

BEACH—SIGHT | To the north of South Caicos, uninhabited East Caicos has an exquisite 17-mile (27-km) beach on its north coast. The island was once a cattle range and the site of a major sisal-growing industry. Today, it's accessible only by boat, most easily from Middle Caicos but also from South Caicos. Visiting is best in the summer months when the winds die down, making boat access more comfortable. From South, the man to take you there is Captain Tim Hamilton with his son, Tamal, of T&V Tours. His service is excellent, and he knows the waters like no other. **Amenities:** none. **Best for:** solitude; swimming; walking.

Long Cay

BEACH—SIGHT | This endless stretch of beach can be susceptible to rough surf. However, on calmer days during the summer months, you'll feel like you're on a deserted island with no one in sight. **Amenities:** none. **Best for:** solitude; walking.

A Tail of a Dive

In the 1970s, during the height of the drug-running days, planes from Colombia landed all the time on South Caicos. One plane, a Convair 29A (the size of a DC-3), ran out of gas as it approached the runway. The pilot survived, but the plane did not. The wings and body stayed intact, but the nose and tail broke off as the plane crashed into the ocean. The pieces now sit in about 50 feet of water, and they are almost completely encrusted with coral. The dive site is in two parts: "The Plane" is the main hub with the body and wings, and the "Warhead" is the tail of the wreck a few yards away. Usually there are schools of snapper and jacks swimming through the wreck, and at night, sometimes sharks, making it a unique dive. As you land at the airport, you can see the wreck from the air. Multiple hurricanes over the past decade have done more damage to the plane, but it still makes an interesting dive site.

🍴 Restaurants

Restaurant choices on South Caicos are limited: there are really only three that operate independently of the owners' homes. Ask around to find out when (or if) local favorites will be open. A couple of other dining spots are operated directly out of their owners' homes; advance notice must be given so that the proprietor can make preparations. Be sure to bring cash!

Asia's Takeout

$ | **CARIBBEAN** | Lillian Cleare cooks up some incredible local delicacies in the kitchen of her small coral-colored home. As with most places, there's no sign, so just ask around. **Known for:** local cuisine; great way to fill up for a low price; local plants infused in the food. ⑤ *Average main: $8* ⊠ *Stammer St., Cockburn Harbour* ☎ *649/247–3483* ▭ *No credit cards.*

★ Blu

$$$$ | **INTERNATIONAL** | Enjoy local or international cuisine inside the open but fully sheltered restaurant overlooking East Bay Resort's pool and beach. Dinner is served at tables covered with white tablecloths, and the menu is decidedly more upscale than you'd expect to find on this sleepy island. **Known for:** upscale dining with a casual atmosphere; fresh seafood; chef will prepare whatever you catch that day. ⑤ *Average main: $38* ⊠ *East Bay Resort, East Bay* ☎ *649/232–6444.*

The Cove Restaurant + Beach Bar

$$$ | **ECLECTIC** | Situated on the beach on the Caicos Banks side of the Sailrock Resort (it's man-made, but you'd never know it), this casual beach bar is the perfect spot to grab lunch while exploring the island. They rotate three different menus offering a variety of salads, burgers, wraps, and homemade pizzas. **Known for:** beachside dining; upscale twists on traditional favorites; special wellness menu complete with selection of detoxifying and rejuvenating juices. $ *Average main: $28* ⊠ *Sailrock Resort, East Bay* ☎ *649/946–3777* ⊕ *www.sailrockresort.com.*

Dolphin Grill at the Ocean and Beach Resort

$$ | **CARIBBEAN** | Located at South Caicos Ocean and Beach Resort, the grill is the only restaurant that operates oceanside. Here you can find a diverse menu that includes burgers, chicken, and freshly caught fish, as well as some exquisite lobster dishes (when in season). **Known for:** incredible sunset vistas; fresh seafood; down-home island cooking. $ *Average main: $20* ⊠ *Ocean & Beach Resort, Tucker Hill* ☎ *649/242–3134* ⊕ *oceanandbeachresort.com* ▭ *No credit cards.*

★ Great House Restaurant

$$$$ | **ECLECTIC** | With an infinity pool overlooking the Caicos Bank on one side and the Columbus Passage of the Atlantic Ocean on the other, the views up here can't be beat—and neither can the food. It's a culinary experience completely unexpected in such a remote setting. **Known for:** healthy cuisine, including gluten-free and vegetarian options; stunning views; eclectic menu. $ *Average main: $38* ⊠ *Sailrock Resort, East Bay* ☎ *649/946–3777* ⊕ *www. sailrockresort.com.*

★ Sunset Cafe Bar & Grill

$$ | **CARIBBEAN** | Most folks refer to this spot as "Darryl's" after the outgoing owner, who is also the head chef. This casual restaurant features a menu of the day that usually boasts conch and fish that's as fresh as it gets. **Known for:** down-home cooking; fresh seafood prepared a number of ways; a good spot to watch the slow-moving comings and goings of the island. $ *Average main: $12* ⊠ *Stubbs Rd., Tucker Hill* ☎ *649/242–7119* ▭ *No credit cards.*

🛏 Hotels

There are only three hotels to stay in on South Caicos, and each appeals to a completely different style and budget.

★ East Bay Resort

$$ | HOTEL | FAMILY | The newest resort offering on South Caicos occupies one of the island's most spectacular beaches, and with nothing else around, you'll likely have it all to yourself. **Pros:** amazing ocean views from every room; ultimate relaxation and fully appointed rooms; infinity pool with swim up bar. **Cons:** far from everything; requires an extra flight or boat ride from Provo; not much to do once the sun goes down. ⑤ *Rooms from: $290* ✉ *1 Fourth St., East Bay* ☎ *649/232-6444, 866/297-6248* ⊕ *www. eastbayresort.com* ⊙ *Closed Sept.* ⇄ *62 rooms* ⦿| *No meals.*

★ Sailrock

$$$$ | RESORT | FAMILY | This resort's goal is to provide "barefoot luxury" for those that appreciate peaceful solitude and the beauty of the outdoors; every detail has been carefully thought through. **Pros:** absolute privacy; luxury and service you'd never imagine in such a remote setting; nature abounds. **Cons:** may be too remote for some; not much to do; because it is spread over 700 acres, it lacks energy from other guests. ⑤ *Rooms from: $1000* ⊹ *northern extension of the island* ☎ *800/929–7197, 649/946–3777* ⊕ *www. southcaicos.com* ⇄ *30 rooms* ⦿| *No meals.*

South Caicos Ocean & Beach Resort

$ | HOTEL | Rustic and basic—though perfectly acceptable—this locally owned two-story hotel has small balconies or patios and views of the never-ending turquoise water off every room. **Pros:** each room has stunning views of Caicos Bank; it has the only real restaurant on the island; walking distance to pretty much anywhere you'd need to visit. **Cons:** you need cash for everything but your room; it's a 5-minute walk to the nearest beach; not as luxurious as the other two South Caicos hotels. ⑤ *Rooms from: $150* ✉ *Tucker Hill* ☎ *649/946–3219, 877/774–5486 for reservations only, 649/331–7526* ⇄ *60 rooms* ⦿| *No meals.*

🏃 Activities

DIVING

The reef walls that surround South Caicos are part of the third-largest reef system in the world. The reef starts at about 50 feet and then drops dramatically to around 6,000 feet. Most sights on the walls have no names, but you can dive anywhere along them. The visibility is ideal—consistently more than 100 feet and most times beyond that.

The **Caves** on Long Cay (which you can see out your window at the South Caicos Ocean & Beach Resort) are really five caves under the water that were made for exploring. The **Maze,** suitable only for expert divers, will keep you swimming at 105 feet through tunnels before you pop out at 75 feet. The **Arch,** so named because it resembles the kind of natural bridge found on Aruba (only under the water), offers the opportunity to see both eagle rays and sharks.

The **Blue Hole** is similar to the Blue Hole in Belize, but this one is under the ocean rather than on land. It's a natural sinkhole in the middle of the ocean between Middle Caicos and South Caicos on the Caicos Bank that drops to 250 feet. From the air it looks like a dark blue circle in the middle of a turquoise sea.

Sharks, barracuda, octopuses, green morays, eagle rays, and lobster are only some of the sea creatures that are common to these waters. During whale-watching season from mid-January to mid-April you can whale-watch, and you can observe them underwater if you are lucky enough to be in the right place at the right time.

The only dive company is located at East Bay Resort (☎ 649/232–6444).

Big Blue Unlimited

BICYCLING | This company offers everything you need to enjoy these pristine waters (weather permitting). You'll fly from Provo to South Caicos on interCaribbean airlines (flights included in the excursion price) and will be greeted by your Big Blue guide. You'll take a walking tour of Cockburn Town, head out on a local fishing boat, and have lunch at the Sunset Cafe. You can even take a bike or kayak for a bit of additional exploration. ✉ *Leeward* ☎ *649/946–5034* ⊕ *bigblueunlimited.com.*

FISHING

★ Beyond the Blue

FISHING | Beyond the Blue offers bonefishing charters on a specialized airboat, which can operate in less than a foot of water. The owner, Bibo, also offers paddleboard fishing, the perfect option for two people who want to spend the day together even though one of them doesn't fish. Lodging packages are available in conjunction with the Ocean & Beach Resort. ✉ *East Bay* ☎ *321/795–3136* ⊕ *www.beyondtheblue.com.*

T&V Tours

BOATING | Local captain Tim Hamilton offers bonefishing and bottom-fishing charters. His service is impeccable, and his knowledge of the waters surrounding South are unmatched. Tim and his wife, Vonne, are great contacts for local information and also provide boat excursions to nearby cays, island tours, and beach drop-offs for those looking for a day of seclusion, including on East Caicos. ✉ *Godet St., Cockburn Harbour* ☎ *649/345–6616, 649/331–0665.*

TOURS

★ Jeremiah Forbes

GUIDED TOURS | Jeremiah knows everything worth knowing about South Caicos. He works for the East Bay Resort, but is available for private tours when his schedule permits. He'll take you to nooks and crannies you'd otherwise never know existed, ensure you know all the history of the island, and even pull along the side of the road to pick some local bush medicine—and give you a lesson in how the islanders use what looks to most like nothing more than weeds—to help you stay healthy and heal any number of ailments. ⊠ *Cockburn Harbour* ☎ *649/347–6932.*

Shopping

Anthony's Gift Shop

CRAFTS | In the front of his tiny two-room house, you'll find local artist Anthony working on simple crafts fashioned out of whatever he finds. Much of what's for sale is on display on the wall in front, including painted conch shells and coconuts as well as bead necklaces. His most unique item is the big bamboo mug (and yes, it will hold your beer). If you see something you like and you're in town for a few days, he'll custom design whatever you want. He's usually somewhere nearby from 7:30 am until sundown. ⊠ *Stubbs St., Cockburn Harbour* ☎ *649/346–2986.*

Ayur Spa

SPA/BEAUTY | If the slow pace, refreshing breeze, and incredible ocean views aren't enough to relax you, Ayur Spa, located at the East Bay Resort, has just the thing. They offer a full menu of massages, body scrubs and wraps, ayurvedic treatments, and facials. You can even pick a remote beach setting and they'll come to you. ⊠ *East Bay Resort, East Bay* ☎ *649/244–0839* ⊕ *www.spatci.com* ⊘ *Closed Sept.*

Caicos Pride

FOOD/CANDY | If you're staying somewhere with a kitchen or a grill and looking for some fresh seafood to prepare, head to Caicos Pride. The local processing plant has top quality fish that's been properly cleaned and ready for cooking. ⊠ *#1 Baker's Way, Cockburn Harbour* ☎ *649/946–3570.*

Surely Goodness Variety Store

CRAFTS | It's easy to miss this little store, but look for a sign that says "souvenirs." Inside you'll find simple, locally made handicrafts, including burlap bags with raffia designs, painted rocks, shells and old discarded tiles, bead necklaces, and mirrors with shell frames. ⊠ *Pond St.*

GRAND TURK

Updated by
Jessica Robertson

Sights ★★★☆☆ **Restaurants** ★★★☆☆ **Hotels** ★★☆☆☆ **Shopping** ★★★☆☆ **Nightlife** ★★★☆☆

WELCOME TO GRAND TURK

TOP REASONS TO GO

★ **Old Caribbean Charm.** In Grand Turk you'll feel like you've stepped back in time. Bright red bougainvillea creates a stark contrast against old Bermudian walls and white picket fences. Everyone smiles and says hello; some will even stop to chat.

★ **History.** Travel to the more than 150-year-old lighthouse, visit Her Majesty's Prison where the last hanging took place in the 1940s, or check out the Turks and Caicos National Museum to learn about the island's involvement in the space race.

★ **Dive the Wall.** The wall off Grand Turk drops thousands of feet as little as 300 feet offshore and makes for a memorable dive.

★ **Gibbs Cay.** A 20-minute boat ride from Front Street takes you along the shore to the uninhabited Gibbs Cay. The stingrays sense the boat coming and then swim with you.

★ **The Cruise Port.** So you think you can't mix Old Caribbean charm with a 3,000-passenger cruise ship? The beauty of Grand Turk is that despite its small size, these two happily coexist.

1 Cockburn Town. The capital of the Turks and Caicos Islands is home to historic colonial buildings, Her Majesty's Prison, and the national museum.

2 North Ridge. At the top of the island, the Grand Turk Lighthouse stands tall amid cruise zip lines.

3 Pillory Beach. The prettiest beach on Grand Turk has great off-the-beach snorkeling. Bohio Dive Resort is one of the best places to stay on the island.

4 Grand Turk Cruise Terminal. Cruise passengers come in to the southern tip of the island, but a half-mile walk to White Sands Beach will lead you away from the crowds.

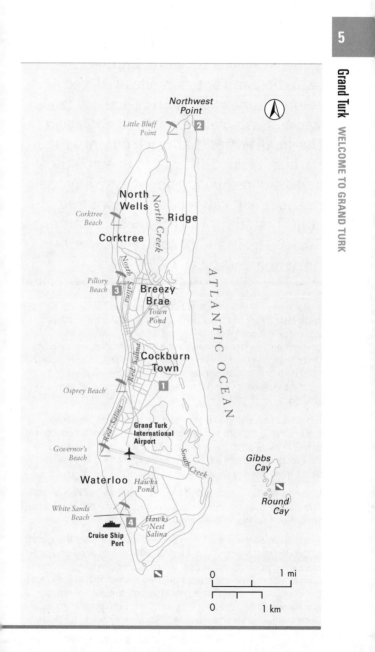

Northwest
Point

Little Bluff
Point

2

North
Wells

Corktree
Beach

Corktree

North Creek

Ridge

North Salina

Pillory
Beach

3

Breezy
Brae

Town
Pond

ATLANTIC OCEAN

Cockburn
Town

1

Red Salina

Osprey Beach

Grand Turk
International
Airport

Governor's
Beach

South Creek

Gibbs
Cay

Round
Cay

Waterloo

Hawks
Pond

White Sands
Beach

4

Hawks
Nest
Salina

Cruise Ship
Port

0   1 mi

0   1 km

Grand Turk is a unique treasure, different from all the other islands in the chain. White-walled courtyards, impressive churches, and bougainvillea-covered colonial inns date back to the early 1800s. Waves crash over the seawall and wash the small jetties that reach out into the harbor; it is not difficult to imagine the small sloops moving about, carrying their precious salt cargo out to the waiting ships bound for North America. Grand Turk is the island of contrasts, where present meets past.

Just 7 miles (11 km) long and a little more than 1 mile (2½ km) wide, Grand Turk has a resident population of approximately 2,500. It's the capital of the Turks and Caicos, with the seat of government, as well as the Crown's representative, residing here. Once a thriving U.S. Navy base, it is now a laid-back community filled with charm. Vacationers looking to simply relax will find much to like about Grand Turk, taking delight in the authentic ambience.

It has been a longtime favorite destination of divers eager to explore the 7,000-foot pristine coral wall that begins its descent only 300 yards offshore. Diving in Grand Turk means seeing Goliath groupers, spotted eagle rays, larger reef shark, and humpbacks from January through April.

On shore the tiny, quiet island has several white-sand beaches. There's also the country's national museum, a historic lighthouse, and several simple, unpretentious beachside bars.

Tourists can also see the Carnival cruise port at the southern end of the island. It brings more than 700,000 visitors per year. There are a variety of high-end shops and the Caribbean's largest Margaritaville-themed bar and restaurant. Despite the dramatic changes this could have made to this peaceful spot, the dock is pretty much self-contained, about 3 miles (5 km) from the tranquility of Cockburn Town. Surprisingly, the influx of tourists has generally had a positive effect on the island, bringing about prosperity and revitalization.

There is still some damage throughout the island caused by Hurricane Ike in 2008 and the double whammy of Irma and Maria in 2017, but the islanders are steadily working on restoring whatever can be saved and rebuilding whatever can't.

Planning

Getting Here and Around

AIR TRAVEL

Unless you're arriving aboard a cruise ship, the only way to get to Grand Turk from Provo is on InterCaribbean or Caicos Express Airways. InterCaribbean also connects South Caicos to Grand Turk, and Caicos Express connects Salt Cay to Grand Turk.

Caicos Express Airways

There are several flights a day between Provo and Grand Turk, which makes it possible to leave Provo in the morning, explore the island, and return by sunset. ⊠ *Southern Shores Plaza, Leeward Hwy.* ☎ *649/941–5730, 305/677–3116* ⊕ *caicosexpress.com.*

InterCaribbean Airways

There are several flights a day between Provo and Grand Turk, making it possible to leave Provo in the morning, explore the island, and return by sunset. InterCaribbean also connects South Caicos and Salt Cay to Grand Turk. ⊠ *Providenciales International Airport, Airport Rd.* ☎ *649/946–4999, 888/957–3223* ⊕ *intercaribbean.com.*

CAR TRAVEL

You can easily walk to several beaches, many of the excursion companies, and to the best restaurants if you're staying anywhere along the waterfront in Cockburn Town. If you wish to explore beyond the town, you'll need a car. There are a couple of local car-rental agencies that offer vehicles for between $60 and $110 for the day, insurance and gas included. There is also the option of hiring a cab for a more personalized tour. You can ask at the airport for assistance if you're visiting just for the day or ask your host if you are staying overnight.

GQ Car Rentals

GQ Car Rentals has a selection of economy, compact, and full-size cars as well as SUVs. Their rate for the day is $100 with a

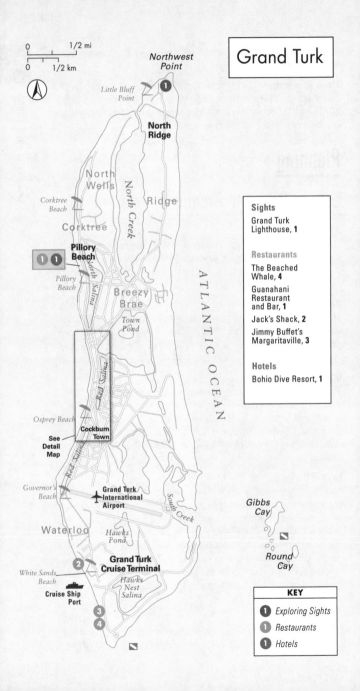

Grand Turk

Northwest Point

Little Bluff Point

North Ridge

North Wells

Corktree Beach

Corktree

Ridge

North Creek

Pillory Beach

Pillory Beach

Breezy Brae

North Salina

Town Pond

ATLANTIC OCEAN

Red Salina

Osprey Beach

Cockburn Town

See Detail Map

Governor's Beach

✈ **Grand Turk International Airport**

Waterloo

Hawks Pond

South Creek

Grand Turk Cruise Terminal

White Sands Beach

Cruise Ship Port

Hawks Nest Salina

Gibbs Cay

Round Cay

Sights

Grand Turk Lighthouse, **1**

Restaurants

The Beached Whale, **4**

Guanahani Restaurant and Bar, **1**

Jack's Shack, **2**

Jimmy Buffet's Margaritaville, **3**

Hotels

Bohio Dive Resort, **1**

KEY

1 *Exploring Sights*

1 *Restaurants*

1 *Hotels*

---

0 — 1/2 mi

0 — 1/2 km

$200 cash deposit. They do not take credit cards. ✉ *Back Salina* ☎ *649/241–7257.*

Island Autos
Neville offers a variety of cars (starting at $65/day), including left-hand and right-hand vehicles. He also has golf carts. You will find him at the Cruise Port Terminal, but he will also deliver to the airport. This company is set up to take credit cards. ✉ *Grand Turk Cruise Terminal* ☎ *649/232–0933.*

Smith's Golf Cart and Jeep Rentals
Some say that it's more fun to get around Grand Turk by golf cart, as the island is quite small and the roads are relatively quiet— much more so than on Provo! Nathan offers carts for two to four people. He also has SUVs to rent. The office is right outside the cruise-ship terminal's gates; on days that a ship is not in, call before reaching Grand Turk so he can meet you at the airport. The day's rental is $80 to $100. ✉ *Outside the gates, Grand Turk Cruise Terminal* ☎ *649/231–4856.*

★ Tony's Car Rental
You can rent a car or jeep from Tony starting at $80, or a scooter at $60, to explore on your own, or you can hire him to give you a guided 90-minute tour in an extended open tram bus. You'll need a group of at least 20 to take the tour, and it seats a maximum of 48. He'll meet you at the airport and get you on your way. He also rents snorkel gear at $30 per day and bicycles for $25. The company takes credit cards. ✉ *Airport* ☎ *649/231–1806* ⊕ *www. tonyscarrental.com.*

Sights

Circling the island is easy, because it's only 7 miles (11 km) long and only 1 mile (2½ km) wide. On a day trip you can have fun for a couple of hours and still have time to relax in the sun that same afternoon. Stroll down Front and Duke streets with their historic buildings; a walking tour leaflet outlines the history behind many of the buildings. You will be able to identify the deck from which the proclamation to abolish slavery was made in 1834, and learn the history behind the families that etched their mark on the island several hundred years ago. Be sure to make time for the national museum—it's an unexpected gem. You can also do some light shopping at the port, but if there's a cruise ship in, go to the lighthouse. If not, dive the crystal-clear waters or swim with the stingrays at Gibbs Cay, or just relax on any one of several beaches. At the end of the day, enjoy a refreshment or island fare at the Sand Bar. It's the epitome of island style.

Beaches

Visitors to Grand Turk will be spoiled when it comes to beach options: sunset strolls along miles of deserted sand, picnics in secluded coves, beachcombing for shells as well as interesting bits of flotsam and jetsam, snorkeling around shallow coral heads close to shore, and simply enjoying the beauty of the surrounding waters. Within Cockburn Town there are small cove beaches in front of Crabtree Apartments and the Osprey Beach Hotel that you will have pretty much to yourself. The best of the small beaches is next to the Sand Bar and in front of Oasis Dive Shop; it's also an excellent place for snorkeling right off the beach. There's a wonderful stretch of beach along the Atlantic side; find your way out there, and you will have miles of coastline to explore.

Hotels

Don't come to Grand Turk expecting five-star resorts with full service and amenities. But as tourism has grown to include a more discerning crowd, lodgings have also evolved. Accommodations include original Bermudian-style inns, more modern but small beachfront hotels, and basic to well-equipped self-catering suites and apartments. Most of the lodgings in Cockburn Town are in buildings that date back to the early 1800s and are filled with character, as well as indoor plumbing, air-conditioning, and other modern conveniences. There are also two small hotels that were built along the west shore post-1980 and some bed-and-breakfasts. Almost all hotels offer dive packages, which are an excellent value. In addition, there are a few private villa-style accommodations to choose from.

Hotel reviews have been shortened. For full information, visit Fodors.com.

Restaurants

The restaurants here are small and charming. They are set either in courtyards under huge trees amid flowering foliage or next to the beach with sweeping views. Most places are associated with hotels or other lodgings, and the ambience is laid-back and relaxing. As the sun sets, most restaurants turn into social venues, where people gather to simply enjoy a rum punch together. You can count on live music several nights a week, as musicians rotate among the more well-known establishments. You won't find quite the same kind of ambience anywhere on Provo anymore.

What It Costs in U.S. Dollars			
$	$$	$$$	$$$$
RESTAURANTS			
under $12	$12–$20	$21–$30	over $30
HOTELS			
under $275	$275–$375	$376–$475	over $475

Shopping

Shopping in Grand Turk is hard to come by—choices are slim. You can get the usual T-shirts and dive trinkets at all the dive shops, and there are two markets on island—one at the cruise terminal and one just north of the museum where you can pick up sea salt from Salt Cay, local hot sauces, and nice artisanal coconut soaps. When a ship is in port, the shops at the pier will be open, increasing your options dramatically. Several little local stores dot the island.

Spa services are definitely new to Grand Turk. You won't find the luxurious refuges found on Provo, but there are a couple of options if you are looking for one of the more common treatments after a day of diving or touring.

Nightlife

Grand Turk is a quiet place where you come to relax and unwind, so most of the nightlife consists of enjoying happy hour at sunset along your favorite stretch of beach or visiting with new friends you've made that day. However, a few spots have incorporated a bit of nightlife into their schedule to keep you busy after dark.

Cockburn Town

◉ Sights

The buildings in the colony's capital and seat of government reflect a 19th-century Bermudian style. Narrow streets, designed just wide enough for horse and cart, are lined with white stone walls and old street lamps. The once-vital salinas have been restored, and covered benches along the sluices offer shady spots for observing wading birds, including flamingos that frequent the

Kids cooling off on a dock in Cockburn Town, Grand Turk.

shallows. Be sure to pick up a copy of the tourist board's Heritage Walk guide to uncover the who and when behind Cockburn Town's Front Street.

Her Majesty's Prison

HISTORIC SITE | This prison was built out of stone in the 1830s to incarcerate men and women who had committed mostly petty crimes. As time passed, the prison expanded, housing even modern-day drug runners until it closed in the 1990s. Tours are currently not available, and there's not much to see from outside the tall limestone walls—but check it out if you happen to pass through the area. ⊠ *Pond St., Cockburn Town* ⊕ *visittci.com* ✉ *$7.*

Open Art Gallery

MUSEUM | The owner of this abandoned building has given his full blessing for local artists to transform the unfinished concrete structure into an open air art gallery with floor-to-ceiling murals depicting historic events and paying homage to important figures in Grand Turk's history. ⊠ *Duke St., Cockburn Town.*

★ Turks and Caicos National Museum

GARDEN | FAMILY | In one of the island's oldest stone buildings, the National Museum houses several interactive exhibits, as well as a super little gift shop with books and local handicrafts. The complete collection of preserved artifacts raised from the noteworthy Molasses Reef Wreck is here. Dating back to the early 1500s, it is the earliest European shipwreck yet excavated in the New World. There is also a natural-history exhibit including artifacts left by the Taíno (or Lucayans), the earliest migrants to settle in the

Turks and Caicos Islands. The museum also has a 3-D coral reef exhibit that complements its presentation on the history of diving. Another gallery is dedicated to Grand Turk's involvement in the Space Race. John Glenn made landfall here after being the first American to orbit Earth. Locals are quite put out that the movie *Hidden Figures* inaccurately portrayed that landing as having taken place in the Bahamas just north of Turks and Caicos. A fascinating display is a collection of "messages in a bottle" that have washed ashore from all over the world. This is the perfect spot to start your walking tour of the historical waterfront. ⊠ *Guinep House, Front St., Cockburn Town* ☎ *649/946–2160, 649/247–2160* ⊕ *www.tcmuseum.org* ✉ *$7* ⊘ *Check sign outside for monthly schedule; opening is based on when ships are in port.*

 Beaches

Governor's Beach

BEACH—SIGHT | Directly in front of the official British governor's residence, known as Waterloo, is a long stretch of beach framed by tall casuarina trees that provide plenty of natural shade. The beach can be a bit crowded on days when cruise ships are in port. There are a couple of picnic tables where you can enjoy a picnic lunch, and there is a decent snorkeling spot just offshore. **Amenities:** none. **Best for:** swimming; walking. ⊹ *20–30-min walk north of the Cruise Center.*

🍴 Restaurants

Conch in every shape and form, freshly grilled snapper and grouper, as well as lobster (in season) are the favorite dishes in the many little laid-back restaurants that dot the Cockburn Town waterfront. As tourism has grown on this sleepy island, a few more upscale restaurants have surfaced, offering a hint of faraway lands to the island fare. Away from these more touristy areas, smaller and less expensive eateries serve chicken and ribs, curried goat, peas and rice, and other native island specialties. In fact, there are spots that have no name, yet serve up some of the best jerk dishes you have ever had. If you have wheels, drive through Palm Grove on a Friday or Saturday night. You'll know when you've found the right spot, as cars will be parked and smoke will be rising from the half-drum barbecues.

Barbie's Restaurant

$ | **CARIBBEAN** | This takeout joint doesn't look like much, but it's a good place to get some local food, as evidenced by the locals who gather here. In addition to conch fritters (the best in town, they say), they also serve real island food like oxtail and griot with fried plantain on Friday and Saturday nights. **Known for:** real local food; popular takeout spot; the island's best conch fritters. ⑤ *Average main: $10* ⊠ *Front St., Cockburn Town* ☎ *649/946–2981* ⊟ *No credit cards.*

Birdcage Bar and Restaurant

$$$ | **CARIBBEAN** | This restaurant is a little more upscale than most of the other dining spots on the island, with a lovely view of the ocean and tablecloths in the evening. There's also a full bar for those looking for a specialty drink. **Known for:** fall-off-the-bone BBQ ribs; sunset views; best spot for live island music. ⑤ *Average main: $30* ⊠ *Osprey Beach Hotel, 1 Duke St., Cockburn Town* ☎ *649/946–1453* ⊕ *www.ospreybeachhotel.com/dining.*

Edith's Fish Fry

$ | **CARIBBEAN** | Look for the brightly colored umbrellas outside this spot just as Front Street merges into West Street for some simple island cooking. The daily menu is written on a small chalkboard behind the bar, but it's still a good idea to ask what's on offer. **Known for:** simple island fare; intoxicating rum punch; a chance to rub shoulders with the locals. ⑤ *Average main: $10* ⊠ *Front St. and West St., Cockburn Town* ⊟ *No credit cards.*

Friskyz Island Grub

$ | **CARIBBEAN** | The left side of this tiny shack is Friskyz, where you can grab a takeout lunch or a light bite of conch fritters or potato wedges. Everything is fried, but that's what makes it all taste so good. **Known for:** tender and tasty cracked conch; good spot for takeout lunch; live music. ⑤ *Average main: $8* ⊠ *Front St., Cockburn Town* ☎ *649/245–8635* ⊟ *No credit cards.*

The Inn Restaurant and Bar

$$$ | **INTERNATIONAL** | Located at the 150-year-old Grand Turk Inn, this restaurant is filled with old-world charm; the rich wood accents have been maintained, as well as much of the architectural detailing, some of it borrowed from decommissioned ships. Meals are served on a covered patio or overlooking the ocean on an elevated terrace, and service is friendly yet efficient—not quite as laid-back as might be experienced in other venues. **Known for:** ocean views; historic charm; simple but tasty food. ⑤ *Average main: $25* ⊠ *Front St., Cockburn Town* ☎ *649/946–2827* ⊘ *Closed Tues.*

Konky Joe's

$ | **CARIBBEAN** | Occupying the right-hand side of the shack that houses Friskyz, this is the spot for conch. In fact, it's basically all they serve—and it's the freshest in town. **Known for:** freshest

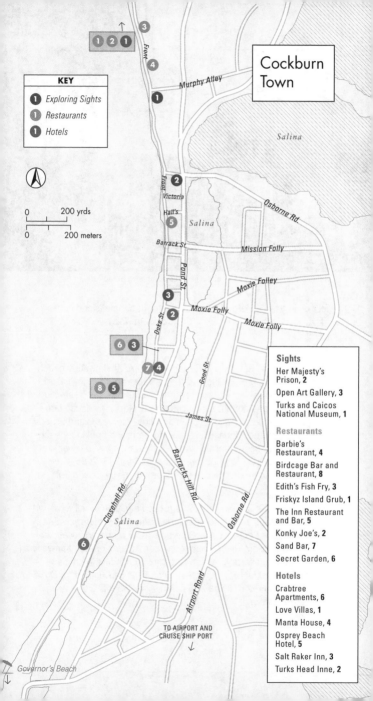

Cockburn Town

KEY

① *Exploring Sights*

① *Restaurants*

① *Hotels*

Salina

Front

Murphy Alley

0 — 200 yrds

0 — 200 meters

Front

Victoria

Hall's

Salina

Osborne Rd.

Barrack St.

Mission Folly

Pond St.

Moxie Folley

Moxie Folly

Moxie Folly

Duke St.

Good St.

James St.

Barracks Hill Rd.

Closehall Rd.

Salina

Osborne Rd.

Airport Road

TO AIRPORT AND CRUISE SHIP PORT

Governor's Beach

Sights

Her Majesty's Prison, **2**

Open Art Gallery, **3**

Turks and Caicos National Museum, **1**

Restaurants

Barbie's Restaurant, **4**

Birdcage Bar and Restaurant, **8**

Edith's Fish Fry, **3**

Friskyz Island Grub, **1**

The Inn Restaurant and Bar, **5**

Konky Joe's, **2**

Sand Bar, **7**

Secret Garden, **6**

Hotels

Crabtree Apartments, **6**

Love Villas, **1**

Manta House, **4**

Osprey Beach Hotel, **5**

Salt Raker Inn, **3**

Turks Head Inne, **2**

Front Street is home to some of the best restaurants on Grand Turk.

conch in town; seafood and only seafood; simple island cooking. *Average main: $10 Front St., Cockburn Town No credit cards.*

★ Sand Bar

$$ | CARIBBEAN | Run by two Canadian sisters, this popular beachside bar is very good value and the perfect spot to enjoy island time—no shoes or shirt required. The menu includes fresh-caught fish, lobster, and conch, as well as typical North American fare—burgers, quesadillas, and chicken and ribs—served island-style with peas and rice. **Known for:** downhome island cooking; beachside dining; sunsets that will take your breath away. *Average main: $20 Duke St., Cockburn Town 649/243–2666 www.grandturk-mantahouse.com No credit cards Closed Sat.*

Secret Garden

$$ | ECLECTIC | This open-air spot is tucked away amid tall tamarind and neem trees in a courtyard garden behind the historical Salt Raker Inn. The Secret Garden serves simply prepared, local dishes such as grilled grouper and snapper, conch, and lobster. **Known for:** homemade desserts; great spot to mix with locals; best place on island for breakfast. *Average main: $18 Salt Raker Inn, Duke St., Cockburn Town 649/946–2260, 649/243–5522 www.saltrakerinn.com.*

🛏 Hotels

Crabtree Apartments

$ | RENTAL | On their own secluded stretch of beach, these three two-bedroom apartments make a quiet getaway that is far enough from the cruise-ship port to give you some peace and quiet but still within walking distance of Duke and Front streets. **Pros:** private beachfront; self-catering; the art on the walls adds a tropical touch. **Cons:** hard to find; a longer walk to restaurants than from hotels in town; five-night minimum makes it hard to use as a base for a quick trip from Provo. $ *Rooms from: $220* ✉ *Close Hall Rd., Cockburn Town* ☎ *978/270–1698* ⊕ *www.grandturkvacationrental. com* 🛏 *3 2-bedroom apartments* ⏀ *No meals* ⚶ *5-night min.*

★ Love Villas

$$ | RENTAL | These three spacious condo-style villas offer upscale amenities that are unmatched on the island. **Pros:** new build; right on the beach; comes with its own electric car. **Cons:** no restaurant on property and no particularly good one nearby; ground floor patio is communal for all three units; only three units means you'll have to book early to guarantee a room. $ *Rooms from: $375* ✉ *West Rd., Cockburn Town* ☎ *649/366-3150* ⊕ *www.lovegrandturk.com* 🛏 *3 units* ⏀ *No meals.*

★ Manta House

$ | HOTEL | Owned by the Canadian sisters who run the Sand Bar across the street, this funky, laid-back island hotel has three units immediately opposite the beach. **Pros:** across the street from the perfect beach to sit and relax; close to all the island's hot spots; you can run a tab at the Sand Bar across the street. **Cons:** no amenities; Sand Bar crowd can get loud; with only three rooms, it can book up fast. $ *Rooms from: $175* ✉ *Duke St., Cockburn Town* ☎ *649/243–2666* ⊕ *www.grandturk-mantahouse.com* 🛏 *3 rooms* ⏀ *No meals.*

Turks Head Inne

$$ | B&B/INN | Staying at this true bed-and-breakfast, one of just a few in all the Turks and Caicos, gives you a feel for the way the Caribbean used to be, without requiring you to give up comfort. **Pros:** charming 150-year-old Caribbean clapboard house; faces the beach; all guests lent a local cell phone. **Cons:** across the street from the beach; not much to do; no extra amenities or activities included. $ *Rooms from: $250* ✉ *Front St., Cockburn Town* ☎ *649/946–2827* 🛏 *5 rooms* ⏀ *No meals.*

Osprey Beach Hotel

$ | HOTEL | You cannot get any closer to the water's edge than this two-story oceanfront hotel and the adjacent guesthouse-style Atrium overlooking a tropical courtyard. **Pros:** within walking distance of several waterfront restaurants, all dive operators, and excursions; affordable and charming, if basic, accommodation; you'll likely have the beach all to yourself. **Cons:** rocky beachfront; very thin walls so privacy can be an issue; courtyard suites lack atmosphere. ⑤ *Rooms from: $165* ✉ *1 Duke St., Cockburn Town* ☎ *649/946–2666* ⊕ *www.ospreybeachhotel.com* ⇄ *33 rooms* ⑩ *No meals.*

Salt Raker Inn

$ | B&B/INN | An unpretentious inn filled with island character and charm, this 19th-century house was built by shipwright Jonathan Glass in the 1850s, complete with its quirky nautical features. **Pros:** ambience and character; an easy walk to everything on the historical waterfront; perfect spot to completely unwind. **Cons:** spotty Wi-Fi; dated furnishings and fittings; no views from ground-floor rooms. ⑤ *Rooms from: $145* ✉ *Duke St., Cockburn Town* ☎ *649/946–2260* ⊕ *www.saltrakerinn.com* ⇄ *13 rooms* ⑩ *No meals.*

Shopping

Island Creations

ART GALLERIES | If you're looking for locally made art and handicrafts, pop into this tiny shop on the side of Blue Water Divers. It's also a good spot for decent espresso. ✉ *next to Blue Water Divers in The Annex, Duke St., Cockburn Town.*

OceanScapes Spa

SPA/BEAUTY | A real spa has finally come to Grand Turk. The OceanScapes Spa is in the Annex of the Osprey Beach Hotel. Services include chair and table massages at $20 for every 15 minutes of service, body scrubs, facials, waxing, and ear candling, as well as pedicures and hair braiding. Services are limited at this location, and groups are encouraged to book online in advance so that no one leaves disappointed. ✉ *Osprey Beach Hotel, The Annex, Duke St., Cockburn Town* ☎ *649/232–6201* ⊕ *oceanscapesspa.com.*

Ripsaw

"Ripsaw" is the official music of Turks and Caicos, known throughout the Bahamas as "rake n' scrape." It's reputed to have started on tiny Cat Island in the Bahamas. TCI's music is made using a guitar, skinned drums (in the Bahamas, the drums are more often made from steel shipping containers), and other "instruments" that are tools you'd find in anyone's home. A carpenter's saw played with a screwdriver is always part of the band, and you might see the occasional washboard played. Its inspiration is the music of Africa, and it's particularly popular on more isolated islands. You can still find ripsaw bands around the islands, but they are more prevalent on Grand Turk and South Caicos.

Nightlife

Osprey Beach Hotel

CAFES—NIGHTLIFE | Every Wednesday and Sunday there's lively local music to add to the ambience of the special barbecue nights. ⊠ *Osprey Beach Hotel, 1 Duke St., Cockburn Town* ☎ *649/946–2666* ⊕ *ospreybeachhotel.com*.

Salt Raker Inn

CAFES—NIGHTLIFE | On Friday local musicians play at the Salt Raker Inn. Many of the local residents gather here for this, so don't miss it if you wish to mingle. ⊠ *Duke St., Cockburn Town* ☎ *649/946–2260* ⊕ *www.hotelsaltraker.com*.

North Ridge

Sights

Grand Turk Lighthouse

HISTORIC SITE | More than 150 years ago, the main structure of the lighthouse was prefabricated in the United Kingdom and then transported to the island; once erected, it helped prevent ships from wrecking on the northern reefs for more than 100 years. It was originally designed to burn whale oil as its light source. You can use this landmark as a starting point for a breezy cliff-top walk by following the donkey trails to the deserted eastern beach. The cruise-ship world has made its mark here, so you'll find the location's solitude can be interrupted and the view has been marred by a zip line. If you are stretched for time, you might want to take a pass. ⌧ *Lighthouse Rd., North Ridge* ⊕ *visittci.com* ✉ *$3.*

Beaches

Long Beach
BEACH—SIGHT | Otherwise known as East Side, Long Beach is more difficult to get to, but it is the perfect spot for individuals wishing to explore. Without the reef as protection, much washes ashore; search for seashells on the seashore or examine decades of flotsam and jetsam that litters the beach, including old bottles and weathered ships' planking. You will be sure to find total solitude on this side of the island. **Amenities:** none. **Best for:** solitude; walking. ⌧ *North Ridge.*

Pillory Beach

Beaches

★ Pillory Beach
BEACH—SIGHT | It's said that Columbus made his New World landfall here, just north of Cockburn Town on the protected west shore. And why not? This is the prettiest beach on Grand Turk; it also has great off-the-beach snorkeling. As you enjoy the powdery white sand, you may be visited by one of the many donkeys that pass by. The Bohio Dive Resort is on Pillory Beach, so you can enjoy a wonderful lunch or a cold drink while there. **Amenities:** food and drink; parking (free); toilets. **Best for:** snorkeling; swimming; walking. ⌧ *Pillory Beach.*

Restaurants

★ Guanahani Restaurant and Bar
$$$ | INTERNATIONAL | Off the town's main drag, this restaurant sits on a stunning but quiet stretch of beach just north of Cockburn Town. The food goes beyond the usual Grand Turk fare and is some of the island's best. **Known for:** English high tea, island-style; Saturday night rake 'n' scrape music and barbecue; Sunday brunch by the beach. ⑨ *Average main: $35* ⌧ *Bohio Dive Resort, Pillory Beach* ☎ *649/231–3572* ⊕ *www.bohioresort.com.*

Of Hurricanes and Wild Weather ◉

The Turks and Caicos has experienced a run of bad luck when it comes to hurricanes and tropical storms, but for the most part, the islands continue to clean up and bounce back, particularly in the more popular tourist spots. In September 2008 the islands received a double whammy: the eye of Category 1 Hanna passed directly over Provo three times and then stayed put for four days, dumping rain nonstop. A week later, Category 4 Hurricane Ike passed through. Most buildings in Provo experienced some minor damage, and the island bounced back quickly. Grand Turk, Salt Cay and South Caicos, however, suffered extensive damage from Hanna and Ike—the damage was so vast it took months to restore power. While the cruise lines that visit Grand Turk sent in the cavalry to get that island ready to receive visitors as quickly as possible, Salt Cay and South Caicos received little assistance. In 2011 Hurricane Irene hit Turks and Caicos as a Category 2, but this time everyone was prepared, and the storm caused no major damage.

And then came 2017, another double whammy. This time, the Turks and Caicos chain was hit hard by Category 5 Irma and Category 1 Maria in the same week. The powerful sucker punch caused widespread structural damage throughout the country, but again, the government and private sector poured money and manpower into getting the key areas up and running; and not long after, in Provo, there were no visible signs that the storms had come through. Many historic buildings suffered damage in Grand Turk, and two years later island residents still await the promised renovations to the island outside of the cruise port. In South Caicos and Salt Cay, you have to ask one of the residents if a particular bit of damage was caused by Irma or simply hadn't been repaired following the 2008 season.

The peak of hurricane season for this region coincides with Turks and Caicos' off-season, which is observed more in the Caicos Cays than in Provo and Grand Turk (where business is dictated by the cruise industry). If you are traveling to the islands during hurricane season, it's always wise to get travel insurance: you are not really in danger visiting TCI, but if the flights are canceled or your hotel closes, you're covered. If a hurricane occurs while you're there, airlines add additional flights so that all wishing to leave can catch a flight out. If you want to ride it out, the resorts will allow guests to stay and are built to withstand the worst these storms deliver. Storms travel quickly, often with beautiful blue days right behind.

Hotels

★ Bohio Dive Resort

$ | **RESORT** | **FAMILY** | Divers are drawn to this basic yet comfortable hotel, whose on-site dive shop means there's no wait for some of the world's best diving. **Pros:** Guanahani is a great restaurant; on a gorgeous beach; steps away from awesome snorkeling year round and whale-watching in the winter. **Cons:** seven-night minimum during holiday season; beach can get crowded when cruise ships are in port; you'll need a bike or car to get around. $ *Rooms from: $240* ✉ *Pillory Beach* ☎ *649/231-3572, 800/494-4310 Toll-free from U.S.* ⊕ *www.bohioresort.com* ⇱ *16 rooms* ○ *No meals.*

 Nightlife

Bohio Dive Resort

CAFES—NIGHTLIFE | On Saturday, local musicians play a bit of rake 'n' scrape at the Bohio so that guests and residents alike can do a bit of dancing oceanside while enjoying their buffet barbecue. It's a little more expensive than the other music combinations, but the food is great and the venue lovely. On Friday nights there's jazz, and Sundays there's a saxophonist. Some might say the music is at Ike and Donkey Beach Bar—that's just the name of the beachside bar at Bohio. ✉ *Bohio Dive Resort, Pillory Beach* ☎ *649/946-2135* ⊕ *www.bohioresort.com.*

Grand Turk Cruise Terminal

🍴 Restaurants

The Beached Whale

$ | **CARIBBEAN** | Head through the outdoor John Glenn landing museum to this laid-back spot for lunch, cocktails, and beach views. They offer the traditional island cuisine, including jerk chicken and pork, as well as burgers and wings. **Known for:** laid-back island vibe; simple island cuisine; a break from the nonstop party on the other side of the cruise port. $ *Average main: $12* ✉ *Grand Turk Cruise Terminal* ☎ *649/946-1514* ⊘ *Closed when no ships are in port.*

★ Jack's Shack

$ | **AMERICAN** | Walk 1,600 feet down the beach from the cruise terminal and you'll find this local beach bar. It gets busy with volleyball players, and offers chair rentals and tropical drinks. **Known for:** jerk chicken; lively bar filled with locals; drinks that don't hold

Grand Turk in a Day 👁

It's easy to take a day trip from Provo to Grand Turk to see this sleepy, colorful island that's completely different from Provo. Make arrangements before going over so that you can have a golf cart, bike, or car waiting at the airport.

From the airport take a right and drive to Front Street. Walk the colorful quiet street with historical houses. Do not miss the small Turks and Caicos National Museum—even if you are not a museum person—as this one is quite fascinating. Stop at Bohio Dive Resort, north past Front Street (take your transportation), to snorkel and to enjoy Pillory Beach. This is also a good place for lunch.

If a cruise ship is in port, you can drive past the airport to the cruise center to check out the shopping and people-watch. The stores at the cruise terminal are the only real shops on island, and there's also a casino nearby. It's a complete contrast to Front Street. You can also tour Her Majesty's Prison.

Set up an excursion to Gibbs Cay and swim with the sting-rays. January through April also brings whales as they migrate past; whale-watching tours are possible to fit in to a single-day visit. Be careful, though, as you'll need to be back at the airport 30 minutes before the flight back to Provo.

back on the alcohol. 🛒 *Average main: $12* ✉ *North of the pier, Grand Turk Cruise Terminal* ☎ *649/232–0099* ⊕ *www.jacksshack.tc* 🕓 *Closed when there's no ship in port.*

Jimmy Buffett's Margaritaville
$$ | AMERICAN | When you're at this branch of the party-loving restaurant chain, you can engage in cruise activities even though you're on land. One of the largest Margaritavilles in the world opens its doors when a cruise ship is parked at the dock. **Known for:** liveliest spot in the entire island chain; margaritas in just about every flavor imaginable; the cheeseburger...in paradise. 🛒 *Average main: $20* ✉ *Grand Turk Cruise Terminal* ☎ *649/946–1880* ⊕ *www. margaritavillecaribbean.com* 🕓 *Closed when no cruise ships are at the pier.*

Grand Turk often welcomes cruise passengers with its soft white sand.

🛍 Shopping

Caribbean Outpost

CLOTHING | Associated with the locally owned Goldsmith shops on Providenciales, this has Grand Turk's largest selection of jewelry, including both fine jewelry and costume pieces. You will also find a variety of clothing, cigars, and more. ✉ *Grand Turk Cruise Terminal* ☎ *649/941–5599.*

★ Dizzy Donkeys

CLOTHING | This pair of shops, right across from each other, is a great spot to pick up high-quality beachwear and beach accessories. They also have locally made jewelry made from sea glass, shells, and other "found" objects from the beach. This is where you go if you are looking for a less expensive something that's a little different, and it's all locally owned and operated. ✉ *Grand Turk Cruise Terminal* ☎ *649/231–3231.*

Piranha Joe's

GIFTS/SOUVENIRS | The T-shirts and jackets here all have "Grand Turk" printed on them. ✉ *Grand Turk Cruise Terminal.*

Ron Jon Surf Shop

GIFTS/SOUVENIRS | The shop sells bathing suits, T-shirts, bumper stickers, and beer mugs with its famous logo on them. ✉ *Grand Turk Cruise Terminal* ⊕ *www.ronjons.com.*

Activities

Adventure Tours

★ Chukka Caribbean Adventures

TOUR—SPORTS | This Jamaican-based adventure-tour operator runs most of the cruise excursions on Grand Turk, but you don't have to be on a cruise ship to take part; if you're staying at a hotel on Grand Turk or are just there for the day, you can still sign up for the activities. Most are offered only if there is a cruise ship moored at the Cruise Centre, but if there's a few of you, they'll likely offer a tour just for you. They offer a horseback ride and swim, snorkeling tours, and a dune-buggy or ATV safari. There's also a zip-line adventure at the lighthouse, as well as a glass-bottom boat excursion and a catamaran party boat. Whether you want to explore Grand Turk by land or by sea, they've got you covered. ⊠ *Grand Turk Cruise Terminal* ☎ *649/332–1339* ⊕ *www.ChukkaCaribbean. com.*

Biking

If you love bicycle riding, then you'll love Grand Turk; it's both small enough and flat enough that it's possible to tour it all by bike. In fact, bicycling is the preferred mode of transportation for some locals. Most roads have hard surfaces, and the slower pace ensures that you don't miss a beat. Be sure to take water with you if you head inland, to the lighthouse, or enjoy an east-side beach; there are few places to stop for refreshments along the way. Most hotels have bicycles available, but you can also rent them from Tony's Rentals *(see rental cars, earlier in the chapter)* or Grand Turk Diving *(see Diving and Snorkeling, below)*. It's not quite a bicycling experience, but Oasis Divers *(see Diving and Snorkeling, below)* offers Segway Tours as something completely different. You are guided throughout Cockburn Town after a brief introduction to Segway driving, complete with a helmet that includes a built-in microphone and headset.

Diving and Snorkeling

Diving Grand Turk is a unique experience. With the wall so close to shore, small skiffs able to hold small dive groups leave the beachfront and within minutes arrive at one of many pristine dive sites. You're sure to see the larger pelagics in the deep blue, along with everything you can expect to see diving Provo. The larger reef sharks, spotted eagle rays, giant manta rays, moray eels, and even enormous jewfish are not uncommon. Although the vertical drops take divers through tunnels and undersea cathedrals, the shallower sands can surprise you with dancing octopuses and "football fields" of garden eels to play with. Even thousands of Atlantic humpback whales swim through en route to their winter breeding grounds (January through April).

Dive outfitters can all be found in the heart of Cockburn Town with the exception of Bohio, on the very far northern end of town. Note that anyone wishing to dive must present a valid certificate card before going out the first time. Two-tank dives generally cost between $90 and $130; gear rentals are extra. Night diving is usually a one-tank dive and costs around $50; there's a minimum number of divers required, so check around to see which company has scheduled dives.

Snorkeling is also an option for those who enjoy the underwater world but don't dive. There are numerous sites around the island that you can safely reach without a boat. Another alternative is to join a guided snorkel trip; Bohio and Blue Water Divers both offer them. Oasis Divers offers an Ultimate Snorkeling Adventure, where they set you up with mask, fins, and snorkel and guide you through your first fish identification ecotour for $45 per person, lasting approximately 1½ hours. If you wish, they also offer a Snuba experience. Snuba is an underwater breathing system that allows users to breathe from long hoses that attach to tanks floating on a pontoon at the surface instead of the traditional tank strapped on the back. Although no experience is required, it often leads to participants' eventually becoming scuba-certified.

Gibbs Cay, just a couple of miles off Grand Turk, makes a great day trip to a small, uninhabited island. Here you can hike around the island, go for a nice beach stroll or beachcomb, and then join in the day's snorkel adventure, culminating in a swim with stingrays. Blue Water Divers, Oasis Divers, and Bohio Dive Resort offer trips here. Oasis Divers also offers a clear-bottom kayak ecosafari where participants learn a little about what's both above and below the surface and how it all works together.

★ Blue Water Divers
SCUBA DIVING | In operation on Grand Turk since 1983, Blue Water Divers is the only PADI Green Star Award recipient-star dive center on the island, priding themselves on their personalized service and small group diving. There won't be more than eight of you headed out for a dive. In addition, Blue Water Divers offers Gibbs Cay snorkel and Salt Cay trips. ⊠ *Osprey Beach Hotel, The*

Atrium, 1 Duke St., Cockburn Town ☎ *649/946–2432* ⊕ *www. grandturkscuba.com.*

Grand Turk Diving

BICYCLING | This company offers full-service dives, as well as trips to nearby Gibbs Cay and Salt Cay. They also offer whale-watching tours January through March when humpback whales migrate from Iceland to the Silver Banks and Turks Bank. In addition, they offer bicycles for hire at $20 for a 24-hour period as well as sunset cruises and the popular champagne tour. ☒ *Duke St., Cockburn Town* ✛ *Across from the Osprey Beach Hotel* ☎ *649/946–1559* ⊕ *www.gtdiving.com.*

Oasis Divers

FISHING | Oasis Divers provides excellent personalized service, with full gear handling and dive site briefing included. In addition, Oasis Divers offers a variety of other tours, including their land-based one on Segways, glass-bottom kayak tours, and whale-watching when the animals migrate past. It's a good spot to rent a kayak or paddleboard for some solo exploration, and if it's fishing you want to do, they offer deep-sea and reef fishing starting at $550 for a half-day charter. ☒ *Duke St., Cockburn Town* ☎ *649/946–1128* ⊕ *www.oasisdivers.com.*

Tours

Deep Blue Charters

BOAT TOURS | If you're eager to do some fishing, Deep Blue is a great choice. They offer private charters, sport fishing and bottom fishing, as well as a Gibb's Cay stingray encounter, snorkeling, and a day trip to Salt Cay. In the winter they can also take you on a humpback whale–watching expedition. ☒ *Grand Turk Cruise Terminal* ☎ *649/243–6096, 649/244–5569* ⊕ *www.deepbluegrandturk.com.*

★ Island Trams

GUIDED TOURS | Hop on this open double tram for a tour of the island's hottest spots. A local will guide the tour with stops at the natural sights, time for some shopping on Front Street, and a chance to taste some local food and drinks. They offer bird-watching tours that will help you see flamingos, ducks, hummingbirds, and the national bird of the Turks and Caicos, the brown pelican. If you're looking for more of a party scene while you explore the island, sign on for the adults-only Rake 'n' Scrape Carnival tour that comes with unlimited rum punch. ☒ *Grand Turk Cruise Terminal* ☎ *649/432–8726* ⊕ *www.islandtrams.com.*

Whale Watching

★ The Humpback Dive Shack

SPECIAL-INTEREST | One of the most unique experiences to be had in the Turks and Caicos is heading out on a small boat to look for migrating humpback whales. Brian and Sabine have mastered the art of identifying a spout of water and approaching a whale with caution in order not to scare it off. If all the conditions are right, you can even hop in the water and swim with them. Whale-watching takes place in the winter months—January to April—and they offer three-hour morning or afternoon excursions. Times can be adjusted to accommodate cruise visitors who want to book a tour. They will pick you up from the beach right where the ships dock. ✉ *Close Haul Rd., Cockburn Town* ☎ *649/347–4921, 649/348–8339* ⊕ *www.humpbackdiveshack.com.*

Chapter 6

SALT CAY

Updated by
Jessica Robertson

⊙ Sights   🍴 Restaurants   🛏 Hotels   🛍 Shopping   🍸 Nightlife

★★★☆☆   ★☆☆☆☆   ★☆☆☆☆   ★☆☆☆☆   ★☆☆☆☆

WELCOME TO SALT CAY

TOP REASONS TO GO

★ **Beaches.** Bar none, North Beach is the best on Salt Cay. Although getting there is not easy, the beach is pure bliss, with bright white sand, absolutely no rocks or seaweed, the perfect hues of greens and blues, and unobstructed views of Grand Turk.

★ **Mollusks and pirates.** Collect bivalves residing in the shallow tidal pools; it's an experience you won't soon forget. When you're finished, head down Victoria Street in search of pirates' graves.

★ **Hanging with the locals.** Since the island has a resident population hovering around 100, chances are pretty good you'll meet most of them during your visit. Soon you'll be hanging out at the Coral Reef Bar & Grill as if you've lived here for years.

★ **Whale-watching.** Take an excursion for your chance to actually swim with whales in season from mid-January to mid-April. Humpbacks migrate past on their way to the Silver Banks and the Mouchoir Banks to mate and calf in warmer waters. Explore Sand Cay, which has the most neon turquoise you'll see.

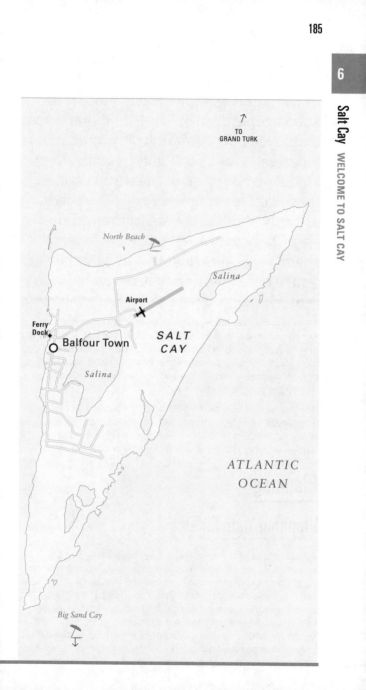

In the 19th century the *salinas* (natural salt ponds) of Salt Cay produced much of the world's supply of salt. More than 1,000 people lived on the island then, most employed in the salt industry, at a time when salt was as valuable as gold. When the salt trade dried up, nearly everyone moved on to other islands. Today there are only about 100 inhabitants on Salt Cay. Chances are you will meet most of them by the end of your stay, whether you're here for one day or several.

As you approach Salt Cay, either by boat or by plane, you may wonder what you've gotten yourself into. The land appears dry and brown, very flat, and too small to occupy you for even a day. Don't worry. Salt Cay has a way of getting into your blood, leaving an everlasting impression. By the end of your first day, you may very well be planning your return trip.

Salt Cay was hit hard by the 2017 hurricane season, and as a result you'll find fewer hotels and shops here than before. However, the island is on the mend, offering opporunities for whale-watching, great restaurants, and plenty of character.

Planning

Planning Your Time

As an island of only 2½ square miles (6 square km), Salt Cay is so small that you can walk around it and soak up its charms in a couple of hours. But we don't recommend that. You'll enjoy yourself more if you take your time, ideally spending at least one night on the island. For some, there can be nothing less than a week to truly unwind and get into the rhythm of island life. You might search for pirate treasure, visit some of the off-the-beaten-path spots on the beautiful north shore, or watch for whales passing by (mid-January through mid-April). If you dive, you must make an appointment with Salt Cay Divers so that you can explore nearby wrecks and the magnificence of "the wall"—the shallow waters surrounding the islands that quickly drop 7,000 feet. Crystal Seas Adventures offers a number of excursions to help you get to know the island, its history, and the waters that surround Salt Cay. You'll be sure to drive past the stately White House dating back to 1835 and the abandoned Governor's Mansion. There are the inland salt ponds, or salinas, with their artifacts left behind to illuminate the history of this tiny island. And you'll notice that many homes have embedded conch shells in their walls, there to keep the donkeys and cows out—you'll find yourself stopping frequently for these seemingly sleepy fellows who rule the roads. If Salt Cay lacks natural beauty, it definitely does not lack character (or is it that it has characters?). By the end of your stay, you will have made some lifelong friends.

Getting Here and Around

Getting to Salt Cay can sometimes feel like an adventure in itself. Although Grand Turk is only a hop, skip, and jump away, it's actually easier to get to Salt Cay from Provo. There's a regularly scheduled flight on Caicos Express (see Travel Smart) and a twice-a-week ferry from Grand Turk (weather permitting). But if you're on Grand Turk and want to travel over, ask at the dive shops to see if someone can take you over in a private boat if the ferry is not running as scheduled. To get to Grand Turk from Salt Cay, ask Salt Cay Divers or contact Crystal Seas Adventures. The 30- to 40-minute boat trip typically costs $300 for a private charter round-trip, but the weather can sometimes put a damper on your travel plans.

Once you reach Salt Cay, you can rent a golf cart ($75/day) or a bicycle through Candy at Pirates Hideaway. A rented cart is a fun way to get out and explore on your own. There's only one named street here, so there's no chance of getting lost—and anyone you meet will be happy to give you directions. Driving through the salt flats to North Beach is an adventure in itself, and stopping for donkeys to cross the road adds to the charm.

CONTACTS Caicos Express Airways. ✉ *Southern Shores, Leeward Hwy., Downtown* ✛ *Across from Grace Bay Auto, just past the Do It Centre as you travel to the airport* ☎ *649/941–5730 main office, 305/677–3116 U.S. number, 649/946–8131 International Airport, 649/946–2178 Grand Turk Airport* ⊕ *www.caicosexpress. com.* **interCaribbean.** ☎ *649/946–4999* ⊕ *www.intercaribbean. com.* **Salt Cay Community Ferry.** ✛ *Departs from Deane's Dock* ☎ *649/241–1009.*

Essentials

HOTELS

The accommodations in Salt Cay are basic, with just enough amenities to keep you comfortable. You'll find private homes, apartments, and a couple of small guesthouse-style accommodations. Most visitors who come to Salt Cay don't mind a little simplicity, as they come here to enjoy the Caribbean of yesteryear as well as the peace and tranquility of their natural surroundings. You won't be roughing it, though. Although most places count on sea breezes for cooling, you'll still find the occasional air conditioner, as well as satellite TV and Wi-Fi. What you do get in every one of our recommended lodgings are pleasant hosts who welcome you like family.

Hotel reviews have been shortened. For full information, visit Fodors.com.

RESTAURANTS

There are only a handful of restaurants on Salt Cay, but the food is generally excellent. Pat's Place is a home-based restaurant, where the menu changes according to what the boats bring in that day. At night Coral Reef Bar & Grill turns into a lively nightspot (by sleepy island standards), and you're likely to see virtually everyone you meet during the day. Reservations for dinner are essential everywhere; the cooks have to plan ahead, so if you just show up, you may not be fed.

What It Costs in U.S. Dollars			
$	$$	$$$	$$$$
RESTAURANTS			
under $12	$12–$20	$21–$30	over $30
HOTELS			
under $275	$275–$375	$376–$475	over $475

◉ Sights

Windmills and salinas are silent reminders of the days when the island was a leading producer of salt. Today the salt ponds attract abundant birdlife. Tour the island by motorized golf cart, by bicycle, or on foot. Many guests choose to visit from mid-January through mid-April, when whales come to mate and give birth to their young in warmer waters.

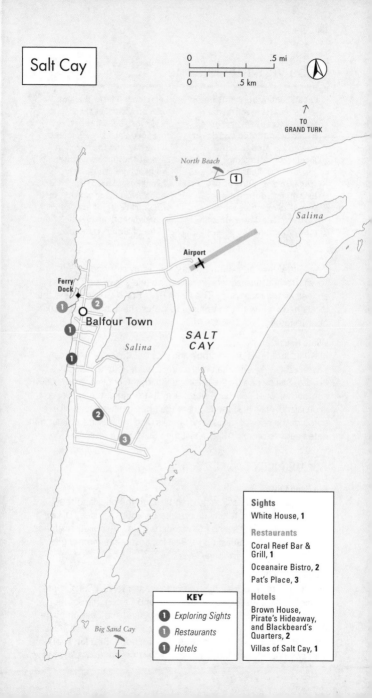

Salt Cay

0   .5 mi

0   .5 km

TO
GRAND TURK

North Beach

Salina

Airport

Ferry
Dock

Balfour Town

SALT
CAY

Salina

Big Sand Cay

Sights

White House, **1**

Restaurants

Coral Reef Bar &
Grill, **1**

Oceanaire Bistro, **2**

Pat's Place, **3**

Hotels

Brown House,
Pirate's Hideaway,
and Blackbeard's
Quarters, **2**

Villas of Salt Cay, **1**

KEY

1   *Exploring Sights*

1   *Restaurants*

1   *Hotels*

The Versatile Islander

On an island this small almost every local is a jack-of-all-trades. Because everything has to be imported and flown in, you will find that the locals have all become very resourceful. Chances are the singer in the band you are listening to during dinner was also your dive master earlier in the day. Your tour guide might be the hotel's electrician. The cabbie you meet on arrival at the airport might also be your boat captain on an excursion later in the day, and the check-in clerk at the airport counter might sell you the jewelry she makes at one of the little shops. After a day or two, you will start recognizing people everywhere from all the different things they do.

What little development there is on Salt Cay is found in Balfour Town. It's home to several small hotels and a few wee shops, as well as the main dock. The Coral Reef Bar & Grill is where the locals hang out with the tourists to watch the sunset and drink a beer together.

White House

HISTORIC SITE | This grand stone and plaster house, which once belonged to a wealthy salt merchant, is testimony to Salt Cay's heyday. Still owned by the descendants of the original family, it's sometimes open for tours when Tim Dunn, one of the successors, is on island. He's pleased to share the house, where you will see some of the original furnishings, books, and a medicine cabinet that dates back to around 1835. ⊠ *Victoria St., Balfour Town* 🖾 *Free*.

Beaches

Big Sand Cay

BEACH—SIGHT | Accessible by boat through the on-island tour operators, this tiny, totally uninhabited island is 7 miles (11 km) south of Salt Cay; it's also known for its long, unspoiled stretches of open sand. **Amenities:** none. **Best for:** solitude; swimming. ✛ *7 miles (11 km) south of Salt Cay*.

★ North Beach

BEACH—SIGHT | This beach is the best reason to visit Salt Cay; it might be the finest beach in the Turks and Caicos. Part of the beauty lies not just in the soft, powdery sand and beautiful blue waters, but also in its isolation; it's very likely that you will have this lovely beach all to yourself. **Amenities:** none. **Best for:** snorkeling; solitude; swimming; walking. ✛ *North shore near Castaways*.

Salt Cay's salt ponds, or salinas, are a reminder of the island's salt producing history.

🍴 Restaurants

Although small in size, the few restaurants on Salt Cay serve food that's big in flavor, with some of the best food in the islands.

Coral Reef Bar & Grill

$$ | CARIBBEAN | Located next to the dock, this small restaurant is Salt Cay's only oceanside café. You can't miss it, as it's painted bright blue and green. ⑤ *Average main: $15* ✉ *Victoria St., Balfour Town* ☎ *649/245–1063* ⊘ *Closed Sept.*

★ Oceanaire Bistro

$$$ | CARIBBEAN | Now fondly thought of as *the* gathering spot, the bistro, a block from the dock and overlooking the salina offers simple but good breakfast, lunch, and dinner that changes depending on what's available. Theme nights (pizza on Friday, ribs on Sunday) are popular with visitors and locals. **Known for:** pizza and ribs theme nights; one of the only spots on the island to get a meal; menu that changes depending on what's available. ⑤ *Average main: $26* ✉ *Dickenson Square, Balfour Town* ☎ *649/341–3363.*

Pat's Place

$$ | CARIBBEAN | Island native Patricia Ann Simmons can give you a lesson in the medicinal qualities of her garden plants and periwinkle flowers, as well as provide excellent native cuisine for a very reasonable price in her comforting Salt Cay home. Home cooking doesn't get any closer to home than this. **Known for:** island-style cooking; reasonable prices; medicinal garden tours. ⑤ *Average main: $18* ✉ *South District* ☎ *649/946–6919* ▭ *No credit cards.*

🛏 Hotels

Salt Cay has no full-service hotels or resorts, but there are many small homes to rent on the island, and many visitors go this route instead of staying in one of the small inns or bed-and-breakfasts. Many rentals are simple yet charming.

Two property managers on island oversee the rental of many of these vacation homes. They can also help you set up tours, take you sightseeing, and troubleshoot anything that may go wrong during your stay. Their multiple hats mean you'll also be calling them to pick you up and drive you to a restaurant.

For expanded hotel reviews, visit Fodors.com.

Candy Herwin
Candy oversees three rental properties on Salt Cay: **Pirates Hideaway by the Sea** is a small boutique guesthouse set only a stone's throw from the shore, with three individual, en-suite bedrooms and full access to a shared pool set amidst a tropical garden (from $150/night). Next door is a modern salt-raker's cottage, referred to as **Blackbeard's Quarters**, with four bedrooms and two bathrooms, a kitchenette, dining area, screened-in relaxation area, and access to the pool, perfect for families or groups (from $450/night). She also manages **Brown House** ($650 nightly for three bedrooms), an original salt merchant's home that's been lovingly restored and furnished with pieces reminiscent of a time gone by. As it is waterfront, guests enjoy the mesmerizing ocean views and cooling tropical breezes; it also has a large kitchen that's perfect for a group traveling together. Candy can regale you with stories about the history of Salt Cay, which will add to your stay. ☎ 649/244–1407 ⊕ *Pirates Hideaway: www.saltcay.tc; Brown House: saltcaywaterfront.com.*

Villas of Salt Cay
$ | RENTAL | Back-to-back hurricanes in 2017 destroyed the main house and cottage, but three oceanfront, one-bedroom cabanas with kitchenettes and amazing sunset views keep this property going. **Pros:** simple and affordable accommodation; on Victoria Street, within walking distance of everything; on a private stretch of beach. **Cons:** no rooms have air-conditioning; rest of property destroyed by hurricane; shared pool. ⑤ *Rooms from: $175* ✉ *Victoria St., Balfour Town* ☎ *649/241–1009* ⌗ *scdivers@tciway.tc* ☺ *Closed Sept.* ⇶ *3 cabanas* ⦿| *No meals.*

🛍 Shopping

There was a time when the only choice for visitors was to rent a boat and head to Grand Turk for basic food supplies and sundries (or have your self-catering accommodations provide provisioning for you). Now it is easier to be self-sufficient in Salt Cay. Ask anyone on the island where to find the shops we list; few streets have names, but it's easy to walk around the few blocks in Balfour Town to find them. However, if there is anything you can't live without, the best advice is to bring it with you from home or make a grocery run on Provo and carry the food with you to Salt Cay.

GENERAL STORE
Elouisa's
CONVENIENCE/GENERAL STORES | Located in the South District, this is a great place to pick up the essentials if you're staying on this end of the island. ✉ *South District, Balfour Town* ☎ *649/343–2158*.

Nettie's Grocery Store
CONVENIENCE/GENERAL STORES | The island's own little bakery produces fresh bread daily, so be sure to go early to get it hot out of the oven. Basic food supplies are also available, including rice and canned goods, as well as toiletries. ✉ *North District*.

Pat's Place
CONVENIENCE/GENERAL STORES | Here you'll find basic island staples—peas (which are actually beans used in the local "peas and rice"), rice, milk, sugar, cream, juices, and bottled water, along with an assortment of canned goods. ✉ *South District* ☎ *649/946–6919*.

SOUVENIRS
Salt Cay Salt Works
FOOD/CANDY | In its heyday, Salt Cay was definitely economically strong, one of the wealthiest islands in the Caribbean because of its salt. Now a team of women lovingly prepare the native salt in colored bottles of different forms so that visitors may purchase them as a keepsake; use it in your bath or for your margaritas! You can buy them at their place, as well as in a variety of shops throughout the country. Keep your eyes open for them. ✉ *Balfour Town* ⊕ *www.saltcaysaltworks.com*.

Splash Boutique
CLOTHING | Affiliated with Salt Cay Divers, this little shop has art prints, clothes, and jewelry. Local handcrafted items include watercolors and acrylics, Haitian art, maps, locally made salsa and hot rubs, Bambarra rum, and Salt Cay beach-glass jewelry. There's also an assortment of souvenirs: shot glasses, caps, and T-shirts.

Whales migrate to Salt Cay between January and April.

If you're a birder, pick up a copy of *The Birds of Turks and Caicos* to help you identify the island's many birds. ☎ *649/241–1009* ⊕ *www.saltcaydivers.tc.*

🏃 Activities

DIVING AND SNORKELING

Salt Cay diving is as laid back as the island itself, with dive sites only 5–10 minutes away. Dives start at 35 feet just offshore, with the wall dropping to 7,000 feet as part of the Columbus Passage. Divers can also explore the *Endymion*, a 140-foot, wooden-hulled British sailing vessel that met its demise in 1790. You can swim over the hull and spot the ship's cannons and anchors off the southern tip of the island. Salt Cay also offers one of the best opportunities in the world to swim with whales as they migrate (mid-January through April).

★ Salt Cay Divers

SCUBA DIVING | Salt Cay Divers conducts daily dive trips and rents out all necessary equipment, with night diving upon request. Snorkeling trips to some amazing sites are also available. The exclusive Cotton Cay private island offers some of the best snorkeling in the entire Turks and Caicos, and SC Divers has the exclusive rights to take guests there for a unique snorkeling and econature tour. In season, SC Divers also offers whale-watching excursions. ✉ *Balfour Town* ☎ *649/245–1063.*

WHALE-WATCHING

During the winter months (January through April), Salt Cay is a center for whale-watching. Approximately 2,500 humpback whales pass close to shore as they migrate through the Silver and Mouchoir Banks for mating and birthing. Today it is thought that many are staying in the waters off Salt Cay instead of moving on. Whale-watching operators have become familiar with their patterns and habits, making up-close observation almost a sure thing.

Crystal Seas Adventures

BOATING | Proprietor Tim Dunn, who is an actual descendent of the original owners of Salt Cay's historic White House, knows the waters around Grand Turk and Salt Cay as well as anybody. His company offers a variety of excursions: swimming with stingrays at Gibbs Cay, excursions to secluded cays, snorkel trips, plus whale-watching from mid-January through mid-April. Crystal Seas Adventures will cater to Salt Cay visitors as well. ✉ *Grand Turk Cruise Terminal* ✛ *Next to the Cruise Terminal* ☎ *649/243–3291, 510/926–3904 in the U.S.* ⊕ *www.crystalseasadventures.com.*

Index

A

Accommodations, 28, 40–41, 48
Adventure tours, 179
Air travel, 30, 32–33, 47
Airport, 102
Alexandra Resort 🖼, 25, 73
Amanyara 🖼, 109
Anani Spa at Grace Bay Club, 83
Anna's and Anna's Too (gallery), 79
Anthony's Gift Shop, 156
Apartment rentals, 41
Aquatic Restaurant & Bar ✕, 137
ArtProvo gallery, 79
Arts and crafts galleries, 79–80, 143, 149, 156, 166, 172
Asia's Takeout ✕, 152
ATMs, 42
Atrium 🖼, 93
Ayur Spa, 156

B

Baci Ristorante ✕, 89–90
Bamberra Beach, 144–145
Banana boats, 28
Banks, 42
Barbie's Restaurant ✕, 167–168
Barracuda Beach Bar ✕, 137, 139
Bars
Caicos and the Cays, 142
Grand Turk, 173, 176
Providenciales, 50, 59–60, 67, 85, 96
Bay Bistro ✕, 62
Beach House Turks and Caicos 🖼, 86, 88
Beached Whale, The ✕, 176
Beaches, 20–21

Caicos and the Cays, 136–137, 144–145, 147, 151
Grand Turk, 164, 167, 174
Providenciales, 55, 85, 92–93, 97, 104, 106–107, 108
Salt Cay, 184, 190
Beaches Turks & Caicos Resort & Spa 🖼, 24, 73–74
Bell Sound, 151
Bella Luna Ristorante ✕, 62
Belmont Car Rental and Tours, 147
Beyond the Blue (fishing tour), 155
Bicycling
Caicos and the Cays, 155
Grand Turk, 179, 181
Providenciales, 109–110, 120
Big Al's Island Grill ✕, 62
Big Blue Collective (kayak tour), 120
Big Blue Unlimited (kayak tour), 141–142, 155
Big Josh Bar & Grill, 142
Big Sand Cay, 190
Bight, The, 50, 85–89
Birdcage Bar and Restaurant ✕, 168
Bird-watching, 22, 26, 147, 149
Blackbeard's Quarters 🖼, 192
Blu ✕, 152
Blue Haven Resort, The Pool Bar, 96
Blue Hills, 51, 107
Blue Mountain, 51, 107
Blue Surf Shop, 80–81
Blue Water Divers, 180–181
Boat and ferry travel, 30, 35–36, 48

Boating, 110–112, 118, 155, 195
Bohio Dive Resort 🖼, 176
Boiling Hole, 151
Bonefishing, 155
Bookstores, 99
Brown House 🖼, 192
Bugaloo's ✕, 12, 103

C

Cabana Bar & Grill ✕, 62–63
Caicos and the Cays, The, 18, 123–156
beaches, 136–137, 144–145, 147, 151
children, attractions for, 28, 136, 154
dining, 127, 137, 139–140, 147, 152–153
exploring, 135–136, 138, 144, 148, 150–151
lodging, 127, 132, 133–134, 141, 147, 153–154
nightlife, 142
prices, 130
shopping, 134, 142–143, 149, 156
spas, 134, 156
sports and the outdoors, 127, 130, 141–142, 147, 149, 154–156
top reasons to go, 124
transportation, 126–127
Caicos Bakery ✕, 63
Caicos Beach Condos 🖼, 141
Caicos Café ✕, 63
Caicos Cyclery, 109
Caicos Dream Tours, 110
Caicos Pride (shop), 156
Caicos Tea, Company, 142–143
Caicos Wear Boutique, 81
Car rentals and travel, 30, 34–35, 47–48, 147

Cardinal Arthur (tours), *147, 149*
Caribbean Cruisin', *142*
Caribbean Outpost (shop), *83, 178*
Casablanca Casino, *85*
Casinos, *85*
Cave tours, *14, 23, 28, 144*
Chalk Sound, *51, 103–106*
beaches, 104
children, attractions for, 104–105
dining, 104–105
lodging, 106
Chalk Sound National Park, *103*
Charter flights, *33–34*
Children, attractions for, *28*
Caicos and the Cays, 28, 136, 154
Grand Turk, 28, 166–167, 176
Providenciales, 28, 69, 73–74, 75–76, 77, 78, 88–89, 93, 97–98, 103–104, 107, 110–111, 112, 114, 115, 116, 118, 120, 121, 122
Chukka Caribbean Adventures, *179*
Climate, *30, 37, 175*
Clothing shops, *80–81, 83, 99, 193–194*
Club Med Turkoise ☷ , *74*
Cockburn Harbour, *151*
Cockburn Town, Grand Turk, *158, 165–173*
beaches, 167
dining, 167–168, 170
exploring, 165–167
lodging, 171–172
nightlife, 173
shopping, 172
Coco Bistro ✕ , *10, 63*
Cocovan ✕ , *63*
Como Shambhala at Parrot Cay, *135*
Conch, *77*
Conch Bar Caves, *144*
Concierge services, *58*
Coral Gardens ☷ , *88*

Coral Reef Bar & Grill ✕ , *191*
Cottage Pond, *135*
Cove Restaurant + Beach Bar, The ✕ , *153*
Coyaba Restaurant ✕ , *63, 66*
Crabtree Apartments ☷ , *171*
Crackpot Kitchen ✕ , *66*
Credit cards, *39*
Crystal Seas Adventures, *195*
Cuban Crafters Cigars, *82*
Cuisine of Turks and Caicos, *38–39*
Currency, *29, 30, 41–42*
Customs and duties, *38*

D

Da Conch Shack ✕ , *107*
Danny Buoy's Irish Pub ✕ , *66, 85*
Deck at Seven Stars ✕ , *66*
Deep Blue Charters, *181*
Dellis Cay, *132–133*
Development, *27*
Dining, *38–40*. ⇨ *Also specific islands*
cuisine of Turks and Caicos, 38–39
paying, 39
prices, 56, 130, 165, 188
reservations and dress, 39
tipping, 31
wines, beer and spirits, 39–40
Discovery Bay, *51, 98–99*
Dive Provo, *114*
Diving and snorkeling, *10, 22*
Caicos and the Cays, 152, 154–155
Grand Turk, 179–181
Providenciales, 112–115
Salt Cay, 194
Dizzy Donkeys (shop), *178*
Dogs, *23, 91*

Dolphin Grill at the Ocean and Beach Resort ✕ , *153*
Downtown, *51, 100–103*
Dragon Cay Resort ☷ , *147*
Driftwood Studio, *79*
Duties, *38*

E

East Bay Resort ☷ , *25, 154*
East Caicos, *151*
Edith's Fish Fry ✕ , *168*
Electricity, *29*
Elouisa's (shop), *193*
Emergencies, *29*

F

Fairways Bar & Grill ✕ , *67*
Fauna, *26*
Festivals and events, *43, 151*
Fire & Ice ✕ , *93*
Fish Fry, *67*
Fishing, *23*
Caicos and the Cays, 155
Grand Turk, 181
Providenciales, 115–116
Fitness, *117*
Five Cays, *51, 102–103*
Flamingo Pond, *135–136*
Flamingos, *100*
Flora, *26*
Food shops, *81–82, 96, 99, 100–101, 156, 193*
Fort George Cay, *132*
FOTTAC (shop), *82*
Four-wheeling, *120*
Frank's Café ✕ , *139*
Fresh Catch ✕ , *67*
Friskyz Island Grub ✕ , *168*

G

Geography of Turks and Caicos, *26*
Glowworms, *15, 108*
Golf, *22, 117–118*
Governor's Beach, *21, 167*

Grace Bay (Providenciales), 12, 50, 61–85
beaches, 20, 61–62
dining, 62–63, 66–73
lodging, 73–79
nightlife, 85
shopping, 79–83
spas, 83–84
Grace Bay Club ⚏ , 24, 74
Grace's Cottage ✕ , 67
Graceway Gourmet (shop), 82
Graceway IGA Supermarket, 99
Graceway Juice & Java ✕ , 68
Grand Turk, 11, 18, 157–182
beaches, 164, 167, 174
children, attractions for, 28, 166–167, 176
dining, 164, 167–168, 170, 174, 176–177
exploring, 163, 165–167, 173–174
lodging, 164, 171–172, 176
nightlife, 165, 173
prices, 165
shopping, 165, 172, 178
spas, 165, 172
sports and the outdoors, 179–182
transportation, 161, 163
Grand Turk Cruise Terminal, 158, 176–178
Grand Turk Diving, 181
Grand Turk Lighthouse, 173–174
Great House Restaurant ✕ , 153
Green Island Café ✕ , 139
Grill at Grace Bay Club, The ✕ , 68–69
Grocers, 68, 143, 193
Guanahani Restaurant & Bar ✕ , 174

H

Half Moon Bay, 10, 20, 92
Harbour Club Villas ⚏ , 98
Haulover Beach, 145

Health concerns, 40
Hemingway's ✕ , 69
Her Majesty's Prison, 166
Hidden Treasures Boutique, 81
History of Turks and Caicos, 16–17
Holidays, 43
Hollywood Beach Suites ⚏ , 141
Homey's ✕ , 100
Horse Stable Beach, 137
Horseback riding, 23, 118
House rentals, 41
Humpback Dive Shack, The, 182
Hurricanes, 30, 175

I

Infiniti ✕ , 69
Inn At Grace Bay ⚏ , 74
Inn Restaurant and Bar, The ✕ , 168
Internet, 29
Island Club, The ⚏ , 74
Island Creations (gallery), 172
Island Trams (tour), 181
Island Vibes, 110–111
Itineraries, 44–46

J

Jack's Shack ✕ , 176–177
Jai's (shop), 82–83
Jeremiah Forbes (tours), 156
Jewelry shops, 82–83, 101
Jimmy Buffet's Margaritaville ✕ , 177

K

Kalooki's ✕ , 69
Kayaking, 22, 120, 122
Kew (North Caicos), 136
Kissing Fish Catering Co., 82
Kitchen 218 ✕ , 86

Kiteboarding, 22, 122
Konky Joe's ✕ , 168, 170

L

La Vista Azul ⚏ , 90
Las Brisas Restaurant & Bar ✕ , 104–105
Last Chance Bar and Grill ✕ , 139
Le Bouchon de Village ✕ , 69
Le Vele ⚏ , 75
Leeward, 50, 91–93, 96
beaches, 92–93
children, attractions for, 93
dining, 93
lodging, 93, 96
nightlife, 96
shopping, 96
Lemon2Go ✕ , 69–70
Lighthouses, 173–174
Liquor shops, 91
Little Water Cay, 130
Lodging, 40–41, 48⇨
Also specific islands
accommodation options, 40
children, 28
coming attractions, 27
concierge services, 58
money-saving tips, 30–31, 105
prices, 57, 130, 165, 188
tipping, 31
villa rentals, 57–58
Long Bay (Providenciales), 50, 97–98
Long Beach (Grand Turk), 174
Long Cay (South Caicos), 151
Love Villas ⚏ , 171
Lower Bight Beach, 21, 85

M

Magnolia Wine Bar and Restaurant ✕ , 90
Making Waves Art Studio, 80
Malcolm's Beach, 21, 108
Mama's (shop), 83
Mango Reef ✕ , 90

Manta House ⬚ , 171
Market, The, 96
Meridian Club ⬚ , 132
Middle Caicos, 143–145,
147–149
beaches, 144–145, 147
children, attractions for,
144
dining, 147
lodging, 147
shopping, 149
sports and the outdoors,
147, 149
Middle Caicos Co-Op,
143, 149
Minigolf, 28
Miss B's ✕ , 139
Money matters, 29,
30–31, 41–42
Mudjin Bar and Grill
✕ , 147
Mudjin Harbour, 20,
28, 145
Museums, 28, 166–167
My Dee's Restaurant,
Bar and Grill ✕ , 140

N

Neptune Villas ⬚ , 106
Nettie's Grocery Store,
193
Nique's Food Mart, 143
North Beach, 190
North Caicos, 134–143
beaches, 136–137
children, attractions for,
136
dining, 137, 139–140
lodging, 141
nightlife, 142
shopping, 142–143
sports and the outdoors,
141–142
transportation, 135
North Caicos Outfitters,
142
North Ridge, 158,
173–174
Northwest Point, 51,
108–109
Northwest Point Resort
⬚ , 109

O

Oasis Divers, 181
Ocean Club ⬚ , 75
Ocean Club West
⬚ , 75
Oceanaire Bistro ✕ ,
191
OceanScapes Spa, 172
Omar's Beach Hut
✕ , 103
Open Art Gallery, 166
Opus Wine-Bar-Grill
✕ , 70
Osprey Beach Hotel
⬚ , 172, 173

P

Packing, 42
Paddleboarding, 13,
22, 118
Palms, The ⬚ , 75–76
Palms Resort and Spa,
The, 83–84
Parallel 23 ✕ , 70
Parasailing, 28, 119
Parrot Cay, 124, 133–134
Parrot Cay By Como
⬚ , 25
Parrot Cay Resort ⬚ ,
133–134
Passports, 37
Pat's Place ✕ , 191
Pat's Place (shop), 193
Pavilion at the Somer-
set, The ✕ , 70
Pelican Bay ✕ , 70–71
Pelican Beach, 21,
92–93
Pelican Beach Hotel
⬚ , 141
Pillory Beach, 158,
174, 176
Pine Cay, 124, 131
Piranha Joe's (shop), 178
Pirates Hideaway by
the Sea ⬚ , 192
Pizza Pizza ✕ , 71
Playgound, 28
Point Grace ⬚ , 76
Ports of Call Resort
⬚ , 76

Potcakes, 23, 91
Price categories, 56, 57,
130, 165, 188
Prisons, 166
Private villas, 57–58
Providenciales, 18,
49–122
beaches, 55, 85, 92–93, 97,
104, 106–107, 108
children, attractions for, 28,
69, 73–74, 75–76, 77,
78, 88–89, 93, 97–98,
103–104, 107, 110–111,
112, 114, 115, 116, 118,
120, 121, 122
dining, 55–56, 62–63,
66–73, 86, 89–90, 93,
97, 100, 103, 104–105,
107, 108
exploring, 55
lodging, 56–58, 73–79,
86, 88–89, 90, 93, 96,
97–98, 106, 109
nightlife, 50, 59–60, 85, 96
prices, 56, 57
shopping, 59, 79–83, 91,
96, 99, 100–101
spas, 83–84
sports and the outdoors,
50, 102, 109–122
top reasons to go, 50
transportation, 53–54,
72, 101
Provo Golf & Country
Club, 117–118

Q

Quality Supermarket,
99

R

Rake-and-scrape
music, 173
ReadyMoney Roadside
Caboose ✕ , 140
Reef Residences ⬚ , 88
Regent Palms ⬚ , 25
Restaurant at Aman-
yara ✕ , 108
Retreat Kitchen ✕ , 71
Rickie's Flamingo Cafe
✕ , 71
Ripsaw music, 173

Ron Jon Surf Shop, *178*
Royal Jewels (shop), *101*
Royal West Indies
  Resort ▦ , *76*
Rumeurs (shop), *83*

S

Safety, *40*
Sailing, *110–113*
Sailrock ▦ , *154*
Salt ✕ , *93*
Salt Cay, *18, 183–195*
  beaches, *184, 190*
  dining, *188, 191*
  exploring, *188, 190*
  lodging, *188, 192*
  prices, *188*
  shopping, *193–194*
  sports and the outdoors,
    184, 194–195
  top reasons to go, *184*
  transportation, *187*
Salt Cay Divers, *194*
Salt Cay Salt Works,
  193
Salt Raker Inn ▦ ,
  172, 173
Sand Bar ✕ , *170*
Sandbox ✕ , *71*
Sands at Grace Bay ▦ ,
  24, 76–77
Sapodilla Bay, *20, 104*
Sapodilla Hill, *103–104*
Scooter Bob's, *109–110*
Scooters, *109–110,
  120–121*
Secret Garden ✕ , *170*
Seven ✕ , *71–72*
Seven Stars ▦ , *25, 77*
Sharkbites Bar & Grill
  ✕ , *90*
Shay on the Beach
  ✕ , *107*
Shopping
  Caicos and the Cays, *134,
    142–143, 149, 156*
  Grand Turk, *165, 172, 178*
  Providenciales, *59, 79–83,
    91, 96, 99, 100–101*
  Salt Cay, *193–194*
Shore Club, The ▦ ,
  97–98

Sibonné Beach Hotel
  ▦ , *77–78*
Silver Deep (fishing
  charter), *116*
Silver Palm Bistro
  ✕ , *140*
Silver Palm Restaurant
  ✕ , *140*
Siren & the Pirate, The,
  (shop), *81*
Smart (market), *100–101*
Snorkeling.⇨ See Div-
  ing and snorkeling
Snuba Turks & Caicos,
  115
Somerset, The ▦ ,
  24, 78
Somewhere Café and
  Lounge ✕ , *86*
South Caicos, *149–156*
  beaches, *151*
  dining, *152–153*
  exploring, *150–151*
  lodging, *153–154*
  shopping, *156*
  sports and the outdoors,
    154–155
  transportation, *150*
South Caicos Ocean &
  Beach Resort ▦ , *154*
Souvenir shops, *80, 83,
  178, 193–194*
Spa Tropique, *84*
Spas, *9, 83–84, 134,
  156, 172*
Splash Boutique,
  193–194
Stelle ✕ , *86*
Stingrays, *14*
Sui-Ren ✕ , *97*
Sun Charters, *111–112*
Sunset Cafe Bar & Grill
  ✕ , *153*
Surely Goodness Vari-
  ety Store, *156*
SURFside Ocean Acad-
  emy (scuba diving), *121*

T

T&V Tours, *155*
Taxes, *42*
Taxis, *31, 36, 101*
  fares, *101*

tipping, *31*
Taylor Bay, *20, 104*
Tennis, *119–120*
Teona Spa, *84*
Thai Orchid Restaurant,
  The ✕ , *72*
Thalasso Spa at Point
  Grace, *84*
Three Mary Cays, *136*
Time, *29*
Tipping, *31*
Tony's Car Rental, *163*
Top o' the Cove New
  York Style Deli ✕ , *89*
Tour options, *120–121,
  181*
Transportation, *30,
  32–36, 47–48*
Turks & Caicos
  National Museum,
  28, 166–167
Turks Head Brewery,
  102
Turks Head Inne ▦ ,
  171
Turks Kebab ✕ , *73*
Turtle Cove, Providen-
  ciales, *50, 51, 89–91*
  dining, *89–90*
  lodging, *90*
  shopping, *91*
Turtle Tail, *98*
Tuscany, The ▦ , *78*

U

Unicorn Bookstore, *99*

V

Venetian on Grace Bay,
  The ▦ , *78*
Venetian Road, *50, 98*
Villa Del Mar ▦ , *78–79*
Villa Renaissance
  ▦ , *79*
Villa rentals, *57–58*
Villas of Salt Cay ▦ ,
  192
Visas, *37*
Visitor information, *48*

W

Wades Green, *136*
Waterskiing and wake-
    boarding, *121*
Weather information,
    30, 37, 175
Weddings, *31*
West Bay Club 🏨 , *88*
West Harbour, *51,
    106–107*
West Harbour Bay,
    106–107
West Harbour Bluff, *21*
Whale-watching, *12, 23,
    182, 184, 195*
When to go, *37*
Whitby Beach, *137*
White House, *190*
Wild Cow Run, *145, 147*
Windsong Resort 🏨 ,
    88–89
Windsurfing, *121*
Wine Cellar (shop), *91*
Wymara Resort & Villas
    🏨 , *89*

Y

Yoshi's Sushi & Grill
    ✕ , *73*

Photo Credits

Front Cover: JoaoBarcelos/iStockphoto. [Description: Drone panorama of pier in beach in Grace Bay, Providenciales, Turks and Caicos.]. **Back cover, from left to right:** BlueOrange Studio/iStockphoto, Vilainecrevette/Shutterstock. Spine: John Wollwerth/Shutterstock. **Interior, from left to right:** Jo Ann Snover/Shutterstock (1). Jo Ann Snover/Shutterstock (2). **Chapter 1: Experience the Turks and Caicos:** jpbarcelos/Shutterstock (6-7). Salt Life Studios/Edouard Zak Photography (8). The Palms Turks & Caicos (9). Brilliant Studios (9). Brilliant Studios (10). National Geographic Image Collection / Alamy Stock Photo (10). Scuba13/Dreamstime (10). Jacquespalut/Dreamstime (10). pablopicasso/Shutterstock (11). Kevin Roland/Salt Cay Divers (12). Bugaloos Conch Crawl (12). Howard Sandler/Dreamstime (12). SUP Provo (13). Steve Passmore (13). Brilliant Studios (14). Dolly MJ/SHutterstock (14). Karen Wunderman/shutterstock (14). Nadia Nice/Shutterstock (15). CG3/Shutterstock (20). JoaoBarcelos/istockphoto (20). Jo Ann Snover/Shutterstock (20). Jo Ann Snover/Dreamstime (20). jcarillet/istock (21). Malley Photography/Shutterstock (22). Brilliant Studios (22). Larry Larsen / Alamy Stock Photo (22). Alexander Kolomietz/Shutterstock (22). Kevin Roland/Salt Cay Divers (23). Grace Bay Resorts (24). LarsenCollinge International (24). The Sands at Gracebay (24). Beaches Resorts (24). The Palms Turks & Caicos (25). Turks & Caicos Collection (25). East Bay Resort. Turks & Caicos (25). Seven Stars Resort & Spa (25). **Chapter 3: Providenciales:** Image Source/Alamy (49). jpbarcelos/Shutterstock (60). Jo Ann Snover/Shutterstock (92). Provo Golf Club (117). **Chapter 4: The Caicos and the Cays:** jpbarcelos/Shutterstock (123). Jo Ann Snover/Shutterstock (131). COMO Hotels and Resorts (134). Robert A. Metcalfe/Shutterstock (146). Karen Wunderman/Shutterstock (149). **Chapter 5: Grand Turk:** KenMorgan/Shutterstock (157). Ian Cumming/agefotostock (166). Walter Bibikow/eStockPhoto (170). mikolajn/istockphoto (178). **Chapter 6: Salt Cay:** Jon Arnold Images Ltd/Alamy (183). Jon Arnold Images Ltd/Alamy (191). Kevin Roland/Salt Cay Divers (194). **About Our Writers:** All photos are courtesy of the writers.

*Every effort has been made to trace the copyright holders, and we apologize in advance for any accidental errors. We would be happy to apply the corrections in the following edition of this publication.

Fodor's InFocus TURKS & CAICOS ISLANDS

Publisher: Stephen Horowitz, *General Manager*

Editorial: Douglas Stallings, *Editorial Director;* Jacinta O'Halloran, Amanda Sadlowski, *Senior Editors;* Kayla Becker, Alexis Kelly, Teddy Minford, Rachael Roth, *Editors*

Design: Tina Malaney, *Design and Production Director;* Jessica Gonzalez, *Graphic Designer;* Mariana Tabares, *Design & Production Intern*

Production: Jennifer DePrima, *Editorial Production Manager;* Carrie Parker, *Senior Production Editor;* Elyse Rozelle, *Production Editor;* Jackson Pranica, *Editorial Production Assistant*

Maps: Rebecca Baer, *Senior Map Editor;* David Lindroth, *Cartographers*

Photography: Viviane Teles, *Senior Photo Editor;* Namrata Aggarwal, Ashok Kumar, Carl Yu, *Photo Editors;* Rebecca Rimmer, *Photo Intern*

Business & Operations: Chuck Hoover, *Chief Marketing Officer;* Robert Ames, *Group General Manager;* Tara McCrillis, *Director of Publishing Operations;* Victor Bernal, *Business Analyst*

Public Relations and Marketing: Joe Ewaskiw, *Senior Director Communications & Public Relations;* Esther Su, *Senior Marketing Manager*

Fodors.com: Jeremy Tarr, *Editorial Director;* Rachael Levitt, *Managing Editor*

Technology: Jon Atkinson, *Director of Technology;* Rudresh Teotia, *Lead Developer;* Jacob Ashpis, *Content Operations Manager*

Writers: Jessica Robertson

Editor: Kayla Becker

Production Editor: Carrie Parker

4th Edition

ISBN 978-1-64097-232-2

ISSN 1946–3049

Library of Congress Control Number 2019952419

SPECIAL SALES

This book is available at special discounts for bulk purchases for sales promotions or premiums. For more information, e-mail SpecialMarkets@fodors.com.

PRINTED IN CANADA

10 9 8 7 6 5 4 3 2 1

About Our Writer

 Born in England and raised in the Bahamas, **Jessica Robertson** has traveled the world for work and play but calls Nassau home. She has visited the Turks and Caicos Islands a number of times and always enjoys the opportunity to actually vacation in a tropical paradise! Jessica is happiest when she's paddling on, diving under or lounging beside the ocean. She updated the entire Turks and Caicos guide.